Spinner in Chief

*How Presidents Sell Their Policies
and Themselves*

Stephen J. Farnsworth

Paradigm Publishers
Boulder · London

green press
INITIATIVE

Paradigm Publishers is committed to preserving ancient forests and natural resources. We elected to print this title on 30% post consumer recycled paper, processed chlorine free. As a result, for this printing, we have saved:

5 Trees (40' tall and 6-8" diameter)
1,962 Gallons of Wastewater
4 million BTU's of Total Energy
252 Pounds of Solid Waste
473 Pounds of Greenhouse Gases

Paradigm Publishers made this paper choice because our printer, Thomson-Shore, Inc., is a member of Green Press Initiative, a nonprofit program dedicated to supporting authors, publishers, and suppliers in their efforts to reduce their use of fiber obtained from endangered forests.

For more information, visit www.greenpressinitiative.org

Environmental impact estimates were made using the Environmental Defense Paper Calculator. For more information visit: www.papercalculator.org.

Copyright © 2009 Stephen J. Farnsworth

Published in the United States by Paradigm Publishers, 3360 Mitchell Lane, Suite E, Boulder, CO 80301 USA.

Paradigm Publishers is the trade name of Birkenkamp & Company, LLC, Dean Birkenkamp, President and Publisher.

Library of Congress Cataloging-in-Publication Data
Farnsworth, Stephen J., 1961–
  Spinner in chief : how presidents sell their policies and themselves / by Stephen J. Farnsworth.
     p. cm.—(Media and power)
  Includes bibliographical references and index.
  ISBN-13: 978-1-59451-267-4 (hc : alk. paper)
   ISBN-13: 978-1-59451-268-1 (pbk. : alk. paper) 1. Presidents—United States.
2. Spin doctors—United States. 3. Communication in politics—United States.
4. Persuasion (Rhetoric). 5. United States—Politics and government. I. Title.
  JK516.F36 2008
  320.97301'4—dc22

                                                            2008018827

Printed and bound in the United States of America on acid-free paper that meets the standards of the American National Standard for Permanence of Paper for Printed Library Materials.

Designed and typeset by Straight Creek Bookmakers.

12 11 10 09 08   1 2 3 4 5

To my parents, who have made all things possible

Contents

Tables

Acknowledgments

This project is the result of support generously offered from many sources. The first debt is owed to Dan Froomkin, author of the White House Watch column on www.washingtonpost.com, who generously allowed me the use of this work's title.

I also wish to express my deep appreciation to my colleagues and students at George Mason University, the University of Mary Washington, Georgetown University's Communication, Culture, and Technology Program, and the McGill Institute for the Study of Canada, who shared with me their reactions to my ideas about presidential communication during the years I worked on this project. In particular, I would like to thank Diana Owen, Jim Lengle, Jack Kramer, Lew Fickett, Jason Davidson, Antonia Maioni, Stuart Soroka, and Bob Lichter for their support and advice.

Jennifer Knerr, the Paradigm editor who first proposed this project and guided this work along the way, and David Paletz, editor of Paradigm's Media and Power series, deserve special thanks for their careful reading of earlier versions of this manuscript as they sought to make this a much stronger work. I also greatly appreciate the rapid and first-rate copyediting and production assistance of Melanie Stafford, Sharon Daugherty, and Kathy Delfosse.

Thanks are also due for the many years of encouragement I have received from my parents and from Tanya DeKona, who in particular has endured much grief as the companion of an anxious academic these many years.

All conclusions in this work, as well as any errors or omissions, are my responsibility.

Stephen J. Farnsworth

Chapter One

The Many Channels of Presidential Spin

Regardless of what the Founders intended, American politics now centers on the White House. Although a modern president is constrained—at least most of the time—by the constitutional system of separate institutions sharing governmental power, today's chief executive dominates modern Washington in a way that was unthinkable a century ago. The most important explanation for this massive shift in the contemporary political environment is today's all-consuming mass media. All a president has to do is start talking and all public attention turns toward the White House. Excessive legislative branch power may have been the chief concern of the Founders, but in modern times Congress has struggled—and mostly failed—even to be heard along with the president's voice, amplified by 24/7 news media.

What modern mass communication systems have wrought is truly amazing. Three-quarters of a century ago, President Franklin Delano Roosevelt (FDR) would sit at his desk surrounded by a few dozen print reporters and regularly hold forth on the issues of the day (Goodwin 1994). When he wanted to go over, under, or around the mass media, he did so through the famous "fireside chats" on the then new medium of radio. These unmediated remarks helped convince an anxious nation that the country was being run by a president who cared and would not rest until the Depression was vanquished (Burns and Dunn 2001).

Roosevelt's mastery of the media helped convince his successors that the best way for the White House to compete in its policy struggles with Congress was through aggressive use of the mass media. An administration's careful determination of what to say and what not to say can help set the political agenda and also frame the debate to the advantage of the White House. Presidential "spin," the selective release of information to win political arguments, did not start with FDR, but his effective use of the mass media led to a new era of presidential marketing, a White House governing advantage that has grown exponentially with the new technologies of television and the Internet.

Today, White House priorities are presented via stage-managed, tightly scripted events before friendly audiences or mute television cameras. Every presidential backdrop and every utterance is precisely designed to shape news coverage and mold the public debate (Kurtz 1998; Waterman, Wright, and St. Clair 1999). CNN and CSPAN broadcast the most important executive branch news briefings live, particularly in times of crisis, and even the White House Web site offers clips and transcripts of presidential speeches, written statements, and administration briefings. The audience for White House communications is far larger as well, as people anywhere in the world can at will tune in or click on the news from 1600 Pennsylvania Avenue.

During the Bill Clinton and George W. Bush presidencies in particular, shaping news coverage has been a vital if not dominant part of presidential operations. Playing to the cameras and the Web has become such an intense White House focus that selling administration priorities to enhance the president's influence may undermine sound policy management. As the examples in this book show, these two presidents and their teams concentrated on how to win daily political debates too often at the expense of the nation's long-term best interests, and sometimes even at great costs to their own long-term political standing. Although presidents have long worried about how they are portrayed by reporters, today's hyperactive executives have turned what was once merely an area of White House concern into an overriding obsession.

The White House Dominates the Discourse

Reporters have grown to prefer to cover the executive branch, and have increasingly turned their attention away from Capitol Hill (Farnsworth and Lichter 2006a, 2006b; Graber 2006; Lichter and Amundson 1994; Rozell 1994). A media-savvy White House offers a single, consistent message that contrasts sharply with the chaotic range of opinions found among the hundreds of members of the U.S. Congress. For a national news program—be it television or, before that, radio—the president's position as a nationally elected officeholder makes him or her a much more recognizable and important figure than the House speaker, who was elected in a district consisting of a fraction of the nation's population, just like everyone else on Capitol Hill. When news producers construct a national newscast, they want familiar faces on the air, and no political figure is more well-known than the president. In the words of more than one news director over the years, nobody watches a nobody. And most Americans could not pick more than a few members of Congress out of a police lineup.

Technological change and increased media attention have helped the White House win public relations battles with Congress. In addition, the modern White House has become more dominant in the wake of an enhanced presidential assertiveness that started during the Great Depression and World War II. From FDR onward, a succession of twentieth-century chief executives chose to be far more active policymakers than their predecessors (Burns and Dunn 2001). Modern presidents have expanded the White House policy agenda and have promoted it through an extensive public relations staff dedicated to caring for and feeding a growing army of Washington reporters (Kumar 2003a, 2003b). These same public relations efforts are designed to help convince Congress and the public to support the president (Kernell 2007). Press conferences, presidential speeches and travel, regular briefings by the press secretary and other top administration hands, official and unofficial leaking of information, and updated-to-the-minute White House Web sites all help transmit and sell the president's message to reporters and citizens (Kumar 2001; Kurtz 1994, 1998).

Few Challenges to White House Media Dominance

The legislative branch can't begin to keep up with the White House's more centralized media management. Since being heard is at least half the battle in politics, in recent decades the less "newsworthy" and less centralized Congress has become less familiar, less significant, and less popular among citizens keeping track of what is going on in Washington (Farnsworth 2003a, 2003b; Hibbing and Theiss-Morse 1995, 1998; Mann and Ornstein 2006).

State governments, another traditional policymaking rival of the national executive branch, cannot compete either. The issues debated in the country have shifted toward the federal government in general and the presidency in particular. Since the New Deal and World War II, the balance of power in the United States has veered strongly, and apparently irreversibly, away from state capitals and toward Washington. In subsequent years, new crises, including the Cold War, the desegregation of public schools, the civil rights movements, and even the war on terror, intensified that pro-Washington shift. Even George W. Bush, a self-proclaimed small-government conservative who vowed as a candidate that he would cut the size and influence of the federal government, expanded its size and reach instead once he became president (Burke 2006).

This trend toward more Washington-based and White House–centered policymaking is particularly prominent in international politics, which has become the dominant concern of the national government over the past half century. This policy focus provides yet another explanation for the president's political communication advantage, since the executive branch provides leadership on international matters. Indeed, the president's effective control of the U.S. Departments of Defense, State, and Homeland Security and the Central Intelligence Agency (CIA) gives him or her a near monopoly on the information that is (or is not) released to Congress and the public (Entman 2004; Norris, Kern, and Just 2003). Although Congress sometimes chafes at executive branch overreach in the international arena, legislators usually care a lot more about domestic matters and hesitate to confront a president on foreign policy (L. Fisher 2004; Norris, Kern, and Just 2003). Only if citizens overwhelmingly reject the president and the president's policies does the White House run the risk of a full-scale confrontation with Congress—and even then the legislative branch may back down (L. Fisher 2004).

Political communication advantages for a president, by themselves, do not guarantee political or legislative success (Edwards 1989, 2003, 2004). Presidential prerogatives are not absolute, and even popular presidents frequently find their domestic policy desires thwarted on Capitol Hill. At the same time Bush's budget requests for the Iraq occupation and the renewal of the PATRIOT Act were endorsed by Congress, the president's proposal for partial privatization of Social Security went nowhere on Capitol Hill—even with Republican majorities in both chambers (Jacobs 2006).

Despite all the executive branch advantages with the modern media—conditions particularly apparent in the years after the 2001 terrorist attacks on the World Trade Center and the Pentagon—presidents continue to struggle in the domestic policymaking realm (Jacobs 2006). The modern media environment, particularly the no-holds-barred coverage found online, may provide the president with new allies but also with enemies in the media world. In other words, what can help a president can also undermine or challenge the White House message.

Even journalists who "rallied 'round the flag" behind President Bush during a crisis, as almost every U.S. reporter did in the wake of 9/11, eventually turned far more critical of him, particularly as the occupation in Iraq grew bloodier (Farnsworth and Lichter 2006a). Presidents may want to change the subject to talk about good news, but events have a way of drawing attention away from what presidents want to emphasize. News content emerges from the struggle between policymakers and reporters over what is important, and the mass media sometimes do not take White House advice about which issues to report on and what to say about those issues, particularly when the president's poll numbers start to slump (and they always do, eventually). In addition, politicians' personal scandals may push substantive policy matters off the front pages as reporters engage in feeding frenzies over allegations of sexual misconduct, corruption, or dishonesty (Sabato 1993; Sabato, Stencel, and Lichter 2000). Presidents, in other words, eye reporters warily, even when presidential influence over media content is at its peak. All of a president's advantages in spinning the news could evaporate in an instant if conditions change.

Looking down Pennsylvania Avenue, the view from Capitol Hill is no more encouraging for countering presidential dominance of policy communication. The aggressive and highly partisan redistricting procedures in nearly all the states means that a president faces a U.S. House composed of only a small number of members who represent swing districts, and who therefore are vulnerable to White House electoral pressure (Jacobson 2001). And senators, with their six-year terms, are experts at wearing down and waiting out presidents when they choose to do so (Pfiffner 2006; Sinclair 2000). Of course, even lawmakers representing "safe" districts keep close tabs on the wishes of their constituents. When public opinion shifts against the White House, lawmakers of the president's party put their own political fortunes ahead of the president's. This was seen most clearly in the Republican debates over how to deal with Iraq after the party lost control of Congress in 2006 (Abramowitz and Weisman 2007; Milbank 2007).

Even within the executive branch, sometimes there are problems for presidents hoping to spin policy options in a consistent fashion. President Bush's troubles with the Republican moderates in his first-term cabinet (Colin Powell, Paul O'Neill, and Christine Todd Whitman) are only the latest examples of cabinet secretaries and other top administration officials who sometimes unenthusiastically pursue or even undermine presidential priorities (Clarke 2004; Suskind 2004). Opponents of administration policies quietly give journalists secret documents in hopes that those unauthorized disclosures (known as "leaks") will expose unpopular ideas and lead to their abandonment in the face of public or legislative pressure (Woodward 1994, 2002, 2006). Or government officials leak information to help build the case for controversial policies resisted by others in the government (Shane 2007a, 2007c). In addition, deeply loyal staffers who pursue White House policies too zealously can also cause problems for an administration, as several recent presidents have come to learn (Ceaser 1988; Clarke 2004; Suskind 2004).

Even with the White House's advantages at spin, presidents sometimes fail to win support for favored policies. The limitations faced by an administration's massive in-house message-shaping staff, particularly over domestic matters, bring us back to where we once began: with Richard Neustadt's (1990: 29) admonition that the real power of presidents is mainly "the power to persuade." Although media and political environments have changed a great deal over time, the central challenge remains. Presidential policymaking is still mainly about conversation and persuasion, and not about unilateral demands (Edwards 1989, 2003).

Taking Spin to a Whole New Level

This book provides a comprehensive look at presidential communication strategies, paying particular attention to the two presidents of the Internet age: Bill Clinton and George W. Bush. These two administrations have been widely celebrated (or condemned, depending on the political orientation of the evaluator) for aggressive political communication operations (Alterman and Green 2004; Kurtz 1998; Sabato, Stencel, and Lichter 2000). But this book is not just about studying recent examples of presidential spin; it also examines the consequences of the modern White House media obsession. The intense focus on marketing a president has been undermining sound policy development in recent years. Although Bill Clinton's and George W. Bush's communication efforts generated some short-term gains, both presidents also suffered from severe longer-term political problems as a result of their public relations strategies—times when the White House endured negative public evaluation and had little control over the process of legislation on Capitol Hill. The temptation to spin has led to overspinning, with troubling results.

Examining how presidents market their priorities and themselves is an essential part of understanding how the modern White House operates. As President Bush stood before one made-for-television backdrop after another—and even once wore a flight suit for a televised landing on an aircraft carrier—we see that White House staffers believed "image is everything" (Waterman, Wright, and St. Clair 1999). Presidents are not the only ones who make news, but they can sometimes replace unfavorable images by making news of their own. When a leaked fall 2006 U.S. government report, the National Intelligence Estimate, made it look as if the Iraq War had increased the threat of terrorism, Bush went from condemning the original leakers to doing some declassifying of his own (also known as "leaking from the top") within just a few days (Mazzetti 2006a, 2006b).

Bush's efforts to buff his image through "Top Gun"–style aircraft carrier landings along with severely limited and deeply misleading release of information that supported his policies represent presidential spin taken to a whole new level (Dean 2004; McClellan 2008). Rarely have presidents sought so aggressively as Bush to clothe himself, literally, as a warrior.

White House teams long have sought to manipulate media coverage, recognizing that a presidency that looks good on television is likely to be a successful one (Kernell 2007). To that end, events are presented in ways designed to maximize media coverage of good news and minimize coverage of bad news. By giving speeches on the war on terror or by traveling around the country to express the need for Social Security reform, President Bush hoped to draw further attention to the issues he wanted to emphasize. Such efforts at public agenda setting are part of the tug of war among political actors and journalists as they collectively shape the national conversation (T. Cook 2005).

In addition to trying to determine what topics are emphasized in the news, the modern White House also tries to substitute administration perspectives for news reporters and producers' framing of political events (Hollihan 2001; Patterson 1994). Putting an issue into context, or saying what a current event resembles, helps shape public response to ongoing events. In the aftermath of 9/11, for example, Bush repeatedly tried to frame the war in Afghanistan and later Iraq as the modern equivalent of World War II (Farnsworth and Lichter 2006a). When he faced potential impeachment, Clinton sought to frame the case against him as the obsessive work of modern-day Puritans who could not accept Clinton's victories at the ballot box (Farnsworth and Lichter 2006a). Because the White House gets to do most of the government's talking on the evening news, administrations often have great ability both to set the agenda and to frame the discussion, guiding public opinion in the direction favored by the White House (Entman 2004). Indeed, even busy lawmakers rely on mass media reports from the White House to learn of the president's priorities and to get some sense of how popular those priorities may be with other Washington policymakers (T. Cook 1989, 2005). Cable

Table 1.1 Media Use Trends, 1992–2006 (percentages)

How have you been getting most of your news about the November elections? [Accept two answers. If only one response is given, probe for one additional response.]

	2006	2004	2002	2000[a]	1996	1992
Television	69	78	66	70	72	82
Newspapers	34	39	33	39	60	57
Radio	17	17	13	15	19	12
Magazines	2	3	1	4	11	11
Internet	15	18	7	11	3	n/a

Note: Because two answers were accepted, columns do not add up to 100 percent.

[a]The 2000 results were based on registered voters only.

Source: Pew Research Center for the People and the Press. 2007. "Election 2006 Online." Pew Internet and American Life Project Report. January 17. http://www. pewinternet.org/pdfs/PIP_Politics_2006.pdf (accessed January 31).

news outlets and the Internet now offer new sources of information for everyone and new opportunities for presidents to promote themselves. Table 1.1 demonstrates the extent to which these new media sources compete with traditional news outlets like network television and newspapers. Television has remained a dominant media source whereas the public attention paid to newspapers has fallen considerably. The Internet remains well below those two traditional media sources in influence.

The Increasingly Mediated Presidency

Presidents have long used the mass media to try to gain public support for themselves, which then helps advance their political fortunes. With today's expansive mass media, presidents who are not aggressive in defining themselves will find their reputations framed by others. For the past half century, nearly every presidential team continued to campaign after it was in the White House, trying to sell the president in the same way it previously had sold the candidate (Tulis 1987). This practice of governing through a permanent campaign offers mixed results. On the positive side, continuing White House solicitation of public support makes politics more focused on public opinion (and less elite-driven) than it was in the days before television and the Internet (Waterman, Wright, and St. Clair 1999). More negatively, presidential marketing may trump substance in the process of lawmaking, favoring short-term benefits over long-term ones—even when the eventual costs outweigh the benefits (Miroff 2006). In addition, the modern media environment encourages presidents to overpromise, leading to deep citizen frustration when results do not live up to expectations (Cronin and Genovese 2004; Lowi 1985).

The Modern Mediated Presidency: Replacing the Founders' Vision

The modern mediated presidency is not at all what the Founders had in mind for the executive branch, which was designed to share power with Congress to a greater degree than has been the norm in recent years (Fisher 2004). Most presidents who served before the advent of national radio and television networks were not publicly oriented politicians. With few exceptions—most notably Thomas Jefferson, Andrew Jackson, and Abraham Lincoln—nineteenth-century chief executives did not routinely go public to win support for their governing agenda (Tulis 1987). Presidents in that era generally served in the political background, much like modern city managers who try to implement the policies developed largely by others. Before the twentieth century, presidents did not campaign for office as aggressively as modern candidates do, so that even successfully elected candidates such as Franklin Pierce and James Buchanan completed their campaigns without becoming skilled in what we now call public relations. There was no 24/7 mass media then, so few candidates found it necessary to develop citizen-friendly media styles. For these reasons few people in the 1850s knew—or even cared—exactly what Pierce and Buchanan were thinking. For most of the nineteenth century, real power rested in Congress, so media and public attention during that era focused on the legislative branch (cf., Cook 2005; Wayne 2006).

Even the few publicly oriented presidents elected during the early years of the republic did not have the field of imagemaking to themselves. Consider the cases of Thomas Jefferson and Andrew Jackson, who stood out among antebellum presidents in their efforts to build populist approaches to politics (Genovese 2001; Remini 1967). Both relied on the efforts of sympathetic, partisan newspapers to enhance their reputations with voters. But their efforts were blunted by opposing partisan newspapers that attacked these populist candidates as libertines, as would-be dictators, as mentally unbalanced, and even, in the case of Jefferson, as being pro-French—a harsh insult throughout most of U.S. history (Genovese 2001).

Among the early presidents, probably only George Washington, who cultivated an image of himself as largely above the squabbles between partisans of Alexander Hamilton on one side and of Jefferson on the other, did not face substantial challenges to his reputation while in public life (Genovese 2001). Although Lincoln may be revered by latter-day Americans, he was subject to aggressive personal attacks during his political career. Before the outbreak of the Civil War, critics routinely ridiculed his rustic background and his visage, a homely face that television journalists of a later generation might describe as "made for radio."

Early twentieth century presidents began to offer a hint of what was to come in modern presidential media relations. Theodore Roosevelt, who imagined a much greater role for the United States—and for its chief executive—on the international stage, was an unusually media-oriented public figure. Roosevelt had grabbed headlines as the head of a key cavalry charge in the Spanish-American War of 1898, and the resulting good press helped secure his place as the vice presidential nominee on the 1900 GOP ticket (J. Cooper 1983). After the assassination of William McKinley in 1901 made him president, Roosevelt used the office, which he termed "a bully pulpit," to create a new, more activist role for the nation's chief executive (Tulis 1987). Theodore Roosevelt's aggressiveness was rewarded with a series of legislative accomplishments for his presidential priorities, including improved consumer health and safety protections and the establishment of a massive system of national parks (Burns and Dunn 2001).

A few years later, President Woodrow Wilson revived Theodore Roosevelt's vision of a public presidency, most notably through his ambitious whistle-stop railroad tour to convince citizens to support U.S. entry into the League of Nations (J. Cooper 1983). But Wilson's failure to move the Senate on that issue demonstrated the limitations of public appeals designed, like a bank shot in pool, to influence Congress by first persuading citizens to back a president's policy. Wilson worked himself , almost to his death, to secure U.S. entry into the League of Nations, but he could not secure Senate passage of the agreement (Wayne 2006). You can reach a lot more people over the airwaves or online than you can over the rails, after all. Had he been president in the television and online age, though, Wilson might have been more successful in moving the public. But modern media outlets, had they existed decades earlier, would also have been Wilson's political undoing. Efforts by Wilson's entourage to hide the severity of his stroke late in his second term could be much more effective when presidents were not seen in public nearly every day (Chandler 2007; Smith 2001).

The role of the president as a key defender of public interests was played most aggressively in the nineteenth century by Jefferson, Jackson, and Lincoln, and in the early twentieth century by Theodore Roosevelt and Wilson. The rise of nationwide radio networks in the 1920s gave the White House new tools to promote the president as the key public representative in government, though it took a while for politicians to appreciate the potential of each new media technology.

Indeed, the president-dominated politics that began in FDR's time were due in large part to the new national mass media—in that time, the radio— that brought the president's voice into living rooms around the country. Roosevelt's famous "fireside chats" connected the patrician president to tens of millions of Americans profoundly anxious about the future (Burns and Dunn 2001). FDR's deliberate efforts to talk to citizens made people believe that a more prosperous future was near or at least that presidents—much more than members of Congress—could make things happen (Goodwin 1994). Citizens rewarded FDR for his activist government with reelection after reelection after reelection—FDR was the only president ever to win four terms (an amendment to the U.S. Constitution now limits presidents to two terms). When Roosevelt died in April 1945, after the United States had vanquished the Depression and was only weeks away from winning World War II in Europe, many Americans had come to feel a close, personal connection with FDR. People wondered how the country could thrive without him (Beschloss 2002).

Although the United States has prospered for most of the years since World War II, presidents ever since have lived in FDR's long and intimidating shadow. Without exception, presidents since FDR have found it difficult, if not impossible, to measure up to the immense public expectations of chief executives serving in the wake of Roosevelt (Gergen 2000; Woodward 1999). Even presidents who enjoyed periods of high public approval—such as

President George W. Bush in the wake of the 2001 terrorist attacks—found that their approval ratings soon returned to earth as public frustrations mounted (Dimock 2004; Pfiffner 2004a, 2004b).

FDR's publicly oriented political leadership, which set a challenging standard for his successors, nevertheless did give subsequent presidents the opportunity to dominate Washington's political discourse. Television, which became commonplace during the late 1950s, gave presidents who mastered that new medium—such as John F. Kennedy and Ronald Reagan—great opportunities to shape the public agenda and create favorable images of themselves. Television and the Internet convey immense communication advantages to the White House, but presidents were not always as effective as they might have been in marketing their policies or themselves (Barber 1992; Brody 1991; Cook 2002; Farnsworth and Lichter 2006a; Gilbert 1989; Gregg 2004; Han 2001; Hertsgaard 1989; Kurtz 1998). Although presidents may not always convince Congress, the citizenry, or the governments of other nations to view a White House policy proposal in the same way as the people at 1600 Pennsylvania Avenue, chief executives can do far more to shape public discourse than can any other political actor (Kernell 2007; Tulis 1987).

The Content Analysis Evidence: Congress Plays Second Fiddle

The propresidency orientation of the mass media is not merely an impression held by government officials and outside observers. Academic studies of media coverage of the federal government repeatedly have confirmed the news media's intense focus on the executive branch. When reporters in Washington try to explain for their viewers and their readers the actions of the national government, the executive branch is the most frequent stop. Presidential actions are also more definite than the incremental developments on Capitol Hill, where nearly every bill fails to clear the cumbersome lawmaking system of House and Senate committees, amendment rules for floor action, potential filibusters, floor action in two chambers, and then successful resolution of interchamber differences in a conference committee (Binder and Smith 1997; Mann and Ornstein 2006). Indeed, the crass and unseemly nature of the horse-trading on Capitol Hill helps explain citizen frustration with the legislative branch (Farnsworth 2001, 2003a, 2003b; Hibbing and Theiss-Morse 1995, 1998).

Given the finality of congressional and presidential actions, and much greater public awareness of presidents, it is no wonder that the White House receives far more coverage than Congress, and has done so throughout the television age (Farnsworth and Lichter 2006a; Graber 2006; Grossman and Kumar 1981; Hess 1981, 1986, 1991, 1996; Kaid and Foote 1985; Lichter and Amundson 1994; Lowi 1985; Waterman, Wright, and St. Clair 1999).

In fact, the White House news coverage advantage is overwhelming. Using content analysis consisting of careful line-by-line dissection of news reports, researchers have found that presidents routinely receive 70 percent or more of news coverage of government (Graber 2006). One study that looked at the entire content of the evening newscasts of ABC, CBS, and NBC for the first years of the presidencies of Ronald Reagan (1981), Bill Clinton (1993) and George W. Bush (2001) found that the executive branch received 76 percent of all government coverage in 1981, 88 percent in 1993, and 82 percent in 2001 (Farnsworth and Lichter 2006a, 33). On average the judicial branch is the focus of about 3 percent of the news coverage, leaving Congress with the rest. In the best year for the legislative branch of those three examined in that study, Congress was outcovered by the executive branch on television by roughly a four-to-one margin (Farnsworth and Lichter 2006a).

Television is not alone in providing a substantial news coverage advantage to the modern executive. The executive branch also received more than 70 percent of the news coverage in the *New York Times* and the *Washington Post* during those same years of 1981, 1993, and 2001 (Farnsworth and Lichter 2006a, 151). Because network television and those two elite newspapers help set the agenda for other media outlets, including cable television, the wire services, other newspapers, and online media outlets, such trends are difficult for the legislative branch to counter in any media venue. When Americans turn to the mass media to try to follow national policy debates, the perspective offered by the media is more the view from the White House than the view from Capitol Hill (Rozell 1994).

The same patterns of executive branch dominance of the mass media are seen in the sources quoted on network newscasts, further enhancing the executive branch's advantages over Congress in setting the agenda and framing the stories that appear on the evening news. In 2001, a total of 45 percent of the sources cited by name or affiliation in the evening newscasts of ABC, CBS, and NBC worked for the executive branch, as compared to 35 percent in 1993 and 48 percent in 1981 (Farnsworth and Lichter 2006a, 39). Legislative branch sources were 12 percent of those identified by name or affiliation in 2001, 19 percent in 1993, and 20 percent in 1981—further evidence of the executive branch's dominance over the legislative in media coverage since the early 1980s (Lichter and Farnsworth 2003, 30).

Although Washington reporters do spend most of their time talking to executive branch officials, that fact does not mean that news coverage of the presidency is overwhelmingly positive. Indeed, network news reporters tend to be equal opportunity offenders, criticizing all presidents regardless of political party. Network news coverage of the first years of the presidencies of Ronald Reagan, Bill Clinton, and George W. Bush showed great similarities in the tone of coverage, with news reports that were 36 percent, 38 percent, and 39 percent positive respectively (Farnsworth and Lichter 2006a, 41).

The study that determined those numbers dropped the few neutral references contained in the news reports—definite statements are more likely to be aired than equivocal ones—which means that news reports from these three presidential first years were over 60 percent negative. On the bright side, though (at least for the executive branch), coverage of Congress is even more harsh—as much as 80 percent negative in some years (Farnsworth and Lichter 2006a, 41).

Conflicting Evidence about Consequences: Does "Going Public" Help?

Mostly negative news coverage may be only part of the president's media problems. Researchers who have looked at the media strategies of modern presidents debate whether the president really can move Congress by first moving public opinion. No doubt presidential administrations try to sell their policies in the media, perhaps because they want to do everything they can to secure passage of their initiatives, but how much presidents actually accomplish with such public appeals is a subject of much debate.

Samuel Kernell, in a widely read 2007 book on presidential efforts to sell citizens on their policies and themselves, wrote that the modern media environment forces presidents to promote their policies publicly, if for no other reason than that a president's opponents will be using media strategies to undermine support for White House initiatives. A president who does not go public runs the risk of appearing weak. Public perceptions of such White House weakness can lead to many problems, according to this theory, including a more combative Congress, increased partisan conflict, more aggressive international adversaries, and perhaps even a one-term presidency.

Perhaps the best case for the effectiveness of going public can be made by examining the presidency of Ronald Reagan, the plainspoken former actor and governor of California who became president in 1981. In his first year, Reagan was able to keep many of his key campaign promises by getting Congress—including a Democrat-controlled House of Representatives—to cut taxes, reduce domestic spending, and increase the Pentagon budget (Kernell 2007). Although Reagan's public standing declined as the 1982 recession arrived, the president was still able to maintain a media and public focus on his core priorities through the use of presidential speeches, public appearances, and a lot of paid television (Farrell 2001; Kernell 2007).

Another example that demonstrates the utility of going public is Bill Clinton's successful effort to redirect media coverage of the Clinton/Lewinsky scandal away from questions of potential presidential lying under oath and toward questions of the credibility of Clinton's attackers, particularly Speaker of the House Newt Gingrich (R-GA) and independent counsel Kenneth Starr (Farnsworth and Lichter 2006a; Newman 2002; Wayne 2000; Zaller

1998). A year of aggressive attacks on Clinton—including the first successful House vote for presidential impeachment in more than a century—failed to undermine public confidence in the president. Bill Clinton's job approval rating stood at a relatively strong 61 percent in November 1997, shortly before the scandal broke. By January 1999, the month he was acquitted by the Senate, Clinton's job approval rating stood even higher, at 69 percent (Cohen 2002a, 2002b). Surveys show that more than half the nation opposed Republican efforts to drive Clinton from office throughout the year-long scandal (Cohen 2002a, 2002b; Wayne 2000).

Kernell (2007) believes that going public helps presidents by building political capital, making it easier for the White House to bargain effectively with Congress. In addition, the process can help bring citizens into the political process, educating and engaging the people on key current issues. But these benefits are not without costs. If engaging citizens means simplifying issues, then public preferences may be distorted by the misleading comments from the White House and other players. Reporters, after all, favor as simple a discussion of politics as possible in order not to drive their viewers and readers elsewhere.

In addition, placing firm presidential issue positions in the public domain is a high-risk strategy, as it makes losing on them a visible event. Compromising on an issue previously identified as a matter of presidential principle carries with it the risk of appearing weak and even unreliable. If presidents don't stand up for their priorities, what do they stand up for?

Of course, little may get passed without compromise in times of ideologically polarized politics. Blocked White House initiatives can hurt the president, particularly when the administration has drawn media and public attention to the topic in the first place (Mayhew 1991; Sinclair 2000, 2006; Wayne 2006). Reporters focus on who is winning and who is losing, and being perceived as weak can hurt the political fortunes of both the president and the president's party. Widely covered failures like Clinton's health-care initiative of 1994 and Bush's unpopular strategies for the Iraq War in 2006 clearly demonstrated how being at the center of media attention can be a mixed blessing (Broder 2006; Skocpol 1997).

Some scholars, most notably political scientist George Edwards (2003, 2004, 2006), believe that presidents accomplish little by going public, and in fact may even make things worse by trying to make law through the media. He notes that President Bush's key second term domestic priority—partial privatization of Social Security—failed to generate enthusiasm among citizens or even among the Republicans who controlled 109th Congress (Edwards 2006). Bush's efforts to sell his international initiatives did not fare well either, according to Edwards. By mid-2006, roughly two-thirds of Americans thought that Iraq was not connected to the war on terror, despite the continual efforts by the Bush administration to make the case for the link between Saddam Hussein and 9/11. In addition, Bush's own efforts to sell himself as a competent and visionary leader also fell short, and his approval numbers sank into the mid-30s as the midterm elections approached (Balz and Cohen 2006; Nagourney and Elder 2006a, 2006b. In the 2006 midterm elections the GOP was clobbered, losing six seats in the Senate and thirty in the House, the party's worst midterm defeat since the catastrophic Watergate election of 1974 (Broder 2006; Hetherington and Keefe 2007).

Critics of the going public strategy also note that Bush's marketing efforts did not move public opinion regarding his 2001 tax cut plan or the 2003 war in Iraq. According to polls, support for Bush's proposed tax cuts in 2001 ranged in polls between 53 percent in February 2001 and 56 percent in April of that year—a time when Bush made dozens of campaign-style appeals for the cuts (Edwards 2003). Similarly, public support for the invasion of Iraq ranged between 52 percent and 59 percent between August 2002, when discussion of the issue began to be a key part of discussions surrounding the 2002 midterm elections, and January 2003, shortly before the invasion of Iraq began (Edwards 2003). In fact, the final Gallup poll of the sixteen-survey series over those six months showed the lowest support for the Iraq War (52 percent) despite the Bush administration's efforts to build public support for the invasion throughout that period. The poll figure for January 23 to 25, 2003, was seven points below the high of 59 percent support registered in a poll conducted November 8 to 10, 2002 (Edwards 2003). Although even the best-conducted polls are only an approximation of public opinion (a 1,000-person national survey is only reliable within a range of three points above or below the stated figure), those studies suggest that Bush had little to show for his marketing efforts—even for the foreign policy issue he deemed a top priority of 2002 (Edwards 2003, 2004).

The Modern White House Media Operation

Whether going public actually pays off, presidents and their administrations frequently employ public relations strategies to "spin" public discussions and build citizen support for their initiatives. At the center of the administration's communications operations, of course, is the president. When the president speaks about almost any topic it remains or becomes news, and citizens can learn of the president's remarks from a variety of outlets: online news, television, radio, newspapers, and even the White House Web page. Whether the topic is Iraq, Social Security, 9/11, tax cuts, health care, or even Monica Lewinsky, a president makes news any time he speaks. What the president talks about today, Americans talk about tonight and tomorrow. Presidents seeking to build support for policy initiatives can use a variety of tools to increase news coverage of the topic they want to emphasize: prime-time television addresses, press conferences, and presidential travel and speeches. In the following chapters I look at how Bush and Clinton in particular have used these various approaches, choosing specific media strategies to help tailor the message in ways favorable to the White House.

Of course, presidential press conferences and prime-time speeches are as big, politically speaking, as the space shuttle. They are not something a chief executive would use for everyday communication efforts, the political equivalent of a trip to the grocery store. As a result, presidential administrations routinely use other government officials to disseminate the president's lower-priority public messages. Ever since John F. Kennedy used live televised press conferences as a major part of his administration's communications efforts, administrations have worried about presidential overexposure, which could lead to diminished effectiveness for future presidential appeals to citizens.

Day-to-day dissemination of administration policy to the mass media is handled by the press secretary, the White House official in charge of responding to reporters' questions. Different press secretaries have different strategies, and depending on the situation the same press secretary may employ different strategies for different topics and for dealing with different reporters. Some press secretaries criticize questions and reporters they do not like, and others employ noncommittal responses to questions the administration does not want to answer (Shane 2007c). Even calling upon reporters selectively can be a news management strategy. In the White House briefing room, a few journalistic "characters" can be counted on to change the subject or provide comic relief, and a spokesperson getting pummeled with unappealing questions during a major controversy will turn to them to reduce the pressure.

Although the press secretary usually does most of the routine talking for the administration, the White House often provides experts in particular areas to handle briefings on such highly technical matters as national security, health policy, or economic policy. Various parts of the administration have their own briefings—the State Department and the Pentagon are among the most visible alternative sources of executive branch news and comment—and other agencies can provide briefings as needed by the White House. Handing off discussion of highly controversial issues to cabinet agencies can help pull unpleasant topics away from the White House. Press secretaries routinely try to downplay stories that portray the administration in a negative light and try to shift blame away from the president by sending reporters to the agencies for bad news (Shane 2007c). Bush was better off when the Federal Emergency Management Agency (FEMA) was made the most visible point of contact with reporters for the government's response to Hurricane Katrina, which devastated New Orleans and much of the Gulf

Coast during 2005. (Of course the reality of the government's bungled relief effort was so bad that Bush himself went to New Orleans to take personal charge of the situation—and to try to turn around the negative news coverage of FEMA's response to the disaster.)

The president's press secretary is the first responder to a crisis, sort of like a firefighting crew that is first on the scene of a car crash. And over the course of a news briefing, there may be other car crashes to deal with—most of them occur at familiar problem intersections such as the Iraqi resistance to the U.S. military occupation. But many other collisions occur on unfamiliar stretches of road, such as the sudden public disclosure shortly before the 2006 midterm elections of inappropriate contacts between U.S. Representative Mark Foley (R-FL) and several teenage boys working as pages at the U.S. Capitol (Nagourney and Elder 2006b).

Like a firefighter entering a burning building, a press secretary has to be careful where he or she steps. Full disclosure of the administration's shortcomings generally is not seen as a good idea by those responsible for those policies—this book is filled with examples of administrations that resisted telling the whole truth about controversial topics. But one can only go so far; consistently unrealistically optimistic portrayals of a policy undermine the believability of the White House spin. The last thing any administration needs is a credibility gap between the actual reality perceived in the country and what the government maintains is the reality.

For a press secretary, any major misstep can be fatal. A press secretary who says too much may anger the president or the chief of staff, and a press secretary who says too little may anger reporters, which can lead to negative news coverage of the White House (Kumar 2001). If a press secretary is dishonest or uninformed, his or her credibility may be compromised to such a degree that a replacement is needed (Kumar 2001; Nelson 2006). With all of these potential pitfalls, even the best press secretaries find it hard to remain effective in the job for more than a few years. Some press secretaries even leave office filled with recriminations for the tales they have spun (McClellan 2008).

No one appreciates the dangers reporters pose for press secretaries and politicians more clearly than Joe Trippi, who ran Howard Dean's 2004 presidential campaign. Although Dean never made it to the White House, his campaign was a perfect example of how devastating media mismanagement can be. Trippi (2004) said that every time a campaign worker picked up a phone to talk to a reporter it was like putting a loaded gun to one's head—a sort of Russian roulette of presidential politics. Of course the shot that killed the Dean campaign was fired by the candidate himself, the so-called "I have a scream" event at a campaign rally the night of the 2004 Iowa caucus, where Dean energetically exhorted his followers to take his campaign to the contests that followed (Ceaser and Busch 2005). Although

Dean and his supporters argued that what was shown on television news repeatedly was a distortion caused by a noise-canceling microphone used on stage, the media moment of Dean's apparently unhinged appeal raised questions for some about his suitability for the White House (Ceaser and Busch 2005; Eggerton 2004).

Because the day-to-day demands of White House correspondents are immense, press secretaries find it difficult, almost impossible, to do much long-term message management (Kumar 2001). Their days are spent just keeping ahead of the reporters who bombard the White House press office with wide-ranging questions. Longer-term news media management issues are handled by the director of communications, and for the higher-priority items, by the chief of staff (Kumar 2001, 2003a). These long-term planning efforts are designed to showcase the president, highlight the most important issues, and draw attention to administration accomplishments. These efforts also are designed to improve the president's standing in public opinion polls, which is particularly important if an election or a controversial policy debate is in the offing (Kumar 2001, 2003a).

One of the best media-managed presidents in recent decades was Ronald Reagan, who had been a movie actor and a pitchman for General Electric before entering elective politics. Reagan was strong when it came to delivering one-liners, like his famous putdown of President Jimmy Carter—"There you go again"—in the 1980 presidential debate and his joke during the 1984 presidential debates that the elderly president would not exploit the "youth and inexperience" of Democratic rival Walter Mondale, a former vice president and senator (Gergen 2000). But Reagan was at his best in communicating a sense of optimism about what the United States had accomplished and could accomplish in the future (Alford 1988). Whether he was standing on the shores of Normandy commemorating the sacrifices of the U.S. troops who liberated France in World War II, standing before the Statue of Liberty commemorating the bicentennial of the U.S. Constitution, or addressing a joint session of Congress, Reagan always appeared personable and confident, and as a result he was politically effective (Farrell 2001; Gergen 2000). Much of the credit for Reagan's image success was owed to Michael Deaver, a public relations executive who honed Reagan's public presentations to ensure the most effective backdrop and lighting for television (Fitzwater 1995).

George W. Bush lacked Reagan's theatrical talents. The new president's first public responses to the tragedy of 9/11 were uneven, including his decision to remain in a Florida classroom for several minutes after first learning of the attack, his shaky media statement on a military base a few hours later, and then his speech to the nation that night (Frum 2003). But Bush clearly found his voice a few days later when he stood atop a mangled fire truck in Lower Manhattan and vowed that "the people who knocked

down these buildings will hear all of us soon" (Frum 2003, 140). Much of
the credit for Bush's public relations success was due to Karl Rove, a political
consultant who engineered Bush's political rise in Texas, and Karen Hughes,
a Texas television reporter turned presidential imagemaker (Minutaglio
1999). Both had a keen eye for ways to present the Connecticut-born Bush
as a plainspoken westerner and the Vietnam War combat-evader as a determined, effective commander in chief. The Bush administration media
strategies, together with the approaches used by Bill Clinton and his team,
are examined in greater detail in the chapters that follow.

Spinner in Chief: An Overview

This first chapter focuses on the various ways administrations try to make
their views heard through the mass media, and to increase the chances
that the rest of the nation and the world will view political matters from
the same perspective as those at 1600 Pennsylvania Avenue. This chapter
surveys past writings on White House political communication and examines
past administration strategies in getting out the White House message. It
traces as well how presidents have coped with that rapidly changing media
environment.

Chapter 2 focuses on presidential efforts to use the media to build support for White House priorities on Capitol Hill. Many presidential initiatives,
particularly domestic policies such as Social Security and health-care reform,
never become law because of Congress' great interest—and differing views—
about those topics (Jacobs 2006; Skocpol 1997). This discussion of how the
executive branch tries to talk the legislative branch into doing the White
House's bidding includes an examination of presidential lobbying operations
and administration efforts to try to frame the news coverage in ways that can
help convince Congress to support White House proposals. Media strategies
designed to convince an increasingly reluctant Congress to "stay the course"
as casualties mount in Iraq, along with the failed efforts to build support
for Bush's Social Security reform and Clinton's health-care reform, are key
examples considered here. Presidents also have to sell their priorities within
a sometimes skeptical federal bureaucracy, and those promotional efforts
aimed at executive branch subordinates will also be examined here.

Chapter 3 turns to presidential efforts to seek public approval for White
House initiatives. If Congress hesitates to do as the president wishes, perhaps the public can be enlisted to persuade reluctant lawmakers to see
things as the White House does. All modern presidents have tried to use
the mass media to cultivate a close connection with citizens, if for no other
purpose than to use the public as leverage in the many legislative struggles
on Capitol Hill. But the sometimes slavish White House attempts to court

public opinion can create real problems for presidents, particularly when administrations promise more than they can deliver. White House media strategies tend to create a boom or bust cycle in public opinion, as incumbent presidents invariably disappoint (Lowi 1985). Incumbent presidents who have frustrated citizens eventually are replaced by new presidents who also overpromise and in turn fail to deliver on those inflated promises as the cycle continues. And contemporary 24/7 coverage in the many media outlets now operating can create even greater temptations to make too many promises and to increase the stakes when inflated expectations are deflated by actual events.

Chapter 4 focuses most directly on the new news media, the journalism of cable television, talk radio, and above all the Internet. These media outlets offer expanded and sometimes high-risk opportunities for presidential spin cycles. The many partisan outlets found online and on cable television can tempt presidents to segment their messages, offering centrist rhetoric for mainstream channels and a far more divisive message in channels used by more partisan news consumers. The new news media can cause problems for the White House as well. The more horizontal media environment sometimes allows individual bloggers to drive the national media agenda in ways that may undermine a president's message. So far, at least, the most effective users of the new news media are not presidents and their teams but rather the presidential candidates, and their efforts in 2004 and the early stages of the 2008 nomination season are examined here.

The fifth and final chapter focuses on the consequences for effective long-term publicly oriented lawmaking in the face of spin-dominant politics. The short-term marketing focus so common at the White House—worsened by the 24/7 nature of modern media—creates negative long-term policy consequences for the nation. The chapter examines ways to recognize and perhaps limit the dangers of White House spin. It also considers ways to improve political communication between the government and the public.

Chapter Two

Spinning Congress and the Rest of the Government

Persuasion (or Not) along Pennsylvania Avenue

The key power presidents have, Richard Neustadt (1990) wrote, is the power to persuade. Of course some people are more persuadable than others. Among the people presidents find most difficult to convince are members of Congress, who have long viewed themselves as part of a coequal branch of the federal government. Although the modern media environment helps presidents, substantial policy disagreements remain between Congress and the executive branch. Lawmakers on Capitol Hill are often unwilling to support presidential priorities, regardless of partisan loyalty or what reporters are saying about those initiatives. Even if a lawmaker considers the presidential proposal a good idea, he or she may still demand payback before actually voting for it. Presidents who want the support of a majority of lawmakers may find it necessary to amend the original plan, agree to support another initiative, or even undertake a presidential fund-raising visit to the districts of wavering lawmakers.

This give-and-take lawmaking exists regardless of the existing media technology, who is president, or how much attention is paid to any particular issue. For example, in order to get fellow Democrats to sign up for his first-term economic policies, Bill Clinton had to make many promises to members of his own party that weakened those plans (Woodward 1994). During 2005 and 2006, when the Republican Party controlled Congress, George W. Bush could not make a deal with fellow Republicans over his proposal to privatize a portion of Social Security (Jacobs 2006). Republicans worried that enacting the president's plan would hurt their own reelection prospects, and polls suggested they were probably correct (Confessore 2005). Media-focused presidential efforts to promote such policies as essential to the nation's future did not move Congress.

Lawmakers object to presidential policy initiatives for three main reasons: (1) they may view the proposal as a bad policy, (2) they may think the policy would hurt the lawmakers' political party, or (3) they may view the proposal as bad for individual members' reelection prospects. There is also another reason that sometimes comes into play: (4) lawmakers may view a presidential proposal as an effort to weaken Congress in its power struggles with the executive. This fourth justification is mainly relevant for measures that expand presidential authority in some fashion. Any one of these four reasons may be sufficient for a lawmaker to oppose a bill, so it is no wonder presidents find it difficult to be persuasive on Capitol Hill, despite their media advantage (Pfiffner 2006).

Bush's Social Security privatization plan is a good example of how difficult it can be for a president to persuade Congress. A Republican lawmaker would have rejected Bush's appeals if the representative believed at least one of the following: (1) the plan was bad for the country overall, (2) the Republican Party would be punished for the plan by losing the next presidential election, or (3) the individual representative fears that his or her own reelection would be hurt by angry senior citizens who feared any change to a system upon which many of them depend. Since senior citizens are a high turnout group, congressional support of Bush on this proposal might be politically risky. In fact, Bush himself did not really push a specific partial privatization plan until he was beyond the reach of the voters in his final term of office. He tried to sell it with predictions of the demise of entitlements and high-profile, stage-managed public appearances, but Bush's attempts to persuade lawmakers fell flat even though Republicans controlled both the House and the Senate at the time (Confessore 2005).

Other priority items have faced similar obstacles on Capitol Hill. Bill Clinton failed to persuade his party's legislative majority to support a health-care reform plan when the Democrats controlled Congress in the early 1990s. At the time, Democratic lawmakers worried they would be punished by middle-class voters with private insurance who worried that the quality of their own health care would suffer if tens of millions of previously uninsured Americans became covered by a government health-care plan (Skocpol 1997). Republicans scored huge gains in the 1994 midterm elections because Bill and Hillary Clinton could not persuade fellow Democrats to support the controversial proposal either; on that issue, the more effective media strategies were implemented by the plan's critics (Skocpol 1997).

The odds are long on Capitol Hill for presidents, even persuasive ones, seeking to change the status quo. This challenge is particularly daunting for domestic policy initiatives, an area in which members of Congress generally have great interest and find it easier to collect their own information. The differences between the president's ability to influence foreign and domestic policies are so great that scholars often speak of "two presidencies." Traditionally, three factors are used to explain this difference: (1) presidents have greater constitutional authority over foreign policy, (2) the executive branch can act more quickly in a crisis, and (3) Congress traditionally has deferred to the executive in international matters (Oldfield and Wildavsky 1989; Sullivan 1991). It appears there is also a fourth factor: domestic policy issues tend to be less dependent on information obtained by the executive branch, making it harder for a president to spin news coverage on such matters to the White House's advantage.

There are, of course, additional barriers to cooperation between the executive and legislative branches. Opposing parties often do battle with each other, demonstrated by the budget wars between Clinton and the Republican Congress of 1995–1996 along with Republican efforts to drive Clinton from office during the Clinton-Lewinsky impeachment saga of 1998–1999 (Blaney and Benoit 2001; Blumenthal 2003; Burnham 1996). The Democrat-led 110th Congress that took office in 2007 demonstrated that Bush became the next president to face the conflict often found during periods of closely divided party control of Congress (Schmitt 2007).

In addition to the electoral pressures Congressmembers face that may make them reluctant to cooperate, presidents hoping to talk Congress into supporting White House initiatives also have to navigate a complex, decentralized, and often slow-moving legislative system (Binder and Smith 1997). Influential committee chairs and subcommittee chairs can kill proposals quietly at a number of opportunities, mainly by holding up the measures in a committee or subcommittee. Party leaders can keep legislation from coming up for a vote. Any of these efforts can suffocate media coverage of an initiative, as a lack of action is hardly newsworthy.

More publicly, legislative majorities can kill proposals outright with floor votes that can embarrass presidents. In addition, individual senators possess the right to filibuster, a highly effective means of blocking legislation through the threat of unending debate that can stop all legislative action (Binder and Smith 1997). In practice, a Senate filibuster can be likened to a school bus with 100 sets of brakes—very easy to stop and very hard to keep moving.

Even if the House and Senate somehow manage to pass versions of a president's policy proposal, one other potential roadblock remains. If the versions are not identical—and there are often at least minor differences between the bills passed in one chamber and those in the other—the House and Senate need to reconcile the two measures through a conference committee. This committee, consisting of members of each chamber, offers a new set of hurdles to overcome before a bill goes to the president's desk. The slogging pace of legislative work can discourage news coverage, even this close to possible passage.

With so many political and structural obstacles on Capitol Hill, it is no wonder presidents often try to make the case for their policy preferences in the court of public opinion. Going public, or aggressive outreach by the administration to persuade citizens, is designed to pressure Congress to support White House priorities more readily (Kernell 2007). Although the strategy may not be all that effective, as discussed in Chapter 1, presidents look at the obstacles to success on Capitol Hill and conclude they need to use all available opportunities to promote their legislative agenda (Edwards 2003, 2006; Kernell 2007). Administrations figure that the media, critical though reporters may be, offer better opportunities to change the status quo than do more private approaches aimed at lawmakers.

This chapter looks at direct presidential persuasion on Capitol Hill, and the next chapter looks at presidential efforts to spin policies for citizens, often with the goal of influencing lawmakers indirectly. Since the publicly oriented approach is primarily citizen-directed, I'll save it for Chapter 3.

In this chapter, I focus on how presidents seek to persuade Congress directly. I examine military and foreign policy, toward which lawmakers tend to be receptive, and domestic matters, in which presidential appeals often fall on deaf ears. I look here at the strategies of recent presidents as they appeal to lawmakers, focusing on George W. Bush and Bill Clinton. In this chapter I look both at what presidents do and what they choose not to do as they sell their policies and their presidencies to the legislative branch. I also examine how Congress competes with the executive branch in the struggle for media attention, and how legislators can try to be heard over the president through media-oriented investigations, hearings, and even passage of bills the president opposes.

The Founders' Celebration of Conflict

The Founders designed a system that encourages political conflict, particularly between the executive and legislative branches. By pitting elected officials against each other, the Founders thought they had a remedy for the governmental tyranny so common in the monarchical regimes that ruled the world then (Carey 1989). The best way to secure the loyalty of the citizens, after all, was to govern with their best interests at the center of policymaking. This competition for public affections would keep the executive and the legislative branches estranged from each other, but presumably the citizens would benefit from the competitive public-interest lawmaking that would result (Carey 1989). Journalists also benefit from this competition, as the resulting conflicts give reporters much to write about. The Founders recognized that a centralized political system such as a monarchy can threaten individual liberties, and they willingly traded the efficiency of such a government for the bulwark against tyranny that comes from the separation of powers (Carey 1989). In addition, the Founders specifically shielded reporters from government censorship, once again demonstrating their interest in creating political institutions of limited power and influence (Carey 1989).

For modern presidents, this complex and combative political structure has its advantages and disadvantages. In parliamentary democracies such as the British one, the head of state is generally separate from the head of government, who often comes from the parliament itself. In the United States, the president exercises both of these functions. Presidents' approval ratings can be inflated or deflated by the dual roles as chief executive and as the "personification of the nation," particularly during a national crisis. At such times, citizens, lawmakers, and reporters all look to the White House for information and for reassurance—an ideal opportunity for describing the world from the administration's perspective.

This presidential agenda-setting advantage can help presidents secure passage of crucial legislation, particularly regarding military policy, during times of uncertainty (Polsky 2006). Defying a commander in chief during wartime can seem unpatriotic, if not disloyal, and an aggressive White House will do all it can to emphasize that interpretation as a way of maximizing legislative deference (Allen 2003). Although the old adage that politics stops at the water's edge no longer universally applies (if it ever did), recent presidents have great opportunities to shape foreign policy debates to their liking, given both their dominance of news coverage and their ability to control the release of secret information to Congress and public information to the country and the world (Entman 2004).

Even so, citizens often expect more of presidents than chief executives in a separated system of government can deliver, policywise (Lowi 1985). A president is not a prime minister who comes from parliament and rules a party apparatus devoted to supporting his or her policy program. The president's most powerful legislative weapon—the veto—is primarily a defensive one against an overreaching Congress. Other than being persuasive because of who they are, what they say, or how they compromise, presidents have limited ability to secure legislative victories when the nation is not in crisis. "This framework inhibits presidential leadership of Congress in an era when the public, the press, and to some extent the Congress itself expects and wants that leadership" (Wayne 2006, 60).

When Americans have selected their presidents over the past three decades, they have not turned to candidates with extensive congressional résumés. In fact, four of the nation's last five presidents never served in Congress: Jimmy Carter, Ronald Reagan, Bill Clinton, and George W. Bush had all been governors before being elected to the White House. The one president of the last five who had served in Congress was George H. W. Bush, who spent four years in the U.S. House, a fraction of the time he later served in the federal government as vice president, head of the Central Intelligence Agency, U.S. ambassador to China, and U.S. ambassador to the United Nations. Most recent presidents, in other words, have had to contend not only with structural barriers that limit a president's ability to govern but also with little if any actual experience with Congress.

Battles between the branches are not new. Throughout U.S. history, presidents struggled with hostile Congresses. Even George Washington fought with the first Congresses over access to executive information and over his judicial appointees (Wayne 2006). By the end of the nineteenth century, political scientist and future president Woodrow Wilson (1885) felt confident in describing the U.S. political system as one dominated by the legislative branch. Few scholars today would make such a claim, particularly given the mass media focus on the White House.

Presidential Spin and Policymaking

President Bush's political fortunes, and with them his ability to persuade, have risen and fallen greatly depending on the circumstances, as shown in Table 2.1. The president's highest approval ratings in surveys conducted for the *Washington Post* came in the wake of 9/11, when the United States experienced a "rally 'round the flag" effect following the terrorist attacks. Before the attacks, just over half of the population approved of the job Bush was doing. Shortly afterward, more than nine out of ten Americans spoke favorably about his performance (Balz and Cohen 2007). Bush's approval ratings remained high, and there was an additional upward approval spike around the time of the Iraq War, which started in March 2003. Bush's numbers were much more negative during his second term, and his approval rating failed to reach 50 percent even once during the year before the 2006 midterm elections. The lowest approval rating in the six years of surveys (31

Table 2.1 Public Opinion of President Bush, 2001–2008

Do you approve or disapprove of the way George W. Bush is handling his job as president? Do you approve/disapprove strongly or somewhat?

		Approve			Disapprove		No Opinion
	Net	Strongly	Somewhat	Net	Strongly	Somewhat	
5/11/08	31	15	16	66	14	52	2
4/13/08	33	16	17	64	15	49	2
3/2/08	32	15	17	66	16	50	2
2/1/08	33	17	16	65	14	51	2
1/12/08	32	16	16	66	15	51	2
12/9/07	33	17	16	64	14	50	3
11/1/07	33	17	16	64	13	50	3
9/30/07	33	15	18	64	14	49	3
9/7/07	33	16	17	64	15	49	3
7/21/07	33	16	17	65	13	52	2
6/1/07	35	17	18	62	16	46	3
4/15/07	35	17	18	62	14	49	2
2/25/07	36	19	17	62	12	49	2
1/19/07	33	17	16	65	14	51	2
12/11/06	36	18	18	62	13	49	2
11/4/06	40	24	16	57	12	46	2
10/22/06	37	21	16	60	15	45	3
10/8/06	39	23	16	60	12	48	1
9/7/06	42	24	18	55	12	43	3
8/6/06	40	23	17	58	12	46	2
6/25/06	38	20	18	60	12	48	2
5/15/06	33	17	16	65	18	47	2
4/9/06	38	20	18	60	13	47	1
3/5/06	41	24	17	58	14	44	1
1/26/06	42	25	18	56	14	42	2
1/8/06	46	29	17	52	13	39	2
12/18/05	47	29	17	52	12	40	1
11/2/05	39	20	18	60	10	17	1
10/29/05	39	22	17	58	13	45	3
9/11/05	42	27	15	57	12	45	1
8/28/05	45	27	18	53	12	41	2
6/26/05	48	27	21	51	11	40	1
6/5/05	48	27	21	52	14	38	1
4/24/05	47	25	22	50	13	38	3
3/13/05	50	31	19	48	11	37	3
1/31/05	50	34	15	45	11	34	5
1/16/05	52	33	19	46	11	35	2
12/19/04	48	27	21	49	12	38	2
10/20/04	50	30	20	46	11	35	4
10/17/04 LV	54	35	19	45	9	36	2
10/16/04 LV	54	35	19	44	10	34	2
10/15/04 LV	54	35	19	44	10	34	2

(continues)

Table 2.1 (continued)

	Approve			Disapprove			No Opinion
	Net	Strongly	Somewhat	Net	Strongly	Somewhat	
10/3/04 LV	53	36	17	46	11	34	1
9/26/04	50	33	18	45	13	32	5
9/8/04	52	35	17	43	11	32	5
8/29/04	50	31	19	47	13	34	3
8/1/04	47	28	18	49	13	36	5
7/25/04	50	32	19	47	13	34	3
7/11/04	48	31	17	50	11	39	2
6/20/04	47	30	17	51	13	39	1
5/23/04	47	31	17	50	14	36	3
4/18/04	51	33	18	47	13	34	1
3/7/04	50	32	18	48	12	36	2
2/11/04	50	30	21	47	14	34	2
1/18/04	58	35	24	40	9	30	2
12/21/03	59	39	21	38	15	23	3
12/14/03	57	37	20	39	10	29	5
12/7/03	53	32	21	40	13	27	7
11/16/03	57	34	23	39	11	28	4
10/29/03	56	30	26	42	13	29	2
10/13/03	53	33	20	43	13	29	4
9/30/03	54	34	20	44	15	29	2
9/13/03	58	35	23	40	14	27	2
9/7/03	56	34	22	41	13	28	4
8/11/03	59	37	22	37	14	23	4
7/10/03	59	35	24	38	13	25	3
6/22/03	68	45	23	29	11	18	4
4/30/03	71	50	22	26	17	9	3
4/16/03	74	52	22	23	9	14	3
4/9/03	77	58	19	20	6	14	4
4/3/03	71	54	16	25	7	19	4
3/23/03	68	NA	NA	27	NA	NA	4
3/20/03	67	NA	NA	28	NA	NA	5
3/2/03	62	38	23	35	13	22	4
2/23/03	60	NA	NA	34	NA	NA	6
2/9/03	64	42	21	34	14	20	3
2/1/03	62	41	21	34	13	22	4
1/28/03	62	43	19	36	13	23	2
1/27/03	59	39	21	37	15	22	4
1/20/03	59	36	23	38	16	22	2
12/15/02	66	37	28	32	12	20	2
11/4/02 LV	67	45	23	31	12	20	1
11/3/02 LV	67	45	22	32	12	20	1
11/2/02 LV	67	47	20	32	9	23	1
10/27/02	67	39	28	29	13	16	4

(continues)

In the immediate aftermath of 9/11, Bush encouraged lawmakers and citizens to think of the terrorist attacks as the Pearl Harbor of the twenty-first century. With the cameras rolling, Bush compared Osama bin Laden to Hitler and vowed the Taliban leader would be brought to justice "dead or alive," just like in the "wanted" posters of the Old West. The plainspoken Texan seemed to be taking on the straight-shooting sheriff role that in the movies once might have been played by John Wayne (Frum 2003). Bush's combative sound bites during this period were like catnip to confrontation-loving reporters.

The Bush presidency was transformed overnight by 9/11 (Pfiffner 2004a, 2004b). Bush did not suddenly become twice as good a president in the immediate aftermath of the terrorist attacks, but Americans did become more than twice as scared after that fateful day. As shown in Table 2.1, approval of Bush stood at 55 percent just before the attacks, rising to a high of 92 percent a month after 9/11. Bush's unimpressive early remarks during the first uncertain hours after the attacks gave way to a confident, aggressive president speaking to rescue workers in Lower Manhattan a few days later (Frum 2003). For most Americans, lingering questions about Bush's legitimacy given Florida voting irregularities in 2000 vanished as the Twin Towers fell (Pfiffner 2004a, 2004b).

The intense citizen reactions to 9/11, which secured enough public approval for Congress to authorize the invasion of Iraq, marked an unusual departure from norms of substantial citizen discontent and skepticism with government measured in U.S. public opinion (Farnsworth 2003a). U.S. public opinion tends not to support international interventions, and during the dozen years between the end of the cold war and 9/11, presidents encountered considerable public resistance to peace-keeping missions (Mermin 1997). A genocide in Rwanda drew little U.S. response as the Clinton administration struggled not to define the ethnic killings as "genocide," so it could justify remaining largely on the sidelines (Power 2002) In response to genocide and ethnic cleansing in the Balkans, in 1999 the U.S. military and NATO launched a 33,000 sortie bombing campaign on Serbia, the largest U.S. military response during the Clinton years (L. Berman and Goldman 1996; W. Berman 2001; Goldman and L. Berman 2000). Even so, Congress expressed little support for interventions in these crises (W. Berman 2001).

Politicizing Patriotism

Presidential appeals to patriotism can garner public support for policy action. Americans are a very patriotic people, with surveys showing extremely positive feelings of support for the U.S. political system and for the country's place in the world (Brooks 2006; Farnsworth 2003b). In fact, Americans are far more inclined to see their nation as a positive force in the world than are citizens of other countries. In a June 2003 poll conducted by the BBC, 80 percent of Americans said they believed the U.S. military presence around the world contributed to international peace and security (Brooks 2006). Citizens of even the closest U.S. ally nations felt quite differently: only 49 percent of people in the United Kingdom and 48 percent of Canadians agreed with that statement (Brooks 2006, 14).

Bush's post-9/11 presidency has been marked by considerable legislative branch deference on matters that would otherwise have been nearly impossible to pass, including the Iraq Resolution of 2002 and the PATRIOT Act of 2001 (Baker 2002; Kassop 2003; Lindsay 2003). The antiterrorism measures in particular helped the executive branch expand presidential prerogatives that had been undermined by Watergate, the Iran-Contra scandal, and the Clinton impeachment (Baker 2002; Farnsworth and Lichter 2006a).

The change that 9/11 caused in executive-legislative relations was notable but not unprecedented. The foreign policy pendulum of power has shifted back and forth between Congress and the president many times over the course of U.S. history. The reason for this ebb and flow does not lie in the Constitution. The constitutional allocation of foreign policy powers, which gives important authority both to Congress and to the president, has not changed since it was drafted. Rather, the answer lies in politics. How aggressively Congress exercises its foreign policy powers turns on the critical questions of whether Americans see the country as threatened or secure, and whether the president's policies are succeeding or failing (Lindsay 2003, 531).

Congressional elections occur at two-year intervals, and one of the ways presidents can maximize their influence over Congress is to schedule votes on military action right before lawmakers themselves face the voters. Not all presidents choose to mix electoral politics and military decisionmaking, however. President George H. W. Bush waited until after the 1990 midterm elections before he asked lawmakers to authorize military action to liberate Kuwait (Lindsay 2003).

But George W. Bush had none of his father's commitment to thoughtful lawmaking and concern for long-term consequences. The second President Bush made the potential Iraq War the pivotal issue in the 2002 midterm elections. Congress must, Bush insisted in speeches on behalf of Republican candidates, make a decision on whether to authorize force before the election. Because the 2002 elections occurred only fourteen months after 9/11, Bush's claims that Saddam Hussein was connected to those terrorist attacks and that he was building a nuclear weapons program were powerful arguments. Also, because the Pentagon and the CIA are part of the executive branch, little information emerged to undermine the president's story—even though we later learned that many experts in government objected to the case the president was making (Entman 2004). Bush and his fellow Republicans were able to attack as soft on defense those Democrats who objected or even hesitated to pass Bush's resolution (Fisher 2004). From a military standpoint, there was little need to rush the vote. Bush did not start the war until March 2003, more than four months after the 2002 midterms. From a political standpoint, forcing a preelection vote helped Bush and the GOP defeat some Democratic incumbents.

The second President Bush likewise used the war in Iraq and appeals to patriotism to secure his own reelection in 2004, regularly campaigning at rallies held with the troops during that campaign (Ceaser and Busch 2005). The vacillations of U.S. Senator John Kerry (D-MA), the 2004 Democratic nominee, on how he felt about the war he had earlier voted to authorize helped Bush win a second term (Easton et al. 2004). But there are limits to spin, particularly over time. The undeniable problems of the Iraq occupation made the war a negative factor for Republicans in the midterm elections two years later (Broder 2006; Milkis 2006).

Control the Information Flow

After the Democrats took control of Congress in 2007, Bush's unwillingness to release information to the legislative branch intensified. The Justice Department refused after the 2006 elections to release two secret documents describing CIA interrogation techniques on individuals suspected of terrorist connections. U.S. Senator Patrick Leahy (D-VT), the new chair of the Senate Judiciary Committee, vowed to use the committee's subpoena power to get the information he said was necessary for the Senate to evaluate the incarcerations and interrogations (Schmitt 2007). The Justice Department also stonewalled on providing evidence and testimony regarding a controversial plan to fire several U.S. attorneys for not being sufficiently pro Bush (Johnston and Lipton 2007).

During Bush's first six years in office, his administration worked diligently to control what the legislative branch, reporters, and the public knew by refusing to release information requested by Congress, particularly requests from Democrats. Although congressional committees can force the administration to release information via subpoena, Republican majorities generally blocked efforts by Democrats to compel the Republican White House to release documents (Mann and Ornstein 2006). Subpoenas issued by the new Democratic congressional majorities in 2007 were routinely ignored by the administration, claiming expansive claims of executive privilege (Lichtblau 2007).

Even so, whistle-blowers sometimes emerge to draw attention to the Bush administration's deceit. In one notable case, a Medicare official went public about pressure he received from the Bush administration to provide Congress low estimates of the projected costs of the prescription drug benefit in order to secure its passage (Pear and Stolberg 2004). In another, John DiIulio, hired by the Bush administration to run its faith-based initiatives program, complained after leaving the administration that the Bush team was so obsessed with controlling the message that they were ignorant of and unconcerned with the substance of what they were talking about. "On social policy and related issues, the lack of even basic policy knowledge, and the only casual interest in knowing more, was somewhat breathtaking: discussions by fairly senior people who meant Medicaid but were talking Medicare, near-instant shifts from discussing any actual policy pros and cons to discussing political communication, media strategy, et cetera" (quoted in Mucciaroni and Quirk 2004, 163).

The administration's many problems in managing the Iraqi occupation triggered a number of leaks by top administration officials blaming each other for the problems as well as finger-pointing books blaming others for the problems (Bremer 2006; Eggen 2008; Feith 2008; Sanchez and Phillips 2008; Woodward 2006). But perhaps the most damaging book was written by former White House press secretary Scott McClellan (2008), a longtime member of the Bush inner circle; the book described the political propaganda campaign he said he helped engineer to promote the Iraq War.

Silence and/or Discredit the Critics

If the president says there is danger, that is a major news story, and few members of Congress are willing to stand up and say "I don't think so!" The president has access to far more national security information than does any lawmaker, putting a senator or a representative at a great disadvantage if he or she wants to challenge the White House over an alleged military threat. Although there were a few voices in Congress arguing against going to war in Vietnam and Iraq, they were largely voices crying in the wilderness. Antiwar lawmakers get little media attention given the president's advantage in news coverage, and they often face blistering attacks from political rivals if they do speak up.

Since military policy debates are often shaped by what administration officials say, critical media coverage of the president's preferred policy approach is limited if the White House can keep its critics silent (Entman 2004). U.S. Senator Max Cleland (D-GA), a skeptic of Bush's decision to wage war in Iraq before capturing Osama bin Laden, was defeated in 2002 in a campaign marked by advertising that featured Cleland's face morphing into that of bin Laden, the mastermind of the 9/11 attacks. Cleland, who lost his legs as a soldier in Vietnam, was replaced by Senator Saxby Chambliss (R-GA), a hawk in his public statements but not so in his deeds. Chambliss, like Bush and Cheney, avoided military service in Vietnam as a young man (Halbfinger 2002).

Cleland's defeat haunted the Democrats for years. Even as the number of U.S. casualties in Iraq continued to climb, Democrats in Congress hesitated to challenge Bush directly about the war. U.S. Representative John Murtha (D-PA), a Vietnam veteran who built a career as a pro-Pentagon legislator, publicly turned against the Iraq War in 2005. Despite his longtime hawk credentials, Murtha likewise was attacked by Cheney and others as insufficiently supportive of the troops (Bumiller 2005b; Sanger 2005). But Murtha represented a safe district, and weathered the storm. When the Democrats took over the House in 2007, Murtha became chair of the House Appropriations Committee, one of the most powerful positions in Congress.

Lawmakers are not the only critics the Bush administration sought to silence. Before the Iraq War, one of the major Bush administration claims about Iraq was that Saddam Hussein was obtaining nuclear processing material, known as "yellow cake," from Niger. An investigation in Africa by former U.S. Ambassador Joe Wilson determined that the claims were bogus, and Wilson went public with his findings in a *New York Times* column. A few days later, conservative columnist Robert Novak, a favorite of the Bush White House, quoted unnamed administration officials dismissing Wilson's claim by suggesting his trip was really a product of nepotism that involved his wife, Valerie Plame, a CIA officer (Johnston and Rutenberg 2007; Shane 2007c).

Since Plame had worked undercover, the public disclosure of her CIA employment both violated federal law and put the lives of Plame's Middle East contacts at risk. It would also discourage potential CIA "assets" from working with undercover agents abroad in the future. Novak said he did not know Plame was an undercover agent, and he was not charged in the incident. Scooter Libby, a top Cheney aide, was indicted for perjury in the matter. Testimony in Libby's trial revealed a great deal about Cheney's and Libby's efforts to influence Washington reporters and to discredit Wilson by spinning off-the-record tales to favored reporters (Johnston and Rutenberg 2007; Shane 2007c). Libby was convicted, but Bush commuted his thirty-month prison term, leaving Libby with a $250,000 fine but no jail time (Shane and Lewis 2007). Bush's action, just short of a presidential pardon, eliminated the possibility that Republican loyalist Libby would decide to testify against Cheney or Bush in exchange for a reduced prison sentence.

Even generals worried about staying in the good graces of the Bush administration. Shortly before the Iraq War started, Army Chief of Staff General Eric Shinseki told Congress that the occupation of Iraq would require at least 300,000 troops, roughly twice the number the Bush administration said was necessary (Shanker 2007). For his honest assessment—required by law in congressional testimony—Shinseki was "permitted" to retire early

(Shanker 2007). His career-ending honesty sent a clear message to generals: if they wanted to keep stars on their shoulders they would be wise to keep their doubts and their professional good judgment to themselves. But as the occupation soured, even the risk of becoming the next Shinseki was not enough to keep the generals quiet. In early 2007, when the Bush administration was selling a proposed "surge" in the number of troops—something opposed by many of the U.S. Army's top commanders—the generals who expressed doubts were replaced by more compliant voices (Rutenberg, Sanger, and Gordon 2007).

Although presidents should rely upon generals who agree with the administration's policy—civilian control of the military, after all, is a key component of a free nation—Congress also has a right to acquire honest assessments from the military commanders called to testify about a pending or ongoing war. Bush's rejection of prewar military advice demonstrated that he was not as committed to following the recommendations of the generals as he had claimed. For Bush, winning the war of spin on Iraq seems to be at least as important as finding out what the generals honestly think about the war itself.

Discredit Reporters, Too

Attacking the messenger is an approach frequently employed by the Bush White House against reporters (Auletta 2004). Indeed, the rise of the Internet has given the administration new vehicles—some located within the ranks of the media—to attack reporters seen as too critical of the administration's perspective. (The Internet-oriented aspects of this phenomenon will be discussed in Chapter 4). Particular reporters are singled out for harsh criticism; sometimes the give-and-take of a press briefing can descend to personal attacks.

The White House press room is a place where reporters and administration officials do battle over how to frame stories. The stakes are high, and the competition intense. Reporters who anger the president or the press secretary can be punished in visible ways—presidents can grant interviews with more supportive journalists, for example, and administrations can leak information to reporters with a track record of positive coverage (Kurtz 1994, 1998). An example of this approach was the Bush administration's use of Judith Miller, a national security correspondent for the *New York Times* and a favored conduit for information that the Bush team wanted to make public to help build the case for the Iraq War. A subsequent internal *Times* investigation condemned the paper's performance, saying reporters and editors did not scrutinize the Bush administration's claims aggressively enough (Kurtz 2007d; Orkent 2004).

Journalists have a tough balancing act. Reporters too close to their sources do their readers a disservice by not being critical enough of the information they receive (Kurtz 2007d). Reporters who are too critical of their sources tend not to have sources and may not end up with the journalistic scoops that keep editors happy. In other words, if White House correspondents lend too sympathetic an ear to the president's critics, they may face White House retaliation. The declining productivity of a reporter getting the brush-off from the administration may mean that the reporter may lose a plum White House reporting job (Kurtz 1994).

Sources play favorites, and will tell their tales to the reporters most willing to view the world through the same lenses that the sources themselves use. Playing favorites with journalists is a tempting strategy for the White House in the tug of war with reporters over how to define and describe news developments. If the *Washington Post* seems to the Bush administration to be too hostile, the White House may leak exclusives to a competing news outlet such as the *Wall Street Journal*. It is an old problem in journalism that the people willing to talk to reporters are likely to be treated kindly by those reporters. The wide-ranging media sources present in today's multimedia, online environment make it even easier for government officials to play favorites, taking care of the most progovernment reporters (Mooney 2004).

The "Fait Accompli"

Another way for presidents to work their will over Congress in military policy is to act unilaterally so that the deed is done before Congress can debate and vote on a controversial presidential initiative. Moving quickly also forestalls much media coverage of a topic, since reporters often judge the newsworthiness of a topic by what Congress says about it. That way, lawmakers must either support the president's deployment after the fact or face charges that they failed to support troops already in harm's way. Two centuries ago, Thomas Jefferson sent the U.S. Navy to the Barbary Coast to deal with seized U.S. ships, and he sought to mollify congressional critics by describing the deployment as a defensive action (Polsky 2006). A hundred years later, Theodore Roosevelt sent a navy fleet halfway around the world and dared Congress to refuse to pay for its return (Polsky 2006).

George W. Bush used the same "fait accompli" approach to forestall opposition to his escalation of the Iraq War in January 2007. As the new Democratic majorities in Congress began to peel off Republican congressional support for the president's proposed troop "surge," Bush increased the size of the force in Iraq before Congress could vote on the matter (Pelofsky 2007). When Democrats accused Bush of trying to block congressional decisionmaking, the White House reacted angrily.

The president's plan drew ire from Democrats who saw the November 2006 elections as a mandate to change course in Iraq. House Speaker Nancy Pelosi (D-CA) lashed out in an *ABC News* interview, saying that Bush had "dug a hole so deep he can't even see the light on this" and calling the buildup "a stark blunder."

"The president knows that because the troops are in harm's way, that we won't cut off the resources," Pelosi told ABC. "That's why he's moving so quickly to put them in harm's way, but we will hold the president accountable. He has to answer for his war."

White House officials bristled at Pelosi's comments, with spokeswoman Dana Perino calling them "poisonous." "I think questioning the president's motivations and suggesting that he, for some political reason, is rushing troops into harm's way, is not appropriate, it is not correct, and it is unfortunate because we do have troops in harm's way," Perino said (White 2007b).

Select the Best Salesperson with the Best Background

The best salesperson for military matters is usually the commander in chief. No other political figure can draw the country together in a crisis like a president can. For the past several decades, presidents have relied heavily on televised speeches to justify their proposed actions. John F. Kennedy's October 1962 speeches to the nation during the Cuban Missile Crisis are powerful examples of how presidents can dominate the global media discourse, as well as how effective presidential communication can be in securing public support in a crisis (Kennedy 1969; Kernell 2007).

Subsequent presidents followed Kennedy's example. Reagan, Clinton, and George W. Bush were particularly reliant on national addresses to explain their policies. For a made-for-television event, nothing can beat a presidential State of the Union speech—the most anticipated presidential appearance of the year. Bush used his 2002 State of the Union speech to identify an "axis of evil" composed of Iran, Iraq, and North Korea to convince Congress to agree to attack Iraq (Frum 2003). Clinton used his 1998 speech to demonstrate that he was still president and would govern despite Republican efforts to ruin him over the Clinton-Lewinsky matter (Klein 2002). And Reagan used his speeches effectively to build support for his tax cuts, a popular policy in the short term but one that led to dramatically worsened deficits in subsequent years (Ceaser 1988; Suskind 2004).

Don't Always Use the President

But chief executives are not always the best messengers. Secretary of State Colin Powell, for example, was the ideal delegate to make the difficult sell to the United Nations that the United States should invade Iraq in 2003. Powell's military career, his moderate Republican credentials, and his high public approval ratings made him seem a far better choice than Bush to urge the United Nations to unite against Iraq. Powell also tended to be treated gently by reporters (Farnsworth and Lichter 2006a). Although Powell was probably more persuasive than any other administration figure would have been, key members of the UN Security Council—most notably Russia, China, and France—were not convinced, and objected to the U.S. invasion plans. Those three nations wanted to give UN inspectors more time to uncover the weapons of mass destruction (WMD) programs Bush and Powell claimed were under way in Iraq, but the U.S. government wanted to have the United Nations pull the inspectors out and start the invasion right away. (As of this writing, more than five years after the U.S.-led invasion began, the Bush administration has been unable to prove its prewar claims that Saddam Hussein had a WMD program in 2003 or that the Iraqi dictator was connected to the 9/11 attacks on the United States.) Bush has said he was surprised that no WMD evidence was found, but he did not apologize for leading the United States into a war on what turned out to be false pretenses (Milbank 2003).

By 2007, when Bush, Cheney, and the U.S. military leaders had been thoroughly discredited by their errors in Iraq, the president turned to a new Iraq commander, General David Petraeus, to try to build support on Capitol Hill for Bush's troop surge plan (Baker 2007). Bush had already learned earlier in the new legislative term that his personal appeals were ineffective before Congress and the public (Baker 2007). So he sent General Petraeus—a new media messenger—to sell the policy.

Other presidents also have maximized their chances of political success by delegating highly respected aides to handle sensitive matters. Harry Truman predicted that Republicans in Congress would reject his plans for a massive influx of aid to Europe, so he dispatched General George Marshall to Capitol Hill to lobby for what came to be known as the Marshall Plan (McCullough 1993). As Truman famously observed, a lot can be done in Washington if you let someone else take the credit (McCullough 1993).

Maximize the Estimated Threat

Bush took World War II as his media image for the war on terror. The terrorist attacks of 9/11 were presented as the Pearl Harbor of a new generation. The term *axis of evil* recalls the Axis powers of World War II. By comparing Iraq, Iran, and North Korea to Nazi Germany, Japan, and Italy, Bush hoped to recall the time when Americans came together in rare unity to defeat the enemies. The administration routinely portrayed Bush's goals as crises in order to maximize both the amount of news coverage and the chances that Bush's preferences would be followed (VandeHei 2005).

By maximizing the notion of threat, the Bush administration was able to secure passage of a raft of legislation that expanded presidential power, most notably the PATRIOT Act (Shane and Liptak 2006). Even when Bush's approval ratings fell below 40 percent in 2006, the commander in chief's ability to dominate the legislative branch on war measures remained intact. In September 2006, two months before Democrats won control of both houses of Congress, the House and Senate gave Bush permission to suspend habeas corpus, and effectively authorized the harsh interrogation techniques employed earlier in the war (Shane and Liptak 2006). Despite their complaints while in the minority, Democratic majorities continued to defer to executive power on wiretapping and spying during 2007, fearing the retaliation of even a deeply unpopular president (Risen and Lichtblau 2007).

When the Bush administration didn't like the lukewarm assessments it was getting from the CIA in the months before the Iraq War, Cheney was dispatched repeatedly to the agency's headquarters to make sure that allegedly objective intelligence assessments were adjusted dramatically upward to hype the alleged Iraqi threat (Johnston 2004). As the quick combat victory in Iraq gave way to a contentious Iraqi resistance campaign, Cheney was frequently used before conservative audiences to justify the administration's decisions on Iraq and to attack as disloyal the Democrats who disagreed with the Bush team (Bumiller 2005b; Milbank and Pincus 2003).

Even as the occupation of Iraq soured, the Bush administration continued to argue that improvement was under way. Progress was not apparent, the White House said, because a biased anti-Bush media was preventing Americans from seeing the truth (Rutenberg 2006). But even the White House was working to step back from its earlier pronouncements, and by 2007 had shifted to warning of the catastrophe that would befall Iraq if U.S. troops left rather than the progress that would occur if the troops remained (Rutenberg, Stolberg, and Mazzetti 2007).

Maximize the Estimated Benefits

For the price of what the administration said would be one small, brief, and relatively inexpensive war, lawmakers were told, Saddam Hussein's WMDs—already well under development, the Bush administration said—would never strike the United States (Campbell 2004a, 2004b). The financial costs would be minimal, the Bush administration promised, and even those expenses would be covered by Iraqi oil revenues (Gordon 2003; Rieff 2003; Webb 2003). After a quick occupation, Bush predicted Iraq would hold free elections and the country would rapidly become a peaceful, stable one thankful for U.S. assistance. The nation then would serve as a model of democracy that would be copied by other Muslim nations across the Middle East.

Presidents often use what turned out be rose-colored scenarios to justify controversial measures. The Reagan tax cuts of 1981 and George W. Bush tax cuts of 2001 and 2003 were sold to Congress and the public with estimates of economic growth and revenue expansion that turned out to be false (Quirk 2006). Critics charged that Clinton also used unrealistically optimistic assumptions to assess the projected costs of the president's 1994 health insurance bill (Skocpol 1997). One might note, however, that the stakes are higher when the rosy scenario in question relates to soldiers' lives rather than budget policy. Ironically, though, the media's ability to get to the bottom of administration claims is severely limited in military matters (Entman 2004).

Minimize the Costs

Although Bush may have wanted Americans to think that the war on terror was like World War II, Americans were not expected by him to sacrifice like our grandparents and great grandparents did. During World War II, in addition to the military draft, citizens endured great hardships, including the rationing of necessities like meat, butter, shoes, and gasoline. Patriotic citizens bought war bonds to finance the struggle, and they willingly submitted to curfews. For years, Americans lived without new cars and new appliances as all available industrial production was diverted to the manufacture of war materials. Households even saved grease from kitchen stoves to help with ammunition production (Burns and Dunn 2001; Goodwin 1994).

After 9/11, there were no similar calls for sacrifice. Instead, Bush said Americans should do their patriotic duty and go shopping. The president proposed no draft, no rationing, no call even to reduce one's driving through carpools or mass transit—even though U.S. reliance on oil from the Middle East undermined national security and enriched those who would do (and did) great harm to the United States. Bush did not even propose reversing his tax cuts of 2001 to pay for the war. Those tax cuts—which mostly benefited those making over $200,000 a year—were untouchable even though Bush repeatedly said the Iraq War was comparable in importance to the fight against the Nazis sixty years earlier (Campbell 2004b; Quirk 2006). Soon the Bush administration was running record deficits, even though Bush had been the only president in more than three decades to have inherited a balanced budget from his predecessor (Weisman 2002). In fact, the Bush administration asked for and received additional tax cuts after 9/11, and the costs of the "war on terror" mounted (Sinclair 2008).

The Bush administration argued that the war on terror was equivalent to World War II in terms of the magnitude of the threat and the need to defer to presidential leadership. The administration's policies demonstrated that the new war was even worse than World War II in terms of the necessary limitations on civil liberties. But Bush made sure that the war on terror was nothing like World War II in terms of the financial price most Americans would have to pay, at least during the short term. For families with loved ones in the military, of course, the war became anything but costless or business as usual.

Presidential rhetoric and administration claims that connected the Iraq War to 9/11 were found to be false, and the occupation of Iraq turned out to be much bloodier and far, far more expensive than Bush's team had predicted. The "coalition of the willing," it turned out, was only so willing. More than 80 percent of the troops deployed in the war and more than 90 percent of the allied combat deaths in this war have been American (Fisher 2006; McLean 2004). As time passed, key allies left the coalition. Voters in Spain and Italy threw out the conservative governments that had joined Bush in Iraq and elected new governments that pledged to get their troops out of Iraq (Fisher 2006; McLean 2004). The United Kingdom also reduced its force by roughly half during 2007.

Another way to hide the true costs of the war from the public was by outsourcing many traditional military functions—including food service, supply transport, and even jail management and prisoner interrogation— to private contractors. This transfer of duties traditionally handled by the military reduces the stated number of troops deployed. The government can also keep the total effective deployment a secret, since the White House refuses to say how many private contractors are working in Iraq because of national security concerns. In addition, the behavior of private contractors is not subject to the same scrutiny as that of uniformed military personnel, providing yet another mechanism to limit public disclosure of government activity (Broder 2007).

The true financial costs of the war were obscured through the use of these private contractors. Budget figures show that the amount of money paid for all government contracting doubled during the Bush presidency, up to a total of roughly $400 billion by 2007 (Shane and Nixon 2007). The vast majority of that increase probably went to the Iraq War, but the government refused to release specifics on national security grounds (Shane and Nixon 2007).

Pick Fights the United States Can Win Quickly

The Powell military doctrine employed during the first Persian Gulf War called for massive troop deployments as a way of minimizing casualties. The military force that liberated Kuwait in 1991—roughly 400,000 strong—was comparable in size to the allied force that went ashore at Normandy in World

War II. The planning for the 1991 Persian Gulf War was designed with a specific, limited objective in mind—driving Iraqi forces from Kuwait. It was not designed to topple Saddam Hussein and occupy the whole of Iraq, though of course if the Iraqi dictator fell from power as a result of the humiliating 1991 defeat there would be no tears shed in Washington.

The 1991 Persian Gulf War was a departure from many of the military activities of the post-Vietnam era, which placed a premium on easily secured targets that did not involve such major troop movements. Shortly after barracks of U.S. Marines were blown up in Lebanon, Ronald Reagan spun public attention away from the disaster by "liberating" Grenada, a tiny island thought to face a Marxist threat. The photographs of U.S. citizens returning from the island nation and kissing the ground on their return helped turn people's attention away from the devastating loss in Lebanon and helped promote Reagan's credentials as commander in chief (Entman 2004). Although Reagan's rhetoric was heated—particularly where communism was concerned—his offensive military actions were modest in scope.

Bill Clinton also favored modest military actions—perhaps as a result of the controversies surrounding how he avoided military service during the Vietnam years (Ceaser and Busch 1993). Clinton promised not to use ground troops in Kosovo, a pragmatic response given congressional opposition to such a step. In his final days in office, Clinton sent warships to Haiti to pressure a military junta to step down, and it did so when the U.S. Navy sailed into Port-au-Prince (Polsky 2006).

At first George W. Bush followed the lead of Reagan and Clinton, even after 9/11. In Afghanistan, a relatively small U.S. force assisted a rebel group that engaged in most of the fighting that drove the Taliban from power. The U.S. military provided money, supplies, intelligence, and above all air support for the anti-Taliban forces but put few U.S. troops at risk in the early stages, U.S. officials along with NATO allies helped support the new Afghan government, and the United States soon turned its focus to Iraq without rebuilding the infrastructure it had destroyed in Afghanistan as the Bush administration had promised Iraq, of course, was no Afghanistan. The 200,000 troops deployed in Iraq were roughly half the number used to achieve George H. W. Bush's far more modest goal—the liberation of Kuwait—a dozen years earlier. The Iraqi Army was no match for the U.S. military, but the Vietnam War—as well as the Afghan resistance against the occupying Soviet Army during the 1980s—had demonstrated that guerilla tactics can be effective in wearing down a large occupation army.

When he ran for president in 2000, George W. Bush said he was "not into nation building." Yet as president, Bush sought to redesign nations in the Middle East as if he were the successor of Woodrow Wilson, who tried to reshape Europe after World War I. Bush's efforts to redesign Iraq have become increasingly unpopular in the United States, and have triggered continuing high levels of sectarian violence overseas (Balz and Cohen 2007; Burns and Tavernise 2007).

The Importance of Word Selection and Definition

When does a civil war become a civil war? The Bush administration argued that the media should not say Iraq was fighting a civil war before the Bush administration was ready to use that term. As Iraq descended ever deeper into sectarian violence in 2006, the Bush administration insisted what was occurring was not a civil war. For a long time, administration assertions helped keep that word out of news stories.

When is torture properly called torture? Although President Bush said the U.S. military did not torture its prisoners, Bush refused to define the term publicly. When Congress passed a law banning torture, Bush signed it and said the U.S. government would not torture—but again, as he defined the word (Shane and Liptak 2006; Zernike 2006). The administration again refused to state publicly what constitutes torture, and even key allies such as the United Kingdom fault the United States for continuing to torture suspects as it did at Abu Ghraib and elsewhere (Bonner and Perlez 2007).

The Bush administration originally described the military action in Iraq as "liberation." This term, of course, accurately reflected the reality of Saddam Hussein's bloody rule in Iraq, and recalled, as Bush often chose to do, World War II imagery. Throughout most of the first four years of the occupation, Bush rejected comparisons between Iraq and Vietnam, arguing that the Persian Gulf nation was no military quagmire. In the summer of 2007, though, Bush reversed course and started using a Vietnam analogy of his own, saying that a rapid U.S. military withdrawal from Iraq would unleash the havoc seen after U.S. troops left Vietnam in the 1970s (Rutenberg, Stolberg, and Mazzetti 2007).

In the months before the 2006 elections, as public opposition to the continuing occupation of Iraq deepened, the Bush administration at first defined its policy as "stay the course" (Rutenberg and Cloud 2006). When polls showed that this slogan was not winning the hearts and minds of Americans, Bush claimed that the administration's policy had not been "stay the course." Since Bush had repeatedly used those exact words, journalists could produce the videotape to prove it (Rutenberg and Cloud 2006). As columnist Michael Kinsley once noted, "Bush II administration lies are often so laughably obvious you wonder why they bother" (quoted in Alterman 2006).

As it happens, the Bush administration did not plan to "stay the course" after all. After the Republicans lost the 2006 election—a year marked by overwhelming voter desire to end the Iraq occupation—the Bush team revealed that it actually favored an escalation of the war, though it preferred the term "surge" to describe the troop expansion it had in mind (Burns, Tavernise, and Santora 2007). Bush insisted the Democrats be on record about future Iraqi policy before the 2002 elections, but he did not consider it necessary to make public his own plans to expand the war before the votes of 2006 were cast.

This double standard may have been sound political strategy in the short term, however disrespectful of voters it was. Had the Bush administration revealed its true intentions before the election, subsequent surveys suggest the results for Republicans would have been even worse (Balz and Cohen 2007). Members of Congress and the public do not like being fooled, and Bush's standing in Washington and in the country continued to drop after the midterm elections and Bush's postelection discussion of the surge plan.

Short-term deceit in military matters is not a new approach for presidents or presidential candidates. Lyndon Johnson did not level with the voters about his military plans during the 1964 presidential election, and he dramatically increased the U.S. military presence in Vietnam in 1965. As a presidential candidate in 1968, Richard Nixon said he had a "secret plan" to end the war. But his real secret was that there was no such plan, though that fact did not become clear until after Nixon took office (Dallek 2007). Both Vietnam-era presidents, like George W. Bush, went on to face major credibility gaps as their deceits were exposed by reporters who had previously been less questioning of government claims (Dallek 2007; Sabato 1993).

The sometimes tortured logic and desperate hope that odd terminology can be used to justify whatever the president wants to do is a key part of the White House marketing playbook. It is a favorite strategy of presidents who have had to engage in damage control to preserve their political standing in Washington. Bill Clinton, who endured the nickname "Slick Willie" from his days as a fast-and-loose politician in Arkansas, offered Bush a lesson in how to twist language for public and media consumption. When the world first heard the name Monica Lewinsky in 1998, Bill Clinton issued his forceful denial on global television: "I did not have sexual relations with that woman," he exclaimed. As was later discovered in Kenneth Starr's investigation, Clinton defined sex as intercourse and excluded oral sex from that definition (Berman 2001; Blaney and Benoit 2001; Isikoff 2000; Klein 2002). (I discuss further this scandal and its impact on presidential communication later in this chapter.)

Slick Willie or not, Clinton was hardly the first president to twist common understandings to suit his own purposes. Ronald Reagan described the Nicaraguan contras as "freedom fighters" rather than guerrillas to help build support for the anti-Sandinista movement. Indeed, the Iran-contra affair, which derailed Reagan's second term, involved what was commonly understood to be a trade of armaments for hostages. Commonly understood, that is, by everyone except Ronald Reagan (Neustadt 1990).

Is the President Lying?

Reporters are not sure how to cover the verbal gymnastics in modern presidential public relations. Can one just report that a president is lying? For a reporter, reaching the judgment that the president has lied comes perilously close to expressing one's opinion, and opinions belong on the editorial page, not in the news columns. Many reporters resolve this potential problem by simply placing the current and former statements next to each other in an article, leaving it to readers or viewers to note the clear discrepancy.

> Reporters only like certain lies. Perversely, these tend to be the relatively trivial ones, involving personal matters: Clinton's deceptions about his sex life; Al Gore's talk of having inspired *Love Story*; John Kerry's failure to correct misperceptions that he is Irish. Here the press can strut its skepticism without positioning itself ideologically. The lies reporters dislike, in contrast, center on what are usually more important matters: claims about public policy—taxes, abortion, the environment—where raising questions of truthfulness can seem awfully close to taking sides in a partisan debate. Most of Bush's lies have fallen into this demilitarized zone, where journalists fear to tread. (Greenberg 2003)

The Limits of Presidential Media Management

Many events are outside presidential control. Even as President George W. Bush sought to divert attention away from bin Laden and toward Saddam Hussein in 2002 and 2003, the terrorist mastermind of 9/11 frequently returned to the public eye with new videotapes warning of future attacks. Although those commentaries generally became only brief snippets on evening newscasts and in the daily newspapers, they undermined Bush's efforts to focus on Iraq. Fortunately for Bush, the U.S. television networks were far more interested in what the president had to say, and network television followed Bush's lead in largely dismissing the reclusive terrorist warlord as yesterday's news.

For Bush, focusing on Iraq rather than Afghanistan seemed like a good strategy at first. The rapid victories during the active combat phase of the Iraq War provided for positive television coverage and favorable images, including the famous footage of the statue of Saddam Hussein being brought down in Baghdad (Farnsworth and Lichter 2006a). At first, the Pentagon's decision to "embed" reporters with the combat units seemed like an effective strategy to secure positive coverage of the war. Journalists traveling with military units, spending all day and all night with the troops and depending on those units for their personal safety, might hesitate to portray the troops in a negative light (Graber 2003). Unlike bin Laden, who remains at large more than six years after 9/11, Saddam Hussein was found and eventually executed for his crimes (Burns and Santora 2007).

But as the Iraq occupation faced an ever-growing resistance, the Bush administration's previous focus on Iraq ensured that the White House would find it hard to change the subject. The news coverage became negative in tone, and the in-fighting within the administration over what to do to improve the situation in Iraq spilled over into White House news reports. Although presidents prefer consistent media messages, deep disagreements over how to proceed—and efforts to make sure someone else was blamed for the situation in Iraq—encouraged administration officials to start attacking each other (Milbank 2004b). Naturally, U.S. government officials eventually focused their criticisms on the elected Iraqi government rather than U.S. policy for the problems in Iraq (Mazzetti 2007b, 2007c).

Outside sources likewise can provide more information to contradict the government line, particularly as time passes. People formerly within the administration completed books that blame others for what went wrong (Clarke 2004; Suskind 2004). The United Nations, which recently revealed that more than 34,000 Iraqis died in violent clashes during 2006, directly contradicted claims by the Bush administration and the Maliki government in Iraq that the sectarian violence was under control (Tavernise 2007).

Can Congress Fight Back? Does Congress Want To?

One of the most interesting and, to political scientists, unexpected developments of the Bush years has been the abandonment by the Republican majorities in Congress of the legislative branch's traditional oversight functions (Mann and Ornstein 2006). The largely unquestioned acceptance of Bush's controversial Iraq War and ongoing strategy during those years marked a departure from previous Congresses that kept presidents under close scrutiny even in wartime. During the depths of World War II, Democratic majorities in the House and Senate aggressively investigated the Roosevelt administration's conduct of the war. In fact, an obscure Democratic Missouri senator named Harry Truman built himself a national reputation by rooting out wartime corruption in government contracts and contractors. Public approval of his activities led to his being chosen as FDR's vice presidential running mate in 1944 (Beschloss 2002).

The Bush Republicans had no Senator Truman of their own. Unlike the Democrats who investigated their party's president with vigor during World War II, the Republicans in Congress gave George W. Bush wide, almost unquestioned, latitude to conduct the Iraq War as he saw fit (Lindsay 2003). By fall 2006, when public opinion was running against them, many Republicans started saying they had doubts about Bush's "stay the course" strategy (Rutenberg and Cloud 2006). But it was too late for many of them, and in the November 2006 elections Democrats won control of both houses of Congress (Broder 2006).

During their years in the minority, Democrats had little ability to collect information about the Bush administration's approach to the war. That minority status also meant the Democrats received little media attention, and the president's position remained largely unchallenged. Members may have had a few minutes during hearings to question Defense Secretary Donald Rumsfeld, generals, and other top administration officials from time to time, but such hearings do not generate much television news coverage if the person testifying chooses not to make news. Experienced government operatives like Rumsfeld usually deflected critical inquiries from minority legislators without much trouble (Cook 1989, 2005; Entman 2004). In addition, Democrats were divided on the war throughout the first few several years of the occupation. Many of the party's most prominent elected officials—including Senators Hillary Clinton (D-NY), John Kerry (D-MA), John Edwards (D-NC), and Joseph Lieberman (D-CT)—voted for the war and continued to support their earlier votes through the 2004 elections. In addition, the Republican Party's electoral successes in 2002 and 2004 were largely a result of Bush's hawkish approach to foreign policy, and his efforts to portray the Democrats as weak on defense (Ceaser and Busch 2005; Easton 2004). For their part, the Democrats feared another round of presidential spin, even though two-thirds of Americans said they opposed Bush's Middle East policies.

The New Democratic-Led Congress and Iraq

As soon as the Democrats took control of Congress in January 2007, they embarked on a deliberate media and political strategy to strengthen opposition to Bush's plans for increasing the number of troops in Iraq (Sanger 2007; Schmitt 2007; Weisman 2007). They vowed to erase the president's traditional agenda-setting advantage in the media. In the first days of Democratic control, House Speaker Nancy Pelosi (D-CA) and the five committee chairs whose responsibilities included aspects of the Iraq situation started planning how to maximize the Democratic Party's use of investigatory power and hearings to discredit Bush's policies (Hulse 2007). Pelosi herself used her first Sunday as speaker to grant an exclusive interview to CBS' *Face the Nation*, an influential weekend interview show. In that interview, Pelosi vowed an aggressive challenge to Bush's plan to expand the war, and described the situation in Iraq as "complete chaos" (Tyson 2007). Saying that she was representing the will of the voters who tried to send the Bush administration a message in the November 2006 elections, Pelosi declared on CBS: "If the president wants to add to this mission, he is going to have to justify it" (Tyson 2007). Pelosi said that Congress would not cut off funding for the troops already in Iraq, but would be highly skeptical of Bush's plans to expand the force there (Tyson 2007).

Pelosi's January 7, 2007, interview was a savvy effort on the part of one of the party's most powerful officials to try to compete with the president in the battle to define the situation in Iraq in the news media. The news program devoted its entire half-hour broadcast to the interview with the speaker, and Pelosi's remarks were reported in other media that Sunday—traditionally a time of little breaking news (Tyson 2007).

The new Democratic majorities had the wind of public opinion at their backs as they started their first session in a dozen years with complete control of Congress. As shown in Table 2.2, citizens surveyed in January 2007 were far more positively disposed to the Democrats and the new speaker than they were to Bush (Balz and Cohen 2007). This is an unusual result, as presidents normally have higher public opinion ratings than Congress (Farnsworth 2003a; Hibbing and Theiss-Morse 1998).

By a margin of more than two to one, U.S. citizens said they wanted the country to go in the direction proposed by the Democrats, not by Bush. By a margin of 52 percent to 40 percent, respondents said that they trusted the Democrats to do a better job in fighting the war on terror, previously a key Republican advantage over Democrats. Sixty percent or more said that the Democrats should take the lead in Iraq, with the economy, and with the federal budget (Balz and Cohen 2007).

How effective the Democrats would be in the face of a determined administration remained to be seen, but as 2007 dawned the Democrats vowed they would be more organized and more critical than in the past. And the formerly dominant Republicans seemed discouraged at the start of Bush's final two years in office. Even U.S. Senator Mitch McConnell (R-KY), a highly partisan leader speaking in the friendly conservative confines of *Fox News*, found it difficult to be enthusiastic about the proposed temporary escalation (Tyson 2007). But stronger Democratic resolve may not have been sufficient, given the executive branch's great ability to shape the national political conversation.

Senator James Webb: An Early Response and Responder

An early sign of the new Democratic congressional majority's improved media savvy came in mid-January 2007, when the party announced that newly elected Senator James Webb (D-VA) would deliver his party's response to Bush's 2007 State of the Union speech. Webb, a tough-talking former

Table 2.2 Public Opinion: President Bush versus the Democrats, January 2007

Do you approve or disapprove of the way George W. Bush is handling his job as president? Do you approve/disapprove strongly or somewhat?

	Approve			Disapprove		No Opinion
Net	Strongly	Somewhat	Net	Strongly	Somewhat	
33	17	16	65	14	51	2

Do you approve or disapprove of the way Bush is handling (ITEM)?

	Approve	Disapprove	No Opinion
a. The situation in Iraq	29	70	1
b. The U.S. campaign against terrorism	46	52	2
c. The economy	41	57	2
d. Global warming	27	61	13

Do you approve or disapprove of the way (ITEM)?

	Approve	Disapprove	No Opinion
a. The U.S. Congress is doing its job	43	50	8
b. Nancy Pelosi is handling her job as Speaker of the House	54	25	21

Do you think things in this country (are generally going in the right direction) or do you feel things (have gotten pretty seriously off on the wrong track)?

Right direction	Wrong track	No Opinion
26	71	3

Do you think the country should go in the direction (Bush wants to lead it), go in the direction (the Democrats in Congress want to lead it), or what?

Bush	Democrats	Other (vol.)	Neither (vol.)	No dif. (vol.)	No Opinion
25	57	4	8	2	4

(continues)

Table 2.2 (continued)

Who do you trust to do a better job handling (ITEM), (Bush) or (the Democrats in Congress)?

	Bush	Democrats	Both (vol.)	Neither (vol.)	No Opinion
a. The situation in Iraq	33	60	1	4	2
b. The U.S. campaign against terrorism	40	52	1	5	2
c. The economy	32	60	1	4	2
d. The federal budget	28	62	1	6	3

Note: This *Washington Post–ABC News* poll was conducted by telephone January 16–19, 2007, among a random nationwide sample of 1,000 adults. The margin of sampling error is plus or minus 3 percentage points for full-sample questions. TNS of Horsham, Pa., conducted the sampling and data collection.

Vol. stands for volunteered.

Question words in paretheses above are exchanged to place response options in different order.

Source: Dan Balz and Jon Cohen. 2007. "Confidence in Bush Leadership at All-Time Low, Poll Finds." *Washington Post,* January 22.

U.S. Marine who served in Vietnam and later as secretary of the U.S. Navy under Ronald Reagan, was a particularly effective Democratic spokesperson against Bush's plans for an escalation of the war in Iraq (Dionne 2007). Webb's own military and political credentials were unassailable; the new senator was a former Republican who turned Democrat, and who could hardly be presented as a far-left dove (Shear 2007a). Webb's background and no-nonsense demeanor made him a "folk hero among liberals and Democratic bloggers," and his aggressive condemnation of the president's military policies only endeared him further to the party's most liberal factions (Shear 2007a, 2007b).

The Bush administration made a tactical mistake in talking to reporters about a strained early encounter between the president and Webb. As senator-elect, Webb had refused to stand in line for a customary photograph with the president at a White House holiday reception. When Bush sought him out, he asked how Webb's son was doing in Iraq. "That's between me and my boy," Webb replied bluntly (quoted in Zeleny 2007).

Many liberal bloggers have long wished the party would take a more confrontational approach, and Webb's Democratic response to the State of the Union did not disappoint the party's anti-Bush activists.

On Iraq, Webb did not mince words about Bush's responsibility. "The president took us into this war recklessly," he declared. Instead of qualifying this strong statement, Webb backed it up: "He disregarded warnings from the national security adviser during the first Gulf War, the chief of staff of the Army, [and] two former commanding generals of the Central Command." The list more than supported Webb's next thought that "we are now, as a nation, held hostage to the predictable—and predicted—disarray that has followed" (Dionne 2007).

Choosing one's adversaries wisely is an important part of prevailing in political debates. Bush's publicized confrontation with Webb helped make the new senator an even more appealing media presence to Bush critics who relished the contrast between the combat-wounded Webb and Bush, who avoided service in Vietnam by joining the Texas Air National Guard (Zeleny 2007). Far better for the Bush administration to have built up in the media a Democratic rival who could have been stereotyped as an effete liberal—the way the Republicans portrayed Kerry in the 2004 campaign (Easton et al. 2004; Nagourney 2004; Wilgoren 2004).

Domestic Politics: The Limits of Congressional Deference

Congress is far more willing to engage opponents over domestic policy matters, particularly during times of divided government. Although in the majority during part of 2001 and 2002, for example, Senate Democrats blocked Bush's economic stimulus plan and his proposal to drill in the Arctic Wildlife Refuge and filibustered some of his more controversial judicial nominees (Lindsay 2003), although they later failed to do so in the case of his Supreme Court nominees.

Sometimes unified party majorities are combative too. When Republicans took over the Senate after the 2002 midterms, the party killed Bush's nomination of Harriet Miers to the Supreme Court over worries she was not conservative enough and not experienced enough, and rejected Bush's plan for providing illegal aliens a path to U.S. citizenship (Farnsworth and Lichter 2006b). But one is hard-pressed to argue that the cases of domestic policy assertiveness by Republicans in recent years are comparable in importance to what the Republicans did not do: investigate aggressively the White House's intelligence failures and its shortcomings in the management of the occupation of Iraq.

As a newly assertive Democratic majority took control of Capitol Hill in January 2007, Bush sought to draw attention to a topic other than Iraq: the federal budget deficit (Andrews 2007). Budget deficits used to be anathema to the GOP, but Bush's tax cuts and the expenses of his wars in Afghanistan and Iraq led to massive deficits during his tenure with few GOP objections. Bush himself drew little attention to the mounting deficits during the years of Republican control, and he never proposed a balanced budget as president. In January 2007, though, Bush called on the new Democratic majorities on Capitol Hill to restrain spending. Democrats generally dismissed Bush's newfound concern over deficits as political posturing and tried to counterspin by wondering aloud why he did not veto a single Republican spending bill during the first six years of his presidency (Andrews 2007).

Defiance in the Republican Senate:
Bush's Failed Nomination of Harriet Miers

Few presidential actions have more lasting consequences than appointments to the Supreme Court (O'Brien 1996, 2005). No one knows this better than George W. Bush, whose own victory in the Florida vote-counting dispute of the 2000 presidential election was secured by a contentious and partisan five-to-four Supreme Court decision that stopped the vote counting in the Sunshine State (Bugliosi 2001; Ceaser and Busch 2001).

Presidents can find it difficult to secure Senate confirmation of controversial nominees during times of divided government, as the failed nomination of Robert Bork in 1987 demonstrated (Maltese 1995). But other controversial nominees—such as Clarence Thomas, accused of being a sexual harasser—can survive the confirmation process despite opposition party control of the U.S. Senate and a media frenzy (Davis 1994a, 1994b; Mayer and Abrahamson 1994).

Since the Senate was firmly in Republican hands in 2005, and White House Counsel Harriet Miers was a long-time Bush loyalist without a hint of corruption, the Bush team expected a quiet and easy confirmation. But Senate Republicans turned on Miers with a harshness that shocked the White House (Nagourney 2005). A content analysis of ABC, CBS, and NBC evening news coverage, along with reporting on the nominee that appeared in the *New York Times* during the twenty-four days Miers was a nominee, found that sources identified by reporters as Republican and/or conservative were only positive toward Miers 43 percent of the time, far less than the 91 percent positive assessments offered by those same sources on John Roberts, who had been nominated for chief justice earlier that year (Farnsworth and Lichter 2006b). Criticism by Senate Republicans doomed her nomination. Bush then nominated Samuel Alito, an appeals court judge with a more established conservative record and an extensive history on the federal bench, and he was confirmed easily (Wittes 2006).

Miers offers a rare example of how legislative spin can trump presidential marketing efforts. The Republican Senate was able to dominate the executive in this unusual case for two reasons: because the senators possessed the will to do so, and because Supreme Court nominations require explicit Senate confirmation, with minimal presidential influence over the process after a nominee has been proposed. The circumstances are quite different from ordinary lawmaking.

Defiance in the Republican House: Bush's Failed Immigration Plan

One of the few areas in which Bush attempted to legislate as the "compassionate conservative" he promised he would be was on immigration issues (Mucciaroni and Quirk 2004). Bush's comprehensive plan for dealing with massive illegal immigration into the United States from Mexico and other Latin American nations involved a tightening of the border and a program that allowed people who have been in the United States illegally for several years to start on a path to citizenship. Many House Republicans, anxious to try to redirect the public's attention away from Iraq, thought a tough stance on immigration would secure their reelections in 2006, a difficult year for GOP candidates (Lipton 2006b). The party's need to change the subject became acute as the fall progressed, particularly following the emergence of a scandal involving Representative Mark Foley (R-FL) and his inappropriate contact with male pages, high school students who come to Capitol Hill to run errands for lawmakers (Hulse and Hernandez 2006). News reports on the scandal revealed that House Republican leaders had known of Foley's troubling behavior for more than a year and had covered up the problems (Hulse and Hernandez 2006). Many Christian conservative voters, a key GOP constituency, faulted the House leaders for failing to protect their young charges from a predatory lawmaker, especially a gay one (Purnick 2006).

Foley resigned, and public attention returned to the immigration issue. In the end, Congress held firm, and Bush signed an immigration bill built largely according to the dictates of the House Republicans. The bill contained plans to build an additional 700 miles of fencing along the U.S.-Mexico border (Lipton 2006b). But this House rebellion did not matter much to an electorate far more concerned about Iraq than immigration, and the GOP House lost its majority several weeks later (Balz and Cohen 2007).

The Republican Majorities and Bill Clinton

These rather modest efforts by congressional Republicans to tinker at the margins of George W. Bush's political agenda stand in sharp contrast to the way they treated Bill Clinton, who faced Republican majorities for the last six of his eight years as president. In a 1995 battle with House Speaker Newt Gingrich (R-GA), Clinton rejected what he considered draconian government service cuts (Ceaser and Busch 1997). After both sides failed to reach an agreement, the federal government was shut down for several weeks. Media coverage of the conflict was extensive, and polls showed that citizens blamed the Republicans for the impasse. A chastened Gingrich compromised on the budget and allowed the government to reopen. The

Republican majority's actions backfired, and Clinton coasted to an easy reelection in 1996 (Ceaser and Busch 1997).

The Republicans again had Clinton in their sights in January 1998, when Americans first learned the name Monica Lewinsky, the former White House intern who became infamous for her sexual dalliance with Clinton (Berman 2001; Blaney and Benoit 2001; Blumenthal 2003; Isikoff 2000; Sabato, Stencel, and Lichter 2000). Again the GOP's attempts to defeat Clinton backfired, though they did generate lots of media coverage of that presidential scandal.

The first and most important lesson to draw from the political communication aspects of the impeachment controversy is that presidents have a great advantage in agenda setting and framing of news, even in the midst of a congressional investigation into their own behavior. Clinton clearly misled the country about his relationship with Lewinsky, but the White House's news management advantages enabled Clinton to turn the story of his misconduct into an attack on Republican extremists portrayed as out to wreck a presidency for partisan gain (Farnsworth and Lichter 2006a). When presidents do battle with Congress over media messages, presidents usually win, even when they are very much in the wrong, as Clinton was.

The second important lesson is how important character definition is to modern presidential communication. The fact that many Americans liked Clinton helped him survive the scandal coverage. Republicans mistakenly thought that Clinton's conduct would be sufficiently offensive that he would be forced from office one way or another after journalists started reporting on his misdeeds. But emphasizing Clinton's misbehavior did help the Republicans in the 2000 election. Because of the impeachment controversy, Al Gore, the 2000 Democratic nominee, hesitated to use the polarizing president on the campaign trail and spoke little about the Clinton-Gore record of peace and prosperity, reducing the advantage of incumbency (Ceaser and Busch 2001). In addition, Republican members of Congress who attacked Clinton for his infidelity paved the way for George W. Bush, who had close ties to the evangelical Christian movement, to campaign for centrist voters by promising higher moral standards in Washington (Ceaser and Busch 2001).

What about the Courts?

Sometimes lawmakers pass popular legislation of dubious constitutionality because the measures are popular with voters. This is a bipartisan pastime as presidents and Congress agree to do the popular but illegal thing in the short term and leave it to the courts to take the unpopular and legal steps later on. President Clinton signed a bill that contained strict content regulation standards on the Internet even though it was widely expected the courts would throw out the law as a violation of constitutional guarantees of free speech—as they eventually did (O'Brien 2005). Clinton's action was the latest in a series of political decisions in recent years by elected officials to trumpet their populism before the cameras and to leave tough issues—like the treatment of criminal defendants, illegal immigrants, and prisoners—to the courts (O'Brien 2005).

George W. Bush, with the assistance of the U.S. Department of Justice, argued for a far more expansive vision of presidential authority and more aggressive treatment of terrorism suspects in custody than in the past. The courts sometimes have claimed the administration acted illegally. In *Hamdan v. Rumsfeld* (2006), for example, the Supreme Court rejected rules for military commissions to try unlawful combatants (Shane 2007b). In some matters, such as warrantless wiretapping, the Bush administration reversed course and deferred to the courts before it lost other cases (Lichtblau and Johnston 2007). Although Bush faulted the *New York Times* for releasing details of the administration's decision in 2005 to bypass the special anti-terrorist courts (known as Foreign Intelligence Surveillance Act [FISA] Courts), in early 2007 the Bush administration capitulated on the controversial "unilateral executive" strategy and allowed judicial oversight of alleged terrorists in custody (Lichtblau and Johnston 2007; Risen 2006). In August 2007, Democrats in Congress helped pass Bush's proposed expansion of the warrantless wiretapping program, enraging Democratic partisans who faulted that party's elected officials for backing down even when Bush was highly unpopular (Hulse and Andrews 2007).

For the White House, and for Capitol Hill, passing popular laws later found to be illegal is win-win. First, they generate headlines and win public support for passing the law, and if the courts rule against the law, they can use the media to attack the courts as out-of-touch elitists who don't understand what the people want as well as elected officials do. Passing obviously illegal measures and otherwise leaving complex issues to the courts do not constitute responsible lawmaking, but these tactics do pay valuable electoral dividends. Few elected officials are going to lose elections for being too tough on criminal defendants, on Internet porn, or on people suspected of wanting to kill Americans. And, by the time the issue is finally resolved in the courts, reporters probably have long since moved on to another story anyway.

Conclusion

As this chapter shows, presidents have many advantages over Congress when it comes to political communication. When the president wants to set the agenda and frame key stories in certain ways, he or she has far greater opportunity to do so than do members of Congress, a branch that receives only a fraction of the network news, cable airtime, and column inches lavished on the White House. Although members of Congress can—and do—try to be heard, the legislative branch cannot compete effectively for public attention. Nor can lawmakers on Capitol Hill compete effectively with a president for the public's affections (Farnsworth 2001, 2003a, 2003b; Hibbing and Theiss-Morse 1995, 1998).

On issues, presidents often do better than Congress in making the case for a policy because of the media's focus on the White House. White House control over the bureaucracy also helps maximize the president's control over what information becomes public, as well as what leading voices across the government are saying about the policy in question. Those advantages are particularly important in foreign policy matters, where the president's—that is, the commander in chief's—control over intelligence disclosures is particularly important in shaping perceptions of ongoing international developments. Congressional investigations and sharp legislative rhetoric can generate a headline from time to time, but Capitol Hill is too diverse and too disorganized to mount an effective media counterattack to presidential spin over the long haul.

White House media dominance has become so widespread that many people outside of government hardly even notice that Congress has become a second-class branch on television. In addition, ordinary citizens are not likely to spend a lot of time focusing on the details of most policies. Only the highest-priority items—like wars and the economy—are likely to command public attention for long (Lewis-Beck and Rice 1992). When presidents go public and to try to sell public policies to citizens, they are hoping to demonstrate that the public wants a certain policy shift and that Congress would be wise to go along. Given many citizens' limited knowledge about most polices, any success from going public may have as much to do with how citizens feel about the president as the merits of the proposal itself. In Chapter 3, I examine this phenomenon: how presidents use the media to communicate character and policy preferences to the public.

This chapter demonstrates that Bill Clinton and George W. Bush tried to spin policies in similar ways, though Bush generally went further then Clinton did when it came to spin. They use similar techniques and in particular rely on the greater media attention they receive to outspin legislative branch efforts to construct counterframes. The president elected in 2008, whoever that might be, will likely be the next chief executive to make the media the center of selling a policy agenda. Like Bush, and like Clinton before him, future presidents can exploit the short-term advantages of spin-based policymaking. But they may be just as tempted to win by spin, and by doing so later face the troubling long-term consequences that became apparent in the two previous presidencies.

Chapter Three

Presidents and Citizens

Spinning for Public Approval

The rise of a national mass media since the mid-twentieth century has dramatically enhanced a president's ability to communicate policy preferences to the public. Members of Congress may be able to spend a lot of time in their districts during work periods, and may be quoted in the local news media, but modern presidents get to be on national television news just about any time they want to be (Cook 1989, 2005; Farnsworth and Lichter 2006a). Chief executives have become dominant national figures in conversations on war, peace, health care, and other domestic policies, a sharp contrast from most of the presidents who served before television and Internet news became commonplace. Running for president has become an intensely personal affair, as candidates sell themselves in the media first on the basis of their character, and then later on the basis of their issue positions.

The rise in presidential visibility in the media and the increase in public expectations of the chief executive often lead to eventual citizen disappointment with a president who struggles to function as a modern legislator in chief (Jones 1994, 1995; Lowi 1985). When policy accomplishment is limited, and it almost always is, presidential administrations increasingly turn to public relations to keep public goodwill, trying to spin a mountain of success where only a molehill exists. A shortage of substance, in other words, is obscured by spin. In addition to direct White House efforts to sell policies to Congress by controlling the terms of the debate in the media, the subject of the previous chapter, modern White House teams frequently try to use the media to enlist public support to give the president leverage in convincing Congress to back the White House. When successful, this strategy involves two steps: presidents sell their policies and themselves to the public; then the citizens who receive these media messages encourage lawmakers to support the president's policy agenda (Kernell 2007). Although results of the going public strategy are mixed at best, presidents devote enormous energies to selling themselves and their presidencies to the public (Edwards 2003, 2004, 2006). Perhaps they are optimistic that marketing will work better this time. But selling the public on policies, which are only marginally interesting to many citizens and not much more interesting to reporters trying to satisfy public demand for news, comes second. Presidents, and presidential candidates before that, start by selling themselves.

Communicating Presidential Character

One of the biggest problems with the White House strategy of going public is that attention for most policy matters is limited. Citizens have many pressing concerns in their daily lives, including jobs, parenting responsibilities, and other obligations, and those matters cut into the time they spend watching CSPAN or even a thirty-minute evening news program. For many citizens, budgets are boring, lawmaking is tedious and international problems often seem distant. Less than two-thirds of American adults vote in presidential elections, the biggest national political event of all. Reporters must respond to public indifference and sometimes disaffection with politics if they hope to attract readers and viewers.

Given this limited public attention to government, much White House political communication aimed at citizens is not explicitly issue-based. Rather it is designed to generate a positive assessment of the president. Savvy White House operators do not bore citizens with the intricacies of budgetary authorizations; instead administrations spend time demonstrating that the president's character and overall performance are praiseworthy. Although there are exceptions—9/11, the war in Iraq, and the Clinton/ Lewinsky story all drew substantial public attention—most issues do not trigger sustained citizen interest (Pew Research Center for the People and the Press 2000, 2004a, 2004b). So White House communication teams place great importance on explaining why people should like the president, and in doing all they can to make sure people do. White House officials then hope that media coverage of the president makes Congress shrink from confrontations with a popular executive.

In many ways, the modern White House's strategies of spin represent a permanent campaign (Cook 2002; Edwards 2000). Even for presidents already in office, White House teams manage aggressively the presentation of the president's personality. The stakes may be higher for first-term presidents, who are less well known when they take office. Second-term administrations focus on the presentation of character as well, even though nearly all Americans have decided how they feel about a president after a few years, if not sooner.

Character Counts in Presidential Politics

Defining character is a difficult business. U.S. politicians, particularly presidential candidates, need to be likable to win an election (Barber 1992; Brooks 2006). Vice President Al Gore certainly was experienced enough and smart enough to have been an effective president, but many voters in 2000 had their doubts about the vice president's character. These public concerns were amplified—if not created—by media coverage focusing on the vice president's temperament. Was the real Gore the aggressive attack dog of the first presidential debate of that year's campaign, the more passive bureaucrat who appeared in the second debate, or some mixture of the two? Voters are electing a commander, not a chameleon, and the media focus on Gore's shape-shifting personality throughout 2000 raised doubts among the millions of voters for whom character matters a great deal when they cast their ballots (Ceaser and Busch 2001).

Bush, in contrast, seemed clearly comfortable with who he was, a back-slapping, middle-aged former fraternity brother who developed deep religious convictions after becoming a father (Ceaser and Busch 2001). Americans have a fondness for presidents who are like them, who have   or at least appear to have—the common touch (Brooks 2006). That genuine connection with the public was something Al Gore, often derided as a wooden know-it-all, struggled to display during the 2000 campaign (Ceaser and Busch 2001).

In the 1996 campaign, Republican Bob Dole famously asked Americans which candidate they would prefer to babysit their kids—the grandfatherly Dole or the scandal-plagued Bill Clinton? Of course Dole's own personality—a bit acidic, one might say—was somewhat off-putting, so a character competition with Clinton might not have been a good comparison for the Kansas Republican to encourage (Pomper 1997).

But Dole's highlighting of character and its relevance to politics was not far off. A better question to ask about the president-public connection might be, Which politician would a voter most want to have at a family backyard barbecue? George W. Bush, one could easily imagine, would be great with the kids, and more than willing to take a turn flipping hamburgers at the charcoal grill. Based on his public persona, voters might imagine that Gore would not be nearly as friendly or easygoing, and could even turn tiresome if he started talking about how charcoal production contributes to global warming.

In U.S. presidential elections, character routinely trumps experience. People want to like their president, perhaps because television and Internet news makes the chief executive a regular fixture in the nation's living rooms. Reporters, particularly those working in television, find it easier and more interesting to write about character than issues. Consequently, many incumbent presidents have lost to more personable challengers during the television age. Gerald Ford was beaten in 1976 by Jimmy Carter, a one-term governor of Georgia who possessed a thin political resume but more importantly offered a winning smile and a friendly, honest nature (Brinkley 1988). Carter, in turn, was beaten four years later by Ronald Reagan, a former movie actor and governor of California who routinely stumbled from gaffe to gaffe when he talked about policymaking but was solid gold when the cameras were on (Barber 1992; Hunt 1981).

Whatever his public policy missteps, the camera-ready Reagan seemed like a confident, relaxed chief executive, a sharp contrast to the apparently tightly wound Carter (Alford 1988; Robinson and Sheehan 1983). In 1984, Democratic presidential nominee Walter Mondale told the policy truth—that Ronald Reagan's massive tax cuts would require a tax increase to balance the budget—but Americans remained loyal to the great communicator, even as the deficits mounted (Pomper 1985).

In 1988, Vice President George H. W. Bush was fortunate to draw Massachusetts governor Michael Dukakis as his opponent. Bush's own limited ability to project a winning personality through the mass media was not really a liability (Hershey 1989). Dukakis, it turned out, was even stiffer before the cameras than Al Gore would be a dozen years later.

But the elder Bush's limitations as a personable media figure were on full display in 1992, when the incumbent president was defeated by Bill Clinton, a Democratic populist from Arkansas whose accent and demeanor gave the image of a working-class hero from a place called Hope, Arkansas. Like the second president Bush, Clinton also projected the character of an affable frat boy, which helped him on the campaign trail (Ceaser and Busch 2001; Drew 1994; Edwards 1996).

Scholars believe questions of character are important for understanding presidents and their connections to the public (Barber 1992). Many presidencies have become mired in scandals that may have been worsened by responses that seemed to flow from paranoia or stubbornness. Richard Nixon might have survived as president if he had been willing, early on, to lay the blame for Watergate at the feet of his top aides, and Clinton may have forestalled the year-long impeachment war of 1998 had he been honest and contrite about his improper relationship with Monica Lewinsky after it became public (Barber 1992; Woodward 1999). But presidential dominance of modern media tempts presidents to try to spin their way out of trouble, and both Nixon ("I am not a crook") and Clinton ("I did not have sexual relations with that woman") tried to do so.

Since many citizens care about the personalities of their leaders as well as their policy positions, presidential candidates and presidents emphasize positive aspects of their characters as they sell themselves to the public in media-infused campaigns. This makes sense for candidates, as issues can be a lot more divisive than appearing good-natured and friendly. As George W. Bush demonstrated, it is wise to describe oneself as a "uniter, not a divider" when soliciting votes, regardless of how you plan to govern. Only after the candidates have won over a significant portion of the voters can they become presidents, and only after presidents have won over a significant portion of citizens can they imagine those citizens will press their legislators to support their administrations' policies.

This chapter focuses on the character definition efforts of George W. Bush and Bill Clinton, both of whom ran White House teams who worked diligently to market presidential personality through the mass media. The presentation of the presidential self is particularly important for presidential efforts to go public, given the relatively minimal citizen attention to public policy specifics. Because citizens do pay attention to high-profile topics, this chapter, like the previous one, contains examples of presidential strategies that maximize a president's chances of winning the policy marketing wars, in this case by selling policies to the public through the mass media.

George W. Bush: One Tough Texan

He may have been born in New Haven, Connecticut, and educated at Yale University and Harvard University Business School, but George W. Bush wanted to portray himself as Texan to the core. His demeanor and accent are more Midland than Massachusetts, more oil patch than Ivy League.

Americans like frontier figures, one of the most heroic types in a century of Hollywood filmmaking (Scott 2000). Presidents who present themselves as tough outdoorspeople tend to be viewed positively by many citizens. Whenever he wanted to emphasize his toughness during the 1980s, Ronald Reagan could be seen cutting brush on his California ranch. George W. Bush also likes to be seen cutting brush on his Texas ranch, even though he, like Reagan, has hired hands for property management. To emphasize further his western credentials, Reagan also liked to be photographed riding a horse. Bush prefers a pickup truck, but for both men the message from those televised images is that the president is a rancher, not a Washington policy wonk. In another way Bush tried to distinguish himself from his predecessor, Bush wants to be portrayed in the media as highly fit—he is no flabby jogger exercising all the way to the nearest McDonald's (Bumiller 2002; Rimer 1994).

Bush's image of personal toughness presaged his muscular approach to foreign policy. When crisis arrives, Bush consistently favors the aggressive response. Indeed, Bush's promise of quick military action in Afghanistan following the terrorist attacks of 9/11 captured the public desire for revenge. When Bush decided to invade Iraq, and justified doing so on the basis of what he said was a weapons of mass destruction (WMD) program as well as links between Saddam Hussein and Osama bin Laden, the U.S. public supported Bush (Edwards 2003). Bush's direct public speaking style fits the mold of the straight-talking, uncomplicated western sheriff or even a Texas Ranger, a popular role in the American imagination (Scott 2000). Bush may be far less articulate than Clinton, but his forceful demeanor helped keep public approval numbers elevated for quite some time after the Iraq War descended into a difficult occupation (Edwards 2003).

Toughness may be easy to portray on screen and appealing to the public, but that quality is not entirely an asset in a president. Bush's aggressive approach appears to come with a side order of stubbornness. Although others might have given more time for the UN arms inspectors to do their job in Iraq, Bush warned them to get out right away. Bush proudly declared that he was a "decider," and that he would not second-guess or otherwise agonize over—or some might say learn from—tough decisions (Stolberg 2006b). When Bush made a decision, he stuck to it—not apologizing for mistakes, nor even admitting that he made any (Kinsley 2003). When voter sentiment turned against the Iraq War in a particularly strong way in 2006, Bush ignored the political setbacks and vowed to escalate the war. Ever confident, at least before the cameras, he said his unpopular approach would be justified by future historians.

Bush's toughness included a strong sense of loyalty to his team. Despite the bad pre-war intelligence and even worse management of the Iraq occupation, Bush refused Secretary of Defense Donald Rumsfeld's many offers to resign, that is until after the Democrats won the 2006 midterm elections (Stolberg and Rutenberg 2006). National Security Advisor Condoleezza Rice was also deeply implicated in the administration's shortcomings both before 9/11 and with the prewar intelligence in Iraq, but she was promoted to secretary of state during Bush's second term (Cooper 2007). Bush bestowed a presidential medal of freedom, the nation's highest civilian honor, on former Central Intelligence Chief George Tenet, who had told Bush that the case that the Iraqis had a WMD program was "a slam dunk" (Sanger 2004).

Although media coverage criticized Bush for promoting and protecting his problem operatives, the president remained loyal to them.

During the 2000 campaign, Bush sought to soften his potentially harsh image by describing himself as a "compassionate conservative" (Hershey 2001). With these words, he sought as well to distinguish himself in the public's imagination from the highly partisan Republicans on Capitol Hill who had impeached Clinton and urged the closure of the U.S. Department of Education. During the 2000 campaign, Bush frequently hinted to reporters that Colin Powell, a leading Republican moderate, would have a top job in his administration. After the 2000 election, Powell was named secretary of state, one of the first of several Republican moderates named to key positions at the start of Bush's first term. That list included former Alcoa chief executive officer Paul O'Neill as treasury secretary and former New Jersey governor Christine Todd Whitman as head of the Environmental Protection Agency. By 2005 these three had been forced out, replaced by far more conservative— and less visible—Republicans (Mucciaroni and Quirk 2004).

From the start of his administration, George W. Bush took good care of conservatives (compassionate or otherwise). Former senator John Ashcroft (R-MO), a favorite of Christian conservatives and an enemy of civil libertarians, was named attorney general (Brown 2003). Bush relied greatly on the advice of Vice President Dick Cheney, one of the most conservative members of his administration (Woodward 2002, 2006). Second-term nominees also did not reflect "compassionate conservative" choices—such as UN Ambassador John Bolton, famous for having said that if the UN headquarters building lost its top ten floors it wouldn't make any difference (Hoge 2006). When even the Republican-majority Senate balked at confirming the undiplomatic diplomat, Bush installed him in a temporary recess appointment. When Bolton's commission expired at the end of 2006, Bush wisely selected another nominee.

Bush's Weakness: Potential Incompetence

From the time George W. Bush first burst on the national stage, reporters and some citizens wondered whether the Texas governor was up to the job of being president. Bush was not a strong student in college, and sometimes found it challenging to pronounce words properly and speak in coherent English sentences. Before entering politics, Bush had failed in the oil business, only to be rescued by his father's friends (Minutaglio 1999). His gaffes during Campaign 2000, such as calling a reporter "a major league asshole" on an open mike, quickly became legend (Kurtz 2000).

Concerns over whether Bush was capable of being president did not entirely evaporate after 9/11. Paul O'Neill, a veteran of several Republican presidential administrations, said many of the Bush team's problems stemmed from the president's own lack of intellectual curiosity.

It's very hard for an organization or an institution to achieve more than the leader can imagine. If you determine to run a five-minute mile, you'll never run a four-minute mile. The leader sets the conditions as to what it is we aspire to. It's not clear to me that you can create a process that will impact whatever the leader brings with him, in terms of his instinct of imagining what could be. I'd like to think that maybe that's not right and think that someone can be a leader and see or smell a new idea and then own it. But there has to be an openness of wanting to do that. There has to be a market there, otherwise you can just spin your wheels all you want to. You can have a lot of great ideas, and if the store is closed, it's not going to make any difference. (quoted in Suskind 2004, 293)

Problems in Iraq and Questions of Competence

Every administration has its so-called kiss-and-tell books, where former administration insiders get even with former political adversaries, sometimes even the president himself. These books become major news events, and often authors give revealing interviews to pump up sales. One particularly newsworthy broadside was launched by Richard Clarke, a former top National Security Council official who criticized the Bush team for its bizarre fixation on Saddam Hussein from its first days in office and for its unwillingness to take the Al-Qaeda threat seriously until after 9/11 (Clarke 2004). The Bush administration's failure to recognize the nation's most serious threats were confirmed by Secretary of the Treasury O'Neill, who described the Bush White House as so obsessed with tax cuts and with Saddam Hussein that it failed to recognize the magnitude of the threat posed by bin Laden (cited in Suskind 2004).

With Bush's declining second-term approval numbers came additional critical inside reports on the administration. As the situation in Iraq worsened, and as bin Laden continued to remain at large, even once largely positive biographers like Bob Woodward (2002, 2006) of the *Washington Post* starting arguing that Bush's management of the occupation was incompetent. Although the Bush team initially praised Woodward's work—recommending one of his earlier books on the White House Web site—when the author turned critical the White House sought to discredit Woodward's reports. When those attempts failed, the Bush administration hoped that the mass media and the American public would move on to other topics, as they did. Unfortunately for the Bush administration, the new topics remained Iraq-related (Balz and Cohen 2007).

By January 2007, Bush's ostensible audience was not the Maliki government, not the generals, not even the Republican officeholders on Capitol Hill. Rather, Bush was trying to market his Iraqi policies to a skeptical American public, which had demonstrated its opposition to continuing the war in Iraq via the 2006 midterm elections. Public opinion polls taken in late 2006 and early 2007 demonstrated that support for Bush continued to deteriorate and that his call for additional troops in Iraq, the so-called surge, decreased voters' approval of the president. In a poll taken immediately after Bush's January 2007 State of the Union speech, only 36 percent of those surveyed favored Bush's troop surge plan, and 53 percent said the Democrats should block the president's new initiative (Abramowitz and Weisman 2007). After a week-long pitch by the president, support for Bush's surge was even slightly lower than before (Balz and Cohen 2007).

Perhaps the most stinging rebuke of Bush's 2007 approach was that many Republicans started attacking the surge idea as soon as Bush presented it during a nationally televised speech on January 10, 2007. Longtime supporters of Bush's policies in Iraq—including Senators Sam Brownback (R-KS) and Norm Coleman (R-MN)—joined Democrats in attacking both Bush and the administration team sent to Capitol Hill to sell Bush's plan (Shanker and Cloud 2007). "I've gone along with the president on this, and I bought into his dream," Senator George V. Voinovich (R-OH) told Secretary of State Rice the day after Bush's speech. "And at this stage of the game, I don't think it's going to happen," he said bluntly (quoted in Abramowitz and Weisman 2007). Other Republicans who turned against the president's policies before 2006 were even harsher in their exchanges with Rice. Senator Chuck Hagel (R-NE), a Vietnam veteran, said: "I have to say, Madam Secretary, that I think this speech given last night by this president represents the most dangerous foreign policy blunder in this country since Vietnam" (quoted in Milbank 2007). The level of Republican hostility helped support Democratic claims that the president was living in a virtual bubble, listening only to his most devoted—and hawkish—advisors (Abramowitz and Weisman 2007; Milbank 2007). But critics from both parties hesitated to go too far, worried that the president could use the media against lawmakers who tried to shut down Bush's wars.

Hurricane Katrina, Its Aftermath, and Questions of Competence

Natural disasters, particularly hurricanes, are problematic for any president. The current red-blue division of states in the United States places Florida as much at the center of Electoral College calculations as it does many Atlantic storm trajectories. President George H. W. Bush's limited response to Hurricane Andrew—or so it seemed at the time to the angry residents of Miami—could have been a reminder to his son of the dangers that can come from failing to focus on storm damage (Wines 1992). Indeed, during his first term the junior President Bush paid great attention to the weather troubles that could affect Florida, the key state during the 2000 election. During the summer of 2004, Bush handed out water bottles at a hurricane relief site turned photo-op with his brother, Governor Jeb Bush. By doing so, the president used the media to send out the all-valuable "I care" message so important to public evaluations of a president. This message is particularly important in swing states during presidential election years (Goodnough 2004).

Unfortunately for New Orleans, Louisiana is not a swing state. Unfortunately for New Orleans, Hurricane Katrina made landfall nearly a year after Bush had been elected to his second term. The Bush administration did not appreciate the magnitude of the incoming storm or the vulnerability of the population of New Orleans, strange oversights given that the Federal Emergency Management Agency (FEMA) had long known the likelihood of a severe hurricane hitting this low-lying city. As a result of the preliminary misjudgments, FEMA was not prepared to deal with the devastation. Pictures of bodies floating in bogs, angry crowds standing on freeway overpasses, and the horrific conditions inside the Superdome that created a major public health crisis were a public relations nightmare for the Bush administration (Nagourney 2006; Shane and Lipton 2005). Rarely have pictures been as damaging to the White House as those aired of Katrina's devastation.

Some people may excuse Bush for FEMA's ill-prepared and stumbling response. A president cannot be everywhere, after all. But Bush was responsible for selecting an agency head with no professional experience in emergency management. The FEMA chief when the disaster struck, Michael ("Brownie") Brown, had been a horse show association official and a Republican loyalist before Bush gave him the job of running the nation's chief disaster response agency (Dowd 2005). By selecting someone with so little relevant experience, Bush set the stage for one of his administration's most incompetent performances (Krugman 2006). Bush chose partisan loyalty over professional competence, and he paid the price for his short-sightedness, or rather the citizens of New Orleans did, when disaster struck.

To make matters worse for Bush, he seriously mishandled his own response to the devastation. He was on vacation in Texas when Katrina struck—and did not cut his vacation short to give at least the appearance he was concerned about the unfolding catastrophe (Rich 2005b). In a response to mounting criticism in the media over FEMA's incompetent response and his own absence from New Orleans, Bush allowed himself to be photographed looking out the window of Air Force One as the plane flew over the devastated city on the way from Crawford, Texas, to Washington. (The plane did not land in New Orleans, however.) When Bush finally did make it to New Orleans several days later, he made yet another communications mistake, telling "Brownie" before the television cameras that he was doing "a heckuva job" (Dowd 2005). As Americans continued to be shocked by the magnitude of the devastation and the government's inadequate response, Bush's compliment to his FEMA chief seemed shockingly ill-informed, given the blistering news reports that made New Orleans look like something out of a *Mad Max* movie (Dowd 2005).

As the president's public relations disaster regarding the Katrina aftermath continued to deepen, Bush sought to improve the White House's image by replacing "Brownie" and sending U.S. Army troops to restore order and to help rebuild the stricken city. He made another trip to New Orleans, this time to give a nationally televised address saying that the federal government would see to it the pre-Katrina New Orleans would be restored (Stevenson and Kornblut 2005). But whatever Bush said two weeks after the storm, the haunting images of the citizens of the Gulf Coast and the government's failed response to their needs helped focus the perception among many citizens—a vision already taking shape over the Iraq occupation—that Bush and his team just were not competent (Nagourney 2006).

Several months later, the Bush administration sought to forestall even greater criticism of its handling of Katrina by refusing to release documents relating to the disaster (Shane and Lipton 2005). The Republican majorities in the 109th Congress did not press the administration to provide more details, but the Democratic majorities elected in 2006 have said they will not let the matter rest (Shenon 2007). On the third anniversary of Katrina's landfall, much of the New Orleans region remains a barely occupied disaster area, a mockery of Bush's prime-time television promises that the city would be entirely rebuilt (Brinkley 2007).

Survey Results: Public Assessments of Bush's Character

National public opinion surveys conducted for the *Washington Post* during Bush's second term not only showed declining public evaluations of Bush and his Iraq policy, as discussed in the previous chapter; they also showed substantial declines in public approval of Bush's character. As shown in Table 3.1, assessments of Bush as a person have trended downward during his second term.

By January 2007, 40 percent of those surveyed said they would describe Bush as "honest and trustworthy," far below the 70 percent who agreed to those words to describe Bush in a December 2002 survey. Even as late as May 2004, 53 percent said they would apply those terms to Bush (Balz and Cohen 2007).

Republican efforts to present President Bush as someone with a common touch were less successful post-Katrina. In a January 2007 survey, 32 percent agreed with the statement that Bush "understands the problems of people like you" (Balz and Cohen 2007). More than six out of ten citizens saw Bush as understanding their problems in a January 2002 survey—a few months after 9/11—but an August 2005 survey marked the last time that at least four citizens in ten would apply that statement to Bush.

Other survey results were equally negative for the president. Only 42 percent of those surveyed in January 2007 thought Bush could "be trusted

Table 3.1 Public Opinion on President Bush's Character, January 2007

Please tell me whether the following statement applies to Bush or not.

A. He is honest and trustworthy.

	Yes	No	No Opinion
1/19/07[a]	40	57	3
3/5/06	44	55	1
1/26/06	46	53	*
12/18/05	49	50	1
11/2/05	40	58	2
5/23/04	53	45	2
10/29/03	59	40	2
9/13/03	60	39	2
12/15/02	70	26	4
7/15/02	71	26	3
7/30/01	63	34	3

B. He understands the problems of people like you.

	Yes	No	No Opinion
1/19/07[a]	32	67	2
3/5/06	37	62	1
1/26/06	38	61	1
11/2/05	34	66	1
9/11/05	38	61	1
8/28/05	40	59	1
4/24/05	40	58	2
1/16/05	43	56	1
5/23/04	42	57	1
1/18/04	43	56	1
12/21/03	45	53	2
10/29/03	40	58	2
9/13/03	48	51	1
4/30/03	51	48	1
12/15/02	51	47	2
7/15/02	57	41	2
1/27/02	61	37	2
7/30/01	45	54	2
4/22/01	47	51	2

C. He is an effective leader.

	Yes	No	No Opinion
1/19/07[a]	40	59	1

(continues)

Table 3.1 (continued)

D. He is a strong leader.

	Yes	No	No Opinion
1/19/07[a]	45	54	1
3/5/06	52	48	*
1/26/06	52	48	*
12/18/05	51	49	*
11/2/05	47	53	*
9/11/05	50	50	*
5/23/04	62	37	1
12/21/03	67	32	2
10/29/03	62	37	1
9/13/03	66	34	*
4/30/03	74	25	*
12/15/02	75	23	2
7/15/02	75	24	1
7/30/01	55	43	2

E. He can be trusted in a crisis.

	Yes	No	No Opinion
1/19/07[a]	42	56	2
1/26/06	53	47	1
11/2/05	49	49	2
9/11/05	49	49	2
5/23/04	60	39	1
7/30/01	60	37	3

F. He is willing to listen to different points of view.

	Yes	No	No Opinion
1/19/07[a]	36	63	1
5/23/04	49	50	1

G. He has made the country safer and more secure.

	Yes	No	No Opinion
1/19/07[a]	44	55	1
5/23/04	52	47	1
9/13/03	63	35	2
12/15/02	65	33	2

Note: * = less than 0.5 percent. This *Washington Post–ABC News* poll was conducted by telephone January 16–19, 2007, among a random nationwide sample of 1,000 adults. The margin of sampling error is plus or minus 3 percentage points for full-sample questions. TNS of Horsham, Pa., conducted the sampling and data collection. Earlier responses are provided for points of comparison.

[a]Each question for January 19, 2007, was asked of a half sample.

Source: Dan Balz and Jon Cohen. 2007. "Confidence in Bush Leadership at All-Time Low, Poll Finds." *Washington Post,* January 22.

in a crisis," as compared to 60 percent who said he was trustworthy in a July 2001 survey. Citizens also increasingly saw Bush as stubborn: 36 percent said in January 2007 that they thought the president was "willing to listen to different points of view" as compared to 49 percent who thought that was true in May 2004 (Balz and Cohen 2007). Close to half of those surveyed—45 percent—believed that Bush was a strong leader, but that number also fell a great deal from the 75 percent who said Bush was a strong leader in a December 2002 survey conducted a few months before the start of the Iraq War (Balz and Cohen 2007).

These figures demonstrated that first impressions, or even second impressions, do not last forever. Despite continuing White House efforts to enhance the president's image, the survey numbers demonstrated that media marketing can take one only so far. The longer someone is president, the more actual events color public assessments of the chief executive. Putting a shine on a candidate's character during the "getting to know you" phase of a presidential campaign or a presidential first year is one thing; keeping the shine on a president's reputation as the years go by is quite another.

Bill Clinton: Not Your Parents' Democrat

When he campaigned for president in 1992, Bill Clinton went out of his way to portray himself as a different kind of Democrat. He argued that he was a centrist: moderate enough to win an election and tough enough to stand up to the largely unanswered Republican attacks that four years earlier had savaged Michael Dukakis, the party's 1988 presidential nominee (Hershey 1989). One of the pivotal moments of the 1988 campaign involved a televised debate question that asked what Dukakis, an opponent of the death penalty, would do if his wife were raped and murdered. Dukakis offered a banal response about how the law needs to take its course, raising questions among some voters about whether the governor had a pulse. The clinical response to that question helped finish off Dukakis, as the Massachusetts governor endured campaign advertisements that attacked him as soft on crime (Hershey 1989). One ad focused on Willie Horton, an African American who killed a white Maryland couple while on a prison furlough, and another ad suggested that Massachusetts prisons had revolving doors (West 2001). Dukakis complained that Bush Senior and the media mischaracterized him, but Bush went on to win forty states (Hershey 1989).

When Clinton ran for president four years later, he vowed he would not be the next Dukakis. During the 1992 nomination campaign, the Arkansas governor made a big media splash by suspending his campaign so that he could return to Little Rock to oversee the execution of Ricky Ray Rector.

Rector's case had generated immense international attention, with many people calling for Clinton to stay the execution because of Rector's mental retardation. But Clinton refused to commute the sentence, sending the clear—and politically expedient—message that he was so supportive of the death penalty that he would employ it even against those without the mental capacity to understand what was about to happen to them (Bonner and Rimer 2000). After Rector's execution, Bush's campaign attack dogs could not credibly make Clinton the next soft-on-crime Dukakis.

After he became his party's nominee, Clinton aimed a second message at white moderate voters. With the cameras rolling, he criticized rap star Sister Souljah. As, Reverend Jesse Jackson, at that time the nation's most prominent African American political figure, looked on, Clinton attacked what he termed the negative messages contained in the performer's music (Pareles 1992). Clinton's public slap down of the rapper made it harder for Republicans to portray the 1992 Democratic nominee the way they had portrayed Dukakis four years earlier—as someone more interested in giving African American criminals weekend passes than in protecting white people (West 2001).

Clinton's media-oriented efforts to insulate himself against traditional race-based Republican attacks on Democratic candidates were only part of his plans for defining himself to the U.S. electorate. Another part of his character-based victory strategy involved presenting himself as a southern populist, a "good old boy" who couldn't be further from Dukakis in personality, ideology, and geographic identity. Clinton also presented himself in sharp contrast to the patrician George H. W. Bush, the incumbent president who seemed and sounded far more Connecticut Yankee than Texas oil mogul (Ceaser and Busch 1993).

The key personality contrast between the two men was evident during a televised 1992 presidential debate held in Richmond, Virginia. An African American questioner asked the elder Bush how the nation's economic troubles had affected him personally, and Bush's stumbling, uncertain response gave the impression he did not understand the plight of ordinary voters. Clinton responded with a far more emphatic discussion of the severe hardships many citizens were facing and his commitment to making sure that as president he would get the economy moving again (Germond and Witcover 1993; Gillon 2002; Owen 1995).

Like Bush Junior eight years later, candidate Clinton only wanted to emphasize the populist part of his life story. In order not to be attacked as an eastern elitist, Clinton focused on his "Bubba" identity, and deemphasized the fact that his undergraduate degree was from Georgetown, his law degree was from Yale, and between those two degrees he studied at Oxford University as a Rhodes Scholar (Ceaser and Busch 1993). For Clinton, as for George W. Bush, the road to the White House was built by paving over one's blue-chip credentials. Once again, these different presidents developed similar media strategies regarding their own diverse characters.

Clinton's Weakness: A Potential Undisciplined Libertine

Bill Clinton's 1992 presidential nomination campaign nearly self-destructed over allegations of infidelity. Clinton's early lead in the polls at the start of the year disappeared after Gennifer Flowers appeared before the cameras to declare that she had had a long-term affair with Clinton, who at the time was governor of Arkansas (Rosenstiel 1994). The Flowers bombshell, coupled with allegations that Clinton had not been honest with the public about his efforts to avoid military service in Vietnam, raised the possibility that the smooth-talking southern charmer was too untrustworthy to be president.

Although people who have grown up after the release of Kenneth Starr's report during the Clinton impeachment process may find it hard to believe, not so long ago presidential campaigns were destroyed by extramarital affairs. For example, former senator Gary Hart (D-CO), was forced to withdraw from the 1988 presidential nomination campaign—in which he previously had been the front-runner—after the *Miami Herald* reported that Donna Rice was an overnight houseguest of Hart's in Washington (Pomper 1989; Sabato 1993). Four years later, Clinton might have expected to face the same fate: an abbreviated campaign terminated by news reports of sexual indiscretions. Scandal coverage relating both to Clinton's connection to Flowers and the Vietnam-era draft controversy dominated news reports on Clinton during the early stages of the primary campaign, shaping the identity of the little-known governor as a slippery political opportunist (Farnsworth and Lichter 1999). But Clinton survived the crisis as he and his wife appeared together on CBS' *Sixty Minutes* to quell the controversy by speaking about problems in their marriage (Ceaser and Busch 1993). Hillary Clinton's public support for her husband despite his dalliances helped him become the "comeback kid," a label he used to describe himself after finishing second in the 1992 New Hampshire primary (Farnsworth and Lichter 1999).

A reasonable person would probably say that the Clinton campaign dodged a bullet in 1992. A reasonable person would probably thank his lucky stars to have evaded the Gary Hart ending to his campaign, and lament the harm to one's reputation and one's family by the airing of such dirty laundry. Clinton, however, was not a reasonable person. What did Clinton do once he made it to the Oval Office? Before too long he was spending intimate time with Monica Lewinsky, a White House intern doubling as the pizza delivery girl!

Clinton's first response to the Clinton-Lewinsky scandal was to say that it did not happen. But given the number of allegations of sexual improprieties involving Clinton—the most famous being Gennifer Flowers and

Paula Jones, an Arkansas state employee who said the governor crudely propositioned her at a business conference—a simple denial from Clinton was not likely to be sufficient to quell the controversy (Isikoff 2000).

> The lies were told at first by Clinton and then spread and magnified by every-body around him—his top aides, his lawyers, his spin doctors. The lies were easily rationalized on the grounds that it was Clinton's private life that was at issue. . . . But lying, engaged in often enough, can have a corrosive effect. . . . A culture of concealment had sprung up around Bill Clinton and, I came to believe that summer, it had infected his entire presidency. (Isikoff 2000: 168)

Clinton's second public relations strategy was to discredit his accusers. As with the Clinton-Flowers scandal of 1992, Hillary Clinton had a central role in responding to attacks on her husband (Ceaser and Busch 1993; Sabato, Stencel, and Lichter 2000). On NBC's *Today Show,* Clinton described "a vast right-wing conspiracy that has been conspiring against my husband since the day he announced for president" (quoted in Blaney and Benoit 2001). Clinton's team believed that if they could make his attackers even more dislikable than the president, Clinton could survive the scandal politically. The second strategy was an effective one. Content analysis of network television news coverage during two peak coverage periods of the Clinton-Lewinsky scandal showed that news reports of independent counsel Kenneth Starr, former White House intern Monica Lewinsky, and other scandal figures was about six-to-one negative, as compared to scandal coverage of the president that was about two-to-one negative (Farnsworth and Lichter 2006a, 117).

A third news management strategy emerged when Clinton changed his story in August 1998, admitting to an improper relationship with the former intern. No longer could Clinton credibly deny conservative accusations that he had deceived the country. The Starr report, released that summer, detailed several instances of Clinton and Lewinsky being alone together and reported on a stained blue dress that demonstrated the extent of Clinton's indiscretions (Blaney and Benoit 2001). As impeachment loomed, the president's team then sought to draw a distinction between the president's personal misbehavior and his performance as president. Although the Republicans sought to frame the scandal as a criminal matter of perjury—that is, the felony of lying under oath—the news media generally adopted the frame that the lies were of a philandering husband trying to avoid embarrassing himself and his family, as opposed to a crook. As a result, Clinton emerged from his impeachment trial with a Senate acquittal, high public job performance ratings, and low ratings for his personal conduct (Bennett 2005; Cohen 2002a, 2002b; Klein 2002; Newman 2002; Owen 2000; Wayne 2000).

Once again, when the president and Congress battled over shaping public opinion, the president won. But there were casualties from this media battle. The consequences for presidential staff morale (and their bank statements) were quite damaging. George Stephanopoulos, a top Clinton aide who went on to become host of ABC's Sunday morning news show *This Week,* complained of the high legal expenses many members of the Clinton team had to bear because of Clinton's personal conduct (Stephanopoulos 1999). Other members of the Clinton administration went even further, claiming that Clinton's personal misconduct had hurt the Democratic Party and the progressive political agenda (Reich 1998). Whatever these additional consequences, it was clear that Clinton could and did take good care of himself throughout this ordeal.

Presidents, the Public, and Public Policy

Although presidents spend a great deal of time presenting their personal character to the public, going public efforts sometimes focus on issues. In this next section, I examine briefly the state of Bush's approval ratings for his Iraq policies. Most of the rest of the chapter focuses on the strategies presidents use to sell their preferred policies to the public. Construction of a popular presidential character in the media is the foundation on which presidents construct the more policy-oriented media messages that follow.

Bush and Iraq: Public Approval Ratings

By January 2007, despite all of the Bush team's public relations efforts, the public turned its thumbs down on all major aspects of the president's plan to increase the number of troops in Iraq. Overall, fewer than three people in ten in the United States—29 percent—approved of Bush's handling of the situation in Iraq (Balz and Cohen 2007), a sharp drop from the roughly two-thirds who supported the Iraq War before it started (Entman 2004). Bush's plan to increase the number of troops in Iraq also generated little public support, as shown in Table 3.2. Only 36 percent said they supported the plan in early January 2007 and that dropped to 34 percent support later that month (Balz and Cohen 2007). The difference was too small to be statistically significant, but the two surveys show that Bush's marketing efforts to promote his policies were not changing minds.

Barely more than one out of every four people surveyed—28 percent—believed that the war in Iraq "contributed to the long-term peace and stability in the Middle East," one of the Bush administration's key justifications for the war. Just over one-third of those surveyed—36 percent—believed that the Iraq War encouraged democracy elsewhere in the region, another key

Table 3.2 Public Opinion on President Bush's Iraq Policy, January 2007

Do you approve or disapprove of the way Bush is handling the situation in Iraq?

Approve	Disapprove	No Opinion
29	70	1

Do you support or oppose Bush's proposal to send approximately 22,000 additional U.S. military forces to Iraq? Do you feel that way strongly or somewhat?

	Net	Support Strongly	Somewhat	Net	Oppose Somewhat	Strongly	No Opinion
1/19/07	34	21	13	65	10	56	1
1/10/07	36	25	11	61	9	52	2

Do you think Congress should or should not try to block Bush's plan to send more troops to Iraq?

Should	Should not	No Opinion
59	39	2

Do you think the war with Iraq has or has not (ITEM)? [Asked of half the sample]

		Has		Has not	No Opinion
	Net	Great deal	Somewhat		
a. Contributed to long-term peace and stability in the Mideast	28	9	19	68	4
b. Encouraged democracy in other Arab nations	36	13	23	59	6
c. Helped to improve the lives of the Iraqi people	48	18	30	48	4

Which of these do you think is the better way to address the problems in Iraq: through diplomatic and political efforts, or through military efforts?

Diplomatic / political	Military	Both (vol.)	Neither (vol.)	No Opinion
63	25	8	2	2

Note: This *Washington Post–ABC News* poll was conducted by telephone January 16–19, 2007, among a random nationwide sample of 1,000 adults. The margin of sampling error is plus or minus 3 percentage points for full-sample questions. TNS of Horsham, Pa., conducted the sampling and data collection. Previous survey results are included where available to provide points of comparison.

Vol. stands for a volunteered response, one not offered in the question options read to the respondent.

Source: Dan Balz and Jon Cohen. 2007. "Confidence in Bush Leadership at All-Time Low, Poll Finds." *Washington Post,* January 22.

justification for the war used by the Bush administration. On the question of whether the war helped improve the lives of Iraqis, the survey respondents were split, with 48 percent saying yes and 48 percent saying no (Balz and Cohen 2007).

These results showed the demise of the president's ability to persuade the public by the seventh year of his presidency. Bush had been more much successful at persuasion efforts earlier in his first term. Bush's strongly prowar appeals also helped him win the political debate in 2002, but subsequent events took a heavy toll on the president's credibility. Overpromising and underdelivering may help win short-term political debates, but a president is likely to lose in the longer term, when the extent of White House deception and spin become clearer.

Bush's Continuing Character Construction: Designing Media–Friendly Images

Two of the most famous photographs of the Bush presidency were taken on May 1, 2003. On that day, Bush landed on the USS *Abraham Lincoln,* and emerged from the cockpit wearing a flight suit. Shortly afterward, Bush stood beneath a banner proclaiming "Mission Accomplished" before a highly enthusiastic navy crew headed home from the Middle East (Bumiller 2003).

But the mission in Iraq turned out to be far from accomplished. The occupation killed far more Americans than the war itself did—more than 90 percent of U.S. military casualties in Iraq occurred after Bush stood beneath that sign—and bin Laden remains at large more than six years after 9/11 despite Bush's vow that the terrorist would be captured "dead or alive." The made-for-television event on the aircraft carrier turned out not to do the president any favors. Content analysis of presidential news coverage during 2003 showed that Bush was assessed positively on network news 49 percent of the time during the combat phase of the war, as compared to 32 percent positive coverage during the six months after Bush stood beneath the "Mission Accomplished" banner (Farnsworth and Lichter 2006a, 94).

No item is too small for the media management of the commander in chief in wartime. Not only did the Bush team position the president beneath the banner, but they at first pretended they were not responsible for the banner's development. (It always looks better when someone else is singing your praises.) Under continuing media investigations, administration staffers eventually conceded they had created the banner (Baker 2007b).

White House marketing efforts on the *Lincoln* were not isolated incidents, but rather part of a consistent public relations effort to portray the president, who used the Texas National Guard to avoid service in Vietnam, as a military hero. At a campaign rally in South Dakota, Bush was positioned so that he could be photographed with the stone carvings of

Mount Rushmore in the background, as if Bush were comparable in stature to George Washington, Thomas Jefferson, Abraham Lincoln, and Theodore Roosevelt. Although Bush in a flight suit or at a presidential monument may not alone change public opinion, such media management efforts are part of cumulative strategies to present the president in the media in as favorable a light as possible (Bumiller 2003). The more Americans thought of Bush as a commander in chief, the more popular he could become. The more he was seen in heroic poses as president, the less the public would recall his less-than-heroic approach to military service when he was a young man.

These are extreme examples of the importance presidential media teams place on visual images and backdrops. Although the Bush administration realized that it had little ability to influence news coverage of a presidential speech, it had considerable ability to influence the picture shown on the news. So Presidents Clinton and Bush in particular used camera-friendly "wallpaper" behind them to telegraph the message of their remarks. These temporary backdrops were seen in the pictures taken of the event and helped convey the theme of the day, even if the news reporters themselves were not cooperative in framing the story the way the White House desired (Bumiller 2003). A president's media team may not be able to tell reporters what to say—though staffers do try to influence news content at every possible moment. No matter how critical the press, reporters can't stage presidential appearances. So, at a minimum, even an embattled White House can determine which pictures the television reporters have available on a given day.

The New Potemkin Village:
Party Loyalists Playing "Ordinary Americans"

Little is left to chance at a president's public appearances. Tickets to Bush's "public" events are often by invitation only, even when taxpayers are paying for the trip. Area Republican Party activists control access to these "public" events, and people who might have their doubts about Bush are not even allowed in the room. Lawsuits filed over access to presidential events have uncovered a 2002 White House manual giving presidential staffers extensive instructions about "deterring potential protesters" at Bush's appearances (Baker 2007c). An ACLU lawyer who sued the government on behalf of protesters said the manual demonstrates "that the White House has a policy of excluding or attempting to squelch dissenting viewpoints from presidential events" (quoted in Baker 2007c). According to the manual, advance staffers were to create "rally squads" of volunteers to stand between protesters and news cameras and to shout "USA! USA!" to drown out any protester chants (Baker 2007c).

At a March 2005 Colorado "public" event, three critics of the president who nevertheless obtained tickets to a Bush speech were removed before

Bush arrived on stage. The president's advance team identified the so-called "Denver Three" as potential critics because of a bumper sticker on one's car that said "No blood for oil" (Bumiller 2005a). Although the people who removed the potential protesters said they were with the U.S. Secret Service, the agency later said its personnel were not involved (the three had not said or done anything disruptive before they were forcibly removed). Impersonating a Secret Service agent is a crime, and two Bush loyalists have been charged in the matter (Bumiller 2005a; Frosch 2007). As this book goes to press, the case remains unresolved.

In August 2007, the federal government paid $80,000 to settle a First Amendment free speech case involving two people who were arrested for refusing to cover up their t-shirts at a 2004 Fourth of July Bush speech at the West Virginia Capitol (Baker 2007c). The settlement included no government admission of wrongdoing (Baker 2007c). Several similar cases relating to people being ejected from Bush's other "public" events are pending in the courts (Baker 2007c).

Presidents like invitation-only events because they deprive critics of a public opportunity to question administration policies. As the Bush team manual details, questioners are carefully screened by Republican loyalists ahead of time to make sure that the questions asked will be those the White House staffers want the president to answer. Those who get to be near the stage, for example, must be "extremely supportive of the administration," according to the manual (quoted in Baker 2007c). The audience questions at those events can be so fawning that one wonders whether the president's media handlers have gone so far that the whole event will look like a campaign rally. Will citizens see such events as so scripted that they are dismissed as propaganda? Although some citizens might see these events as a joke—particularly those who watch the extended news footage segments on Bush that are a staple of the *Daily Show* and the *Colbert Report* on Comedy Central—at least some people who see a sound-bite exchange of these planned-to-the-second events on the evening news may feel more positively about the president.

Presidential public relations teams like these scripted, invitation-only events because news reports often create the impression that the president is conversing with ordinary Americans and that few if any presidential critics exist. If "public" events are actually open to the general public—that is, all the people who actually pay for the government—things can quickly get out of the planners' control. During Clinton's second term, his national security team decided to hold a town hall meeting on potential military options against Iraq. The meeting, held at Ohio State University, was a public relations disaster as critics rejected, heckled, and ridiculed administration officials seeking to justify the policy (Bennett 1998). Such unscripted town meetings undermine presidential policy initiatives, for news reports that focus on the protests imply that the president's critics may be more numerous than they actually are. Although the Clinton team was generally effective at spinning the news to its advantage, this public event was a significant failure. The Bush team has worked hard to make sure it did not repeat the Clinton team's public relations mistake.

In addition, a truly open public meeting can also make a president look silly. During a 1994 town hall meeting on MTV, a young citizen asked Bill Clinton if he favored "boxers or briefs" (Kolbert 1994). The question may have been trivial, but it was not without impact. After all, the last thing that political lothario needed was a question that drew further attention to his private life, much less his privates.

Use the Troops

Of course staged backdrops and carefully selected supportive crowds are only part of the image the public sees. Bush has often given televised speeches from military bases before crowds of soldiers who are under orders not to ask rude questions or heckle. Bush's "mission accomplished" appearance is the best remembered, but Bush also made a variety of surprise visits to the troops in Iraq, including a holiday appearance where the president was photographed carrying a cooked turkey—a Norman Rockwell–style image of the commander in chief as national parent.

Military base visits are like gold to White House public relations staffers. Those well-behaved crowds in uniform also remind media viewers of Bush's role as commander in chief. Because polls show that citizens have great respect for the military, politicians appear with the troops for the same reason they appear with children—they hope that the good feelings directed at those in the politician's company will rub off. To appreciate how a military base appearance can enhance the president's reputation—remember that military bases are completely secure locations. The president flies in on Air Force One, gives a talk, and flies back to Washington, D.C., without encountering anyone who was not authorized to enter that high-security environment. The event does not even involve a presidential motorcade driving through the streets of a U.S. city, with the president running the risk of encountering placard-waving demonstrators and facing the consequences of negative pictures on the evening news. Presidents who appear at military bases, in other words, come across on the evening news and hence in public opinion as more popular than they really are. Presidential policies receive a warmer response before a disciplined audience of uniformed subordinates in the chain of command than in the country of civilians located outside the military base.

The troops, though, sometimes can use the made-for-television events to their own advantage and turn the tables on the visiting official. Rank-and-file soldiers used a televised event with Secretary of Defense Donald Rumsfeld to complain about the lack of armored plating for military vehicles, increasing the number of U.S. casualties. Rumsfeld made a bad situation worse when he uttered his impolitic criticism to the troops in Kuwait: "You go to war with the Army you have, not the Army you might want" (E. Schmitt 2004). "The truth is, every side in the war debate uses the troops for political gain. When Bush tearfully presents the Medal of Honor to the family of a slain war hero the morning after announcing his latest strategy for Iraq, then flies off to Fort Benning, he is using the troops as props. Democrats didn't make the absence of body armor a key campaign issue until they had done a lot of poll-testing" (Hiatt 2007).

Although a commander in chief is in the best position to use the troops, others can do so to some extent. Members of the administration and members of Congress on fact-finding missions to military bases can also be photographed in the company of officers and troops. Members of Congress with military backgrounds and combat experience, most notably Senators John McCain (R-AZ), John Warner (R-VA), James Webb (D-VA), and Chuck Hegel (R-NE), along with Representative John Murtha (D-PA), are given particularly respectful hearings by lawmakers and the press when they opine on military matters. But for those outside the military, particularly opposition party members of Congress, the welcome will never be as warm.

Bill Clinton's years in the White House passed without a large war, and the relatively peaceful nature of those years kept him from even contemplating using the troops for public relations in the same way Bush did after 9/11. But there can be little doubt that the media-savvy president would have accentuated his role as commander in chief and would have been equally tough on bin Laden had 9/11 occurred on Bill Clinton's watch.

Ordinary citizens can also use the troops—or a single soldier—to increase the importance of their messages. Cindy Sheehan, the mother of a fallen serviceman in Iraq turned high-visibility antiwar activist, was removed from the visitor's galley of the U.S. House shortly before Bush's 2006 State of the Union address. Although she had a valid ticket, Sheehan was removed because of the t-shirt she wore, which noted that more than 2,000 U.S. troops had died in Iraq by that time. Her expulsion increased news coverage of her continuing efforts to confront the president over his Iraq policies (Stolberg and Kornblut 2006). Sheehan was particularly visible in the online media, and her anti-Bush and antiwar public relations efforts are discussed at greater length in the next chapter.

Pass the Buck

Harry Truman once placed a sign on his White House desk that said "The buck stops here" (cited in McCullough 1993). But politicians often find it advantageous to state that they are acting on the advice of others, even if that is not always so. Passing the buck to subordinates is particularly popular when presidential policies backfire, like the Iraq occupation. From the promises of "Mission Accomplished" in May 2003 through the bloody occupation that followed, Bush sought to deflect questions about his competence by saying, in effect, that "the generals (or the Iraqis) made me do it."

In order to forestall attacks on his Iraq occupation policy as mismanaged, Bush repeatedly told reporters that he was following the advice of his generals. If the generals in Iraq want more troops, they will get more troops, Bush said throughout the occupation. During the 2006 midterm elections, Bush again used the generals to justify his "stay the course" approach (Rutenberg 2006b). Since military personnel are highly regarded in U.S. public opinion, Bush sought to suggest that any attacks on him were also attacks on the military.

But Bush's statement to the country that he was listening to the generals was not entirely true. Before the war started, the administration effectively silenced any critical views from the generals. As discussed earlier, the case of Army Chief of Staff Shinseki demonstrated that the Bush team rejected expert counsel that conflicted with the public relations message of a near-costless war (Shanker 2007). In order not to even hint at the possibility of White House error, Bush rewarded the staffers who made the biggest mistakes, not those with the most discerning judgment. Deputy Secretary of Defense Paul Wolfowitz, who rejected Shinseki's estimate as "wildly off the mark," was rewarded for his misjudgments by being promoted to head of the World Bank (Becker and Sanger 2005; Shanker 2007).

But by the start of 2007, the administration could no longer sustain the claim that Bush was following the advice of his military advisers. After his top generals said that additional U.S. troops would not help the situation, Bush replaced them (Rutenberg, Sanger, and Gordon 2007). Members of the Iraq Study Group, a special panel headed by former secretary of state James Baker and former U.S. Representative Lee Hamilton (D-IN), said that not a single general they interviewed felt that additional troops in the numbers proposed by Bush would be helpful this late in the occupation. Even generals who favored some additional troops suggested a force half as large as Bush's proposed boost of 21,500 troops (Rutenberg, Sanger and Gordon 2007) .

Bush's claim that Iraq was a sovereign government and that the United States was doing what the Iraqi government wanted also fell apart at the start of 2007. Despite Bush's frequent claims to the contrary, the Maliki government did not want additional U.S. troops in Iraq. In fact, the feeble Iraqi government feared that an even larger occupation force would generate an even larger civil uprising (Burns, Tavernise, and Santora 2007). In fact, the Maliki government explicitly requested that the U.S. military presence in Baghdad be reduced, even though that city was at the center of much of the nation's violence (Abramowitz and Baker 2007; Rutenberg, Sanger, and Gordon 2007).

> While senior officials in Washington have presented the new war plan as an American adaptation of proposals that were first put to Mr. Bush by Mr. Maliki when the two men met in the Jordanian capital of Amman in November, the picture that is emerging in Baghdad is quite different. What Mr. Maliki wanted, his officials say, was in at least one crucial respect the opposite of what Mr. Bush decided: a lowering of the American profile in the war, not the increase Mr. Bush has ordered. These Iraqi officials say Mr. Maliki, in the wake of Mr. Bush's setback in the Democratic sweep in November's midterm elections, demanded that American troops be pulled back to the periphery of Baghdad and that the war in the capital, at least, be handed to Iraqi troops. (Burns and Tavernise 2007)

Change the Subject

One of the most striking and successful media strategies to build support for Bush's presidency was the administration's ability to change the subject. In the days after 9/11, Bush presented himself as the national sheriff vowing to capture terrorist mastermind Osama bin Laden "dead or alive." At first it appeared that Bush would be successful in that quest. U.S. military operations in fall 2001 helped the Afghan resistance drive the Taliban from power in Afghanistan, and the internationally recognized figure was believed to be on the run in the porous border area between Afghanistan and Pakistan.

Shortly after the fall of Afghanistan, though, the terrorist leader became "Osama been forgotten." Throughout 2002 Bush turned his attention to Iraq and the threat Bush said Saddam Hussein and his alleged WMD programs posed to the United States. Bin Laden did his best to stay in the world limelight through the regular release of videotapes exhorting his followers (and scaring Americans), but the Bush administration was largely successful in shifting media and public attention to the pending war in Iraq.

As of this writing, more than six years after 9/11, Bush appears no closer to capturing bin Laden than he ever was. As the occupation of Iraq intensified, as the search for the alleged WMDs went nowhere, and as public approval of his performance continued to slide, Bush tried to redirect public attention to what he said were several planned but thwarted terrorist strikes on U.S. soil. Bush's efforts to take credit for what did not happen did not hold up under close scrutiny, however. A *Washington Post* investigation of

Bush's claims found that the Department of Homeland Security's color-coded warning system did not change when those threats were said to have been discovered. In addition, national security sources told the paper those "plots" were in their embryonic stages, not far enough along to have been thwarted by anyone (Goo 2005).

Gay Marriage and Other Divisive Topics

Changing the subject meant much more than pivoting from Afghanistan to Iraq and back as circumstances warrant. During the Bush years, Republicans repeatedly tried to focus on the issue of gay marriage, an issue that divided Democrats but largely united Republicans in opposition. Polls show that Christian conservative voters, a key GOP constituency, are particularly troubled by the prospect of same-sex marriage (Ceaser and Busch 2005). So holding state referendums to ban gay marriage can increase Republican turnout and make the Democrats appear to be divided and outside the American mainstream. During the 2004 election campaign, Bush endorsed a constitutional amendment to ban gay marriage—which at that time was legal only in Massachusetts (Bumiller 2004). When you change the subject, try to change it to a topic that will bedevil your opponent. Although Kerry was opposed to gay marriage, the fact that the Massachusetts senator opposed a constitutional amendment could be used by the Bush team to help convince some voters that only Republicans could be trusted to protect so-called traditional family values (Bumiller 2004).

Gay marriage was a useful alternative topic for Bush to raise as the war in Iraq continued to worsen. But Republicans in 2006 faced a problem about how to keep voters' minds off Iraq: after voters in a state had been energized to pass a ban on gay marriage, they could not pass another one. So the party turned to illegal immigration as a way of raising an alternative issue to the Iraq occupation (Nagourney, Hulse, and Rutenberg 2006). The issue did not turn out to be effective for the party in 2006. Given the attention the Bush administration had placed on Iraq over the previous several years, it was harder to change the subject in 2006 than some Republicans thought (Balz and Cohen 2007). In addition, evangelical Christians cared a lot more about stopping gay marriage than illegal immigration.

Since the 1960s, the Republican Party has been far more effective than the Democratic Party in using the media to exploit divisive issues on the way to electoral victory. In 1968, rather than offer details on his so-called secret plan to end the war in Vietnam, Republican presidential candidate Richard Nixon pursued white, middle-class voters and disaffected Democrats to support his campaign. Talking about the rioting in U.S. cities and capitalizing on racial fears in the wake of the civil rights movement, Nixon's press appearances were designed to convince white southern voters in particular to abandon the Democratic Party, which Nixon argued was too supportive of African Americans (Dallek 2007; McGinnis 1969). Reagan also cross-pressured white voters in his campaign appeals in 1980, arguing that welfare programs were too generous. He made a point of starting his campaign in Philadelphia, Mississippi, home to one of the most vicious murders of voting rights activists (Robinson and Sheehan 1983).

Bill Clinton was one of the few Democrats in recent years who could turn the tables on his Republican tormenters effectively. In 1992, Clinton hammered George H. W. Bush in the press for breaking his 1988 promise not to raise taxes—and for not dealing effectively with the economic problems of the United States in the early 1990s (Ceaser and Busch 1993).

Wag the Dog
When presidents try to redirect the national conversation, they often turn to foreign policy, where the executive branch has a freer hand to make policy. Cynical reporters often bring up a film called *Wag the Dog*, in which political operatives manufacture a military crisis to distract the nation from a presidential scandal.

There is some evidence that following the filmmaker's vision is an effective strategy for changing the subject. During summer 1998, when the Clinton-Lewinsky scandal was the talk of the nation's capital, the president went on a political trip to China. The three major news networks broadcast fifty-eight stories on Clinton's trip between June 24 and July 4, 1998, as compared to only nineteen stories on the scandal (Farnsworth and Lichter 2006a). This period marked one of the few times that year when the volume of coverage of the president's policies was greater than the coverage of the president's personal life. In addition, coverage of the trip was far more positive in tone than run-of-the-mill presidential news coverage. During that eleven-day period, more than four out of five sources quoted on the newscasts evaluated the president's China policies favorably, in sharp contrast to the roughly 60 percent negative coverage presidents normally receive (Farnsworth and Lichter 2006a).

Some of George W. Bush's critics raised the "wag the dog" flag when Bush turned his focus from Afghanistan to Iraq in 2002 following the administration's failure to capture Osama bin Laden. But even Bush critics suggested that was hardly his primary motivation. Treasury Secretary Paul O'Neill, along with Richard Clarke, Bush's first antiterrorism czar, portrayed the president as fixated on Saddam Hussein long before 9/11. Indeed, according to them, the new administration was so obsessed with the Iraqi dictator that it may have missed the warning signs of Al-Qaeda's imminent attack (Clarke 2004; Suskind 2004).

The Challenge of Changing the Subject

Between September 2007 and May 2008, surveys show that concerns over the economy and jobs have become the most important issue for an increasing number of Americans. Indeed, as the violence in Iraq has been reduced, it has steadily become a less important matter to voters. As shown in Table 3.3, by May 2008, 36 percent said that the economy and jobs were the most important matter to consider when electing Bush's successor, compared to 21 percent most focused on Iraq. No other issue comes close: the third most important issue, health care, was a top concern of only 6 percent (Cohen and Balz 2008).

Republicans have tried to make illegal immigration the focus of public discussion in recent years, but the surveys show how little success they had in drawing public attention away from Iraq. Immigration ranked third in importance in the January 2007 survey, with 7 percent considering it a top issue, though that figure is comparable to the 6 percent who considered it a top priority two years earlier before it became the focus of GOP lawmakers. Only 2 percent of those surveyed in May 2008 said the immigration issue would be the most important issue for them when selecting a president in the 2008 presidential election.

Other issues that attract intense followings also do not show signs of being likely to draw large numbers of single-issue voters to the polls. Morals and family values, taxes, the environment, gun control, and abortion are each identified as the top priority for only 1 or 2 percent of the voters in the May 2008 survey.

These results show that despite efforts by John McCain to focus public attention on what he says is the progress being made in Iraq, voters are still inclined to be more concerned with economic matters. Likewise, efforts by Democratic candidates to draw attention to alleged Bush administration shortcomings on honesty in government, education policy, and the budget deficit have largely fallen on deaf ears.

Three Little Words

In today's short-attention-span politics, politicians do not have much time to explain themselves. Forty years ago, the length of time a presidential candidate was given on the evening news to explain himself was roughly forty seconds (Adatto 1990). In 2004, the length of time of unmediated candidate commentary—called a sound bite—has shrunk to fewer than eight seconds (Farnsworth and Lichter 2007). Needless to say, an eight-second sound bite does not give a candidate much time to explain how he or she will fix Social Security or Medicare or deal with the situation in Iraq.

If you look at a watch and start talking, you'll see that it is hard to say more than a sentence or two in eight seconds. There really isn't time to express a complicated thought, and even most simple thoughts may take more time than the average network news sound bite.

Politicians trying to reach voters through the news have to play the cards they are dealt, and television's extremely brief sound bites shortchange

Table 3.3 Public Opinion on Key Government Priorities, 2005–2008

Question (for surveys conducted after February 2007)
Thinking ahead to the November presidential election, what is the single most important issue in your choice for president?

Question (for surveys conducted before February 2007)
What would you say is the one most important problem you would like to see Bush and the Congress deal with this year?

	5/11/08	4/13/08	2/1/08	1/12/08	12/9/07	11/1/07	9/7/07	1/19/07	12/11/06	12/18/05
Economy/Jobs	36	41	39	29	24	14	11	9	10	15
War in Iraq	21	18	19	20	23	29	35	48	44	32
Health care	6	7	8	10	10	13	13	4	6	11
Terrorism/ National security	4	5	5	4	9	5	6	5	4	5
Immigration	2	4	4	4	5	5	5	7	5	6
Ethics/Honesty/ Corruption in Government	3	4	4	5	4	4	6	1	2	1
Education	2	2	2	2	1	2	1	2	4	3
Family values	2	2	2	2	3	3	2	n/a	n/a	n/a
Gas/Oil/ Energy prices	2	1	*	1	n/a	n/a	n/a	2	3	2
Taxes	2	*	1	1	1	1	1	1	2	2
Environment	1	*	1	1	1	2	1	*	1	1
Abortion	1	1	1	1	1	1	1	n/a	n/a	n/a

Foreign policy	1	1	1	2	1	2	1	n/a	n/a	n/a
Guns/Gun control	1	*	*	*	*	n/a	n/a	n/a	n/a	3
Social Security	*	*	*	1	1	2	1	1	2	3
Federal budget deficit	*	*	*	*	*	1	1	1	*	1
Housing/Homelessness	*	*	*	*	*	*	*	2	2	1
Global warming	0	*	*	*	*	*	*	*	1	*
Iran	*	0	0	0	*	0	*	0	n/a	n/a
n/a										
Medicare	n/a	n/a	n/a	n/a	n/a	n/a	n/a	2	1	3
Prescription drug benefits	n/a	n/a	n/a	n/a	n/a	n/a	n/a	1	*	*
Crime	n/a	n/a	n/a	n/a	n/a	n/a	n/a	*	1	1
None	*	*	*	1	*	*	*	0	0	1
Other	7	6	9	7	9	9	7	8	6	6
No opinion	6	7	7	7	8	8	9	3	4	3

* = less than 0.5 percent

Note: This *Washington Post*–ABC News poll was conducted by telephone May 8–11, 2008, among a random national sample of 1,122 adults. The results from the full survey have a margin of sampling error of plus or minus 3 percentage points. Sampling, data collection, and tabulation by TNS of Horsham, Pa. (Earlier survey results are included to provide points of comparison).

Source: Cohen and Balz (2008).

serious discussion of issues. Because candidates want to be heard on the evening news, they have to tailor what they say to the eight-second quotation format. Speeches today are peppered with sound bites for media use, and candidate answers on the stump likewise are offered with the media's insistence on brevity in mind. Candidates who refuse to speak simply, who refuse to abide by the one- or two-sentence conventions of network television sound bites, are giving up free airtime they desperately need to reach voters to promote their campaigns. Elected officials generally have mastered this technique; otherwise they probably would have lost to a more media-oriented candidate. But if elected officials have not mastered the sound bite they better get to it; otherwise they won't be able to compete effectively in the struggle to set the public agenda and frame ongoing events.

Nixon had an uneven reputation as a political communicator. The same president who was spectacularly unsuccessful in drawing media attention away from the youthful John F. Kennedy in 1960 and Watergate more than a dozen years later was nevertheless a highly effective media personality at other times. As a candidate running for reelection in 1972, Nixon demonstrated the strength of the three-word sound bite. After defining the McGovern Democrats as out of touch and his own Republicans as the party of traditional American values, Nixon won forty-nine states, losing only Massachusetts and the District of Columbia to George McGovern (Aitken 1993; Dallek 2007).

One of the best candidates at using three little words to make his case was, ironically, one of the least effective presidential communicators: George H. W. Bush. At the 1988 Republican convention, the presidential candidate electrified the party faithful with the following exhortation: "Read my lips: No new taxes." Bush's "No new taxes" pledge helped define his campaign, demonstrating that he was a worthy successor to Ronald Reagan, the president who aggressively cut taxes (and as a result created huge budget deficits for future generations). The statement was the theme of Bush's campaign and helped secure his victory over Michael Dukakis, a longer-winded Massachusetts governor who did not give good sound bite (Hershey 1989). The Bush 1988 campaign was also aided by a two-word warning that played on racial fears, "Willie Horton," the name of the African American Massachusetts inmate who killed a white Maryland couple during a weekend furlough (West 2001).

In order to focus both his 1992 campaign and the media on Bush's shortcomings, the Clinton team famously lived by a widely reported four-word mantra: "It's the economy, stupid!" (Ceaser and Busch 1993). Other famous one-liners include Ronald Reagan's putdown of Jimmy Carter in a 1980 debate, "There you go again" (Abramson, Aldrich, and Rohde 1982) and Bob Dole's frustrated 1996 campaign response to what he saw as Bill Clinton's inexplicable popularity despite his scandals, "Where's the outrage?" (Abramson, Aldrich, and Rohde 1999). In his 2002 State of the Union speech, George W. Bush relied on the term *axis of evil* as three-word shorthand for the three countries Bush said were aligned against the United States (Frum 2003).

Video News Releases and Paid Favorable Coverage

It is sometimes said that the best defense is a good offense, and the Bush administration certainly followed that strategy when it came to controlling information flow to the public. The Bush administration expanded the use of government-produced videos to trumpet administration policies. Hundreds of these videos were created and packaged as ready for air on local television stations, though the practice generated controversy when some releases failed to say they were produced by the government (Barstow and Stein 2005; Pear 2004). These video news releases were aired on hundreds of local television stations, usually without informing viewers the segments were produced by the government, a serious breach of media ethics (Barstow and Stein 2005). Critics also questioned the legality of using taxpayer funds to promote administration policies in this way (Pear 2004).

The Bush administration apparently believed that the best way to get positive media coverage was to pay for it. In 2005, its communications team came under fire for paying several conservative columnists a total of more than $250,000 to write favorable stories about government policies for the Departments of Education and Health and Human Services. Critics condemned the government for trying to manipulate the media and the columnists for taking the payments but not disclosing them to readers. Since the columnists who received the money, including Armstrong Williams and Maggie Gallagher, are prominent conservatives, critics also considered the payments a waste of taxpayer money since these writers supported the administration anyway. Bush ordered the practice stopped after the controversial government payments came to light (Kornblut 2005a, 2005b).

Several months later, however, the practice resurfaced. The U.S. Environmental Protection Agency came under fire for a proposal to spend $5 million on a media relations program, including ghost-writing articles supportive of agency policies for placement in academic journals (Barringer 2005). This also does not seem like prudent use of taxpayer resources, as anyone who has spent time around graduate students knows that you can get academic writers for hire for almost nothing.

A Friendly Reporter, but Is He Gannon or Guckert?

The Bush administration also gave a party loyalist access to the White House pressroom as a working journalist. Jeff Gannon, whose real name was James

Guckert, and who was employed by Republican media organizations, obtained a White House press pass under his false name, and was frequently called upon during press briefings to ask "soft ball" questions (Rich 2005a; Seelye 2005). White House press passes are highly coveted and are only given to reporters who have passed lengthy background checks, given the national security concerns relating to anyone who works inside the White House (Seelye 2005). The scandal erupted when Guckert was able to get a pass under an assumed name despite his apparent lack of journalistic credentials (Kornblut 2005b; Seelye 2005). The head of the Texas Web site (gopusa.com) that published his work denied that Guckert was a plant for the party and said that he reported under the name Gannon because he preferred the sound of it (R. Blumenthal 2005).

Attempts to Spin Policy Proposals

Bush's efforts to build public support for his presidency were aided by 9/11, by the Iraq War, and by how Bush handled both issues. But the aggressive media management efforts, together with the worsening situation in Iraq during Bush's second term, resulted in a powerful backlash. Bush's presidential approval numbers fell to near-record lows in late 2006 and early 2007, and Congress, traditionally much more negatively regarded than the White House, enjoyed a revival of public esteem.

In 1994, the Republicans gained control of Congress through a list of policy promises called the Contract with America (Gingrich 1995) that gained traction because of the Clinton administration's public and unsuccessful health-care reform proposal. The Democrats gained majority status in Congress a dozen years later largely on the basis of public dissatisfaction with Bush's handling of the Iraq War and occupation (Balz and Cohen 2007). But the Democrats did run on other issues, including greater federal support for embryonic stem-cell research (Saulny 2006). Bush's first presidential veto was of a stem-cell bill when Democrats wanted to loosen current restrictions on federal funding. According to a January 2007 national survey, by a 55 percent to 38 percent margin more people backed the Democratic Congress on this question (Balz and Cohen 2007).

Table 3.4 shows that the Democratic positions on several issues were more positively received than the Bush administration's record. A Democratic priority, increasing the minimum wage from $5.15 to $7.25 an hour, was favored by 86 percent of those surveyed. More than half of that 86 percent favored an even higher minimum wage.

More than three-quarters of those surveyed also agreed that the government should be allowed to negotiate with prescription drug companies to get better prices for medications for senior citizens, a procedure prohibited

Table 3.4 Public Opinion on Domestic Issues, January 2007

Do you support or oppose loosening the current restrictions on federal funding for embryonic stem-cell research?

Support	Oppose	No Opinion
55	38	7

Would you support or oppose raising the minimum wage, which is now five dollars and fifteen cents an hour, to seven dollars and twenty-five cents an hour?

Support	Oppose	No Opinion
86	13	1

[Ask if respondent supports the increase in the minimum wage in the previous question] Is seven twenty-five enough, or should the minimum wage be higher than that?

Enough	Should Be Higher	No Opinion
45	52	3

Some people say the Medicare program should be allowed to negotiate with drug companies to get better prices for prescription drugs for senior citizens. Others say this would give the government too much of a role in the marketplace and prevent drug companies from making the profits they need to develop new drugs. Do you think the Medicare program should or should not be allowed to negotiate prices with drug companies?

Should	Should Not	No Opinion
79	17	4

How concerned are you about the issue of global warming—is that something that worries you a great deal, a good amount, just some, or hardly at all?

| Great Deal / Good Amount | | | | Some / Hardly / Not at All | | | No Opinion |
Net	Great Deal	Good Amount	Net	Just Some	Hardly at All	Not at All (vol.)	
49	26	23	49	24	22	3	3

Note: This *Washington Post–ABC News* poll was conducted by telephone January 16–19, 2007, among a random nationwide sample of 1,000 adults. The margin of sampling error is plus or minus 3 percentage points for full-sample questions. TNS of Horsham, Pa., conducted the sampling and data collection.

Vol. stands for a volunteered response, one not offered in the question options read to the respondent.

Source: Dan Balz and Jon Cohen. 2007. "Confidence in Bush Leadership at All-Time Low, Poll Finds." *Washington Post,* January 22.

by the Bush administration. The public also seemed more concerned than the White House about global warming, with 26 percent saying they worried about global warming "a great deal," 23 percent "a good deal," and 24 percent "some." Only 22 percent said they were "hardly at all" worried by the potential of climate change.

By the middle of his second term, Bush's effort to build public support in all policy areas suffered as a result of public discontent with his Iraq policies and the stagnating economy. As shown in Table 3.3, other issues were not as important to voters, who were far more focused on Iraq and the economy than by anything else. Despite White House advantages in spin, by the middle of Bush's second term public opinion had become more anti-Bush than pro-Congress.

Conclusion

Presidents who seek to win public approval for policies must first win Americans' hearts. From the start of a candidate's public emergence, extreme care is paid to the public presentation of one's personality. Nowhere does the matter of character have more impact than in the White House, where the president—or at least the president's transmitted image—is effectively a frequent guest in Americans' living rooms. A winning personality, which includes a friendly, open, common personal demeanor, in most elections years is a prerequisite for the office. In those rare cases (like 1988) when both parties nominate technocrats, the winning candidate only has to be less off-putting than his rival.

Modern White Houses are engaged in permanent marketing campaigns to build and retain public affection for the president and win over some of the less-committed moderates who can be persuaded to view the president in a positive light. Although today's hyperpartisan politics mean that every president has a core of die-hard supporters who will support nearly everything and a core of die-hard opponents who will reject nearly everything (each group is about one-third of the electorate), there are still significant numbers of voters who could be talked into supporting any president at least some of the time.

Presidents and presidential candidates spend so much time discussing their character because they believe that winning and keeping public approval is essential for presidents trying to govern. Congress may not be easily won over by presidential efforts to market policy alternatives, particularly regarding domestic matters. But presidents who go public imagine they have a trump card—that the public backs the president. Legislators, this theory suggests, fear presidents with strong public support as they worry that opposing a popular president will hurt lawmakers' reelection prospects. Although little evidence suggests that going public is an effective political strategy, we see that presidents nevertheless cultivate their public image and public response with an intensity that borders on obsession.

Although Bush and Clinton had effective media management teams, their strategies sometimes diverged in response to different current events. Bill Clinton never had the public opinion highs Bush did after 9/11, nor did he have a Congress or public so willing to support military interventions as existed after the terrorist attacks. As a result Bush could make far greater use of an administration's inherent advantages in releasing—and not releasing—information to reporters relating to national security questions that dominated public and media attention. Given the issues prominent during his presidency, Clinton could never consistently focus on foreign policy, nor could he control the information flow as effectively as the post 9/11 president could. Neither could Clinton silence his critics on Capitol Hill or in the press by claiming a national emergency during the relatively tranquil 1990s.

The real media management successes of Clinton, therefore, were more defensive in nature. Clinton and his team did an effective job of spinning impeachment as more about radical Republicans than about his own misconduct. Clinton was also quite effective in separating his personal life from his policymaking skills in the public mind—a particularly tough sell given the perjury allegations against him.

Shading the truth, if not committing outright fraud, seems like a particularly high risk strategy. Although it may work to secure some short-term policy goals, the approach can really hurt a president's standing later in one's term. Presidents who sell themselves and their policies through less-than-honest marketing often face an eventual day of reckoning. Bush's credibility was lost shortly after the start of his second term as the Iraq operation turned out to be the opposite of what Bush and his team predicted. Clinton's credibility would have been lost too, except for the lucky break that the Republicans trying to impeach him seemed even less appealing to the voters than the philanderer in chief. Clinton, after all, really was the likable person Americans first discovered in 1992, and that positive early portrayal helped insulate him against the attacks that came later.

The media changes since the 1980s have expanded greatly the media channels for presidents and presidential candidates to communicate with citizens. The now wide-open media landscape also gives citizens greater opportunity to join in the political debate, be it via e-mails, blogging, or even posting videos online. The new media aspects of presidential efforts to spin policies and personalities are the key subjects of the next chapter.

Chapter Four

Modern Media Channels

Presidents and Presidential Candidates
Spin the New Media

In the United States, as in many democratic countries, government officials
have great interest in enlisting the public to support their policies. The previous chapters examined how presidents seek to win over citizens through
media portrayals of their personalities and their policy arguments, all with
the hopes of making those citizens foot soldiers in presidential battles with
Congress. What is most striking about White House marketing efforts thus
far is the extent to which the executive-governed policy discussion takes place
in only one direction, from the administration to citizens. That top-down
approach has existed throughout the various forms of U.S. mass media, as
it has consistently been far easier for presidents to reach the citizens than
the other way around.

This chapter examines how new media outlets may change the nature of
political spin involving a president or a presidential candidate and citizens.
Some new technologies make modern political discourse less mediated, and
other new media outlets can make that political discourse more interactive

than it once was. This chapter examines how leading new media outlets have been increasing or decreasing the ability of presidents and presidential candidates to spin successfully in recent years. Because much of the online news and discussion involves presidential candidates, this chapter will contain more information about candidate media strategies than did previous chapters.

The Past: Largely Top-Down Spin

Before modern mass media, political communication involving the president and the public was largely a one-way street. Presidents could always communicate with citizens through party newspapers and the conversations of local party officials and citizens, but the response from citizens went largely unheard by presidents most of the time. Citizens could express themselves individually with letters to the White House or questions asked of the president's local party representatives; but such idiosyncratic feedback, early citizen attempts to counter government spin, may not have accomplished much.

The most effective early mechanisms for citizens to be heard, of course, were elections. But presidential elections occur once every four years, and they offer only a rough guide to citizen policy preferences. Did George W. Bush's victory in 2004 signify public support for his Iraq policies, for the proposed partial privatization of Social Security, or for a Christian conservative social agenda? Surveys say "no" to all three, but those polls do suggest that people felt comfortable with Bush as a person, whatever their doubts about his policies (Balz and Cohen 2007; Ceaser and Busch 2005). In addition, 2004 exit poll surveys revealed that many voters believed Kerry was not tough enough to be president (Ceaser and Busch 2005).

Although elections obviously helped redirect policy by selecting new policymakers, the once-every-four-years process offers only a blunt, infrequent, and sometimes ineffective instrument for citizens to use in policy matters. Politicians are greatly tempted to interpret elections as they see fit, hearing what they want to hear. Even in the rare situation in which one can view a specific presidential election as a mandate, exactly what citizens endorsed with their votes remains subject to interpretation. In 1932, for example, Franklin Delano Roosevelt (FDR) won in a landslide because citizens wanted a more activist national government to combat the Depression, but the voters did not speak to specific policies (Goodwin 1994).

Indeed, many presidential elections do not take the shape of referenda. Sometimes voters even have expressed opposition to what would come to pass. Woodrow Wilson in 1916 and FDR in 1940 campaigned for reelection on promises to keep the United States out of the world wars then raging in

Europe; and Lyndon Johnson said in 1964 that American boys would not fight on Asian soil. In both of the European examples, the United States entered those wars shortly after those elections—albeit in response to new developments like Pearl Harbor. Within several months of Johnson's 1964 election, roughly half a million Americans were fighting in Vietnam (Beschloss 2002; Burns and Dunn 2001; Cooper 1983).

In other words, the U.S. constitutional order and the practical realities of governing give presidents wide latitude to pursue policies they consider necessary if they are prepared to live with the electoral consequences. As the Founders intended, the political system does not give much short-term authority to citizens, though of course voters can replace all politicians when their terms expire and can pressure their congressional representatives to impeach a president in extreme cases. In practice, presidents often have been able to convince citizens to support the White House, particularly on foreign policy matters (Cronin and Genovese 2004). What presidents do hear from citizens generally seems to them not crucial to their decision-making process.

Traditionally, the only other significant mechanism that could be employed by citizens seeking to be heard collectively was a mass protest rally. Throughout U.S. history—be it the antidraft rallies of the Civil War and the Vietnam war, the suffrage marches of women and civil rights marches of African Americans, the nuclear weapons freeze rallies of the 1980s, the demonstrations against the pending war in Iraq in 2003, or the demonstrations against the Iraq occupation "surge" in 2007—citizens have found it hard to redirect presidential initiatives, even when polls showed support for the demonstrators' positions. Presidents often choose not to listen even to hundreds of thousands of voices outside the White House on the National Mall if they dislike what the masses are saying. Defensive presidents often blame reporters and pollsters for distorting the public voice, in effect justifying their choices to ignore apparent public preferences.

The ever-increasing use of survey research gives presidents and other political figures evidence about what citizens are thinking about and how they view leading issues. Polls are widely reported, giving citizens a clearer sense of the policy preferences of other voters. This increased public knowledge can encourage greater pressure on the White House after people learned that many other citizens agreed with them on controversial policies. In practice, though, collective action against even an unpopular president is sporadic at best.

The consequences of public opinion on a presidential administration are only as great as presidents allow them to be. Sometimes presidents listen and abandon unpopular policies in the face of citizen opposition. Frequently, though, they do not. Discounting public opinion is particularly common in foreign policy, an area in which elites often have strong doubts about the ability of citizens to reach considered judgment (Entman 2004).

In fairness, though, survey research has significant limitations. First, public opinion can be fluid, changing quickly in response to ongoing events. Bush's own presidential approval ratings nearly doubled in the immediate aftermath of 9/11 (Busch 2004; Pew Research Center for the People and the Press 2001). Many surveys ask citizens to give opinions on things they may not know much about, such as international trade agreements or countries they cannot locate on a map. Public opinion is sometimes conflicted, such as when citizens say they want both low taxes and more government services. In addition, responses can depend greatly on question wording, a fact that allows an administration to dismiss as unreliable any poll the White House staff does not like (Entman 2004). Even though considerable research exists to suggest that the public as a collective provides rational assessments of current conditions and adjusts its preferences to ongoing developments, presidents, like other people, are tempted to ignore what they do not want to hear (Page and Shapiro 1992; Popkin 1991).

With these uneven results in the past, survey research did not appear to be a viable means for public influence on White House policies. Given the difficulties involved in reaching the president in a country the size of the United States, and the Founders' explicit efforts to reduce the pressures of public opinion on the president, it should come as no surprise that political observers hoped the technological developments of mass media during the past several decades would trigger an entirely new, more citizen-oriented politics. Whether these new communication vehicles have had a democratizing effect, or merely provided a new mechanism for top-down communication and spin, remains an open question.

The New Media and the New Spin

Television spread across the U.S. landscape in the 1950s, and by the end of the decade could be found in nearly all U.S. homes. The 1960 presidential election, some say, was determined by the new medium, which in televised debates pitted the youthful, optimistic, apparently vigorous Senator John Kennedy (D-MA) against the haggard-looking Vice President Richard Nixon (Druckman 2003; White 1961). After the devices became standard in U.S. homes, and the evening newscasts expanded to the thirty-minute length in the early 1960s, changes in media politics became more evolutionary than revolutionary.

The next dramatic change in the media environment came two decades later with the rise of the Cable News Network (CNN) in the 1980s, which created a 24/7 outlet for news and a demand for a huge volume of news content to fill all that time (Baum and Kernell 1999; Goldberg and Goldber 1995). Shortly after CNN's development, academics started writing abou the so-called CNN effect, the idea that citizens looking at horrific picture of violence from foreign lands would pressure national governments to act Although western governments sometimes intervene (as in Kosovo), they often take insufficient measures to halt mass killings (as in Rwanda and Sudan). Political leaders, at least in the United States, do not seem to face the domestic outcry associated with inaction under this theory (Entman 2000; Kristof 2004; Power 2002).

The creation of CNN was followed shortly by the rise of stridently ideological public affairs programming, first with talk radio hosts such as Rush Limbaugh and then expanding into television with Fox News (Dautrich and Hartley 1999; Davis and Owen 1998; Sella 2001). Liberals tried to fight back with their own ideologically oriented outlets—including liberal talk radio programming and the Air America radio network—but these media outlets suffered from small audiences and minimal revenue (Jensen and Miller 2006; Laufer 1995).

The Internet, of course, represented the biggest technological advancement of the late twentieth century for political communication. Anyone with a Web page or an e-mail account could be a journalist, dramatically expanding the ability of citizens to communicate with one another about politics, to refute presidential spin, or to write about whatever interests them. By the late 1990s, even the mainstream media outlets had put their own news sites online, providing up-to-the-minute coverage of breaking news (Pew Research Center for the People and the Press 2006). Public expectations of free online content made it impossible for most Internet outlets to charge for their material, though a few specialty publications do so (Rainey 2007).

The traditional gatekeeper function of the mainstream media began to break down with the rise of online news, allowing news consumers to tailor their preferences among the nearly infinite number of sources available online (Williams and DelliCarpini 2004). Providing free online content was less of a problem for bloggers, those Internet journalists who post their own opinions and link to reports and news posted on other sites—a low-cost approach to mass public discourse (Drezner and Farrell 2004; Goo 2007; Schudson 2007; Sipress 2007). Because they are not close to government sources, these freelancers are not as constrained in their commentary and may be less reliable than traditional news outlets (Drudge 2000; Schudson 2007).

"The Internet today is like the American West in the 1880s. It's wild, it's crazy, and everybody's got a gun," said Thomas Kunkel, dean of the University of Maryland's journalism school. "There are no rules yet." The common journalistic practices of verifying facts, seeking both sides of a story and subjecting an article to editing are honored mostly in the breach. Innuendo and rumor

Figure 4.1 Clinton Web site

Figure 4.2 shows the White House Web site from a typical day during Bush's second term. The differences between the two Web pages are substantial. Many are the result of faster downloads and the greater ability of today's computers to deal with pictures, video, and links to other Web pages. The pictures are much larger, and Bush is front and center in the Web page's description. Photos of the president doing things the Bush team wants to emphasize are on the front page and throughout the linked sections. The Web page contains handy links to the president's most recent weekly radio address and to the daily press briefing, which is available live on the site or can be accessed later. Many of the features of the new Web site were not realistic during the Clinton administration, as citizens would not have waited for picture-filled and link-heavy pages to materialize on their home computer screens. In fact, it probably would have been faster to wait for delivery of a new computer than to download video clips in those days.

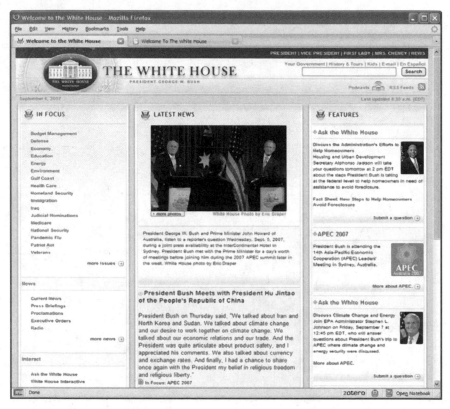

Figure 4.2 Bush Web site

The most significant difference between these two Web sites, however, is one of perspective. In another example of the ever-increasing importance of presidential marketing, the Bush Web page is far more focused on Bush than on the White House. Although the Clinton Web page might have been useful for high school students writing papers on the federal government, the Bush Web page is designed to maximize the promotion of the president and his policies. Several key issues are presented on the Web page, with links to many other current issues available for those who desire more specialized material. In addition, citizens who want regular e-mailed updates can get them by registering their e-mail addresses, and the Web page includes a convenient search function for those desiring specialized material. Other administration officials are also enlisted into Bush's marketing effort on this page. A regular feature, "Ask the White House," showcases presidential priorities by having top administration officials respond to questions sent in by Web page users. Spanish translations are also available for the content.

Reducing clutter is an important part of effective Web page management. The Bush administration has removed the matters relating to routine federal services to a separate Web page (www.usa.gov) that provides useful links to more than 100 online government services. On the Clinton administration Web site, the link to information on government services was one of the most prominent on the page, limiting the ability of the Clinton-Gore team to promote its policy agenda or tout its accomplishments in a more visible way.

As a presidential media management tool, the White House Web site has come a long way over the years. Part of the evolution of the page was based on technological improvements that allowed the George W. Bush team to do far more with the page than the Clinton team ever could. But even more importantly, the Bush team moved far more aggressively to capitalize on the Web page's potential to market the president and his policies in a direct, unmediated way. At the same time, the page is not a free-for-all. Although people can submit information to the White House Internet team, the Bush administration does not offer an open discussion page where citizens can communicate with each other about Bush's policies. In that way, the ostensible public access is less than it appears. The page retains some of the traditional top down presidential political communication elements that are rapidly disappearing on mainstream media Web sites and the Web pages of many bloggers.

Conservative New News Media: Help for the GOP

Matt Drudge

One of the most famous and important online political voices is the Drudge Report (www.drudgereport.com), a collection of news story links and original reporting by Matt Drudge, who critiques politics and the media on his frequently viewed Web site. Two of the major problems with the Drudge Report, according to its critics, are its inaccuracy and bias. Drudge ran a story in 1999, for example, alleging that Bill Clinton had fathered a half–African American son while governor of Arkansas. A week later DNA tests confirmed there was no genetic link between Clinton and the boy. Drudge's influence is magnified, according to critics, because he has functioned as an agenda-setting news source for the mainstream media since the Clinton-Lewinsky scandal. Critics also complain that Drudge's continual focus on sexual matters during those years distracted citizens from more important matters such as international relations (Hall 2001).

Drudge (2000) said that the mainstream press had been too easy on Clinton and failed to scrutinize the president at the level he deserved. Drudge blamed the allegedly cozy coverage on the fact that White House reporters are dependent on the administration for stories and therefore have professional incentives to be kind to those in power. Drudge said he does not need to curry favor with the White House because he is not in the daily journalists' competition for every story.

Even so, Drudge did help the Bush campaign by airing unflattering and sometimes incorrect information about John Kerry, the 2004 Democratic presidential nominee. A variety of negative claims about the Massachusetts senator received wide distribution via the *Drudge Report,* including allegations that Kerry had Botox facial treatments and that he had extramarital relations of his own with an intern. The site also provided a ready platform for the attacks on Kerry's wartime record by the Swift Boat Veterans for Truth (Halperin and Harris 2006).

Content analysis, by the way, refutes Drudge's claim that White House correspondents are routinely soft on the presidents they cover. As discussed earlier, an analysis of all evening network newscasts during the first year of the Ronald Reagan (1981), Bill Clinton (1993), and George W. Bush (2001) presidencies found almost equally negative content relating to the three presidencies on ABC, CBS, and NBC (Farnsworth and Lichter 2006a).

Fox News: Upbeat Coverage of George W. Bush and the Iraq War
Although Fox News programming lags far behind network television news in the size of its audience, Fox programs generate some of the highest ratings on cable television news and commentary. The distinctive ideological approach of Rupert Murdoch's network is apparent to many news viewers, as surveys show that Fox is particularly appealing to conservatives (Pew Research Center for the People and the Press 2004a, 2007). Researchers who have looked at the cable news programs through content analysis have found that viewers turning to Fox for a conservative view on the news are generally not disappointed.

During the 2004 general election campaign, George W. Bush received extraordinarily positive treatment on Fox News' *Special Report with Brit Hume,* the network's flagship hour-long news report (Farnsworth and Lichter 2007). During the two months between Labor Day and Election Day, content analysis reveals that Bush's coverage was 53 percent positive, compared to 21 percent positive for John Kerry, a 32-percentage-point margin favoring the Republican (Farnsworth and Lichter 2007). Bush had substantial advantages over Kerry in all three Fox coverage areas examined: foreign policy (61 percent positive for Bush versus 10 percent positive for Kerry); domestic policy (43 percent positive for Bush versus 33 percent positive for Kerry); and leadership qualities (63 percent positive for Bush and 34 percent positive for Kerry).

Network television treated Kerry more positively than Bush, with a 59 percent positive overall for the challenger versus 37 percent positive overall for the incumbent president. The 2004 network television margin was 22 percentage points, less one-sided than Fox's coverage but far larger than the 3-percentage-point difference that separated Bush and Gore in a similar study of network news content during the 2000 campaign. In 2004 on network television, Kerry won all three of the coverage areas discussed above, but in the key area of foreign policy Kerry's coverage (27 percent positive) was only 2 percentage points better than Bush's (Farnsworth and Lichter 2007, 162).

Fox's markedly pro-Bush coverage was not limited to the election season. A comprehensive study of the tone of Iraq War coverage on Fox from the first missile attacks of March 19, 2003, through the fall of Tikrit on April 14, 2003, examined news on three dimensions: Bush administration Iraq policies, U.S. military performance, and the debate over going to war. On these three dimensions, Fox's news coverage was 60 percent positive, 10 percentage points more positive than the network evening news programs during the same period (Farnsworth and Lichter 2006a, 97).

The pro-GOP spin of Fox News is not lost on its viewers. Republicans are more likely to get their news from Fox than Democrats are. When asked about their most important media sources, 24 percent of those who voted Republican in 2006 said they relied on Fox, as compared to only 10 percent of those who voted Democratic. As shown in Table 4.3, the 14-percentage-point spread in Fox's audience is the largest partisan gap of any of the media outlets examined in the survey (Pew Research Center for the People and the Press 2007).

Overall, television retained its dominant position as a source of campaign news: 69 percent of the Republicans and 74 percent of the Democrats relied on television as one of their two leading news sources. Democrats were slightly more likely to watch network television news, though the difference was generally only a few percentage points between Republicans and Democrats. There was a wider gap for CNN, identified by 17 percent of Democrats and 8 percent of Republicans as a key news source. Republicans favored radio by a margin of 21 percent compared to 14 percent for Democrats, perhaps because of the greater strength of conservative media in the talk radio environment. The Internet was considerably less important to many news consumers than television or newspapers, and slightly less important than radio. But Democrats and Republicans were equally likely to rely on the Web: 17 percent of each partisan group identified the Internet as one of their top two sources of campaign news.

Liberal New Media: Struggling to Catch Up?

Liberal Bloggers Battling Online

Bloggers provide online commentary on the news and usually offer links embedded in the text (hyperlinks) that connect readers to original reporting

Table 4.3 Media Choices of Voters by Party Identification, 2006

How have you been getting most of your news about the November elections? [Accept two answers. If only one response is given, probe for one additional response.]

	Voted Republican (percent)	Voted Democratic (percent)
All forms of television	69	74
Fox Cable	24	10
Local news	22	25
ABC Network	11	13
NBC Network	10	14
CNN Cable	8	17
CBS Network	7	11
MSNBC Cable	3	6
Newspapers	38	44
Radio	21	14
Internet	17	17
Magazines	2	2

Note: Because two answers were accepted, columns do not add up to 100 percent.

Source: Pew Research Center for the People and the Press. January 17, 2007. "Election 2006 Online." Pew Internet and American Life Project Report. http://www.pewinternet.org/pdfs/PIP_Politics_2006.pdf (accessed January 31).

by others. The commentary consists of posts, with the most recent report found at the top of the page (M. Blumenthal 2005; Drezner and Farrell 2004). The liberal bloggers were particularly influential during the 2006 political season, trying to channel public anger over the occupation in Iraq into victories for antiwar Democrats. One of the key targets of the movement was Senator Joseph Lieberman (D-CT), the Democratic senator most supportive of the Bush administration's policies in Iraq. Online commentators such as dailykos.com and moveon.org, leading liberal Web sites, promoted Ned Lamont, a little-known former Democratic local official in Greenwich, who decided to wage a David versus Goliath struggle against the three-term incumbent who had also been the party's 2000 vice presidential nominee (Bai 2006; Grynbaum 2006).

Lamont won the primary in an upset, but Lieberman chose to run as an independent and won the general election in November 2006. Lieberman then caucused with the Democrats, as he had promised to do before the election, giving the Democrats a one-seat majority in the Senate that took office in January 2007.

Markos Moulitsas Zuniga, founder of the Daily Kos, said that Lamont's primary victory was a result of voter discontent with Lieberman, not blogger influence. Blogs "are fairly irrelevant when it comes to generating discontent. We can't generate discontent. We can amplify it" (quoted in Grynbaum 2006).

The audience for liberal bloggers is smaller than that for conservative bloggers. According to TruthLaidBear.com, a leading source of online blog traffic, two of the four most popular bloggers are conservative sites: instapundit.com and michellemalkin.com. As shown in Table 4.4, the most popular liberal Web sites—dailykos.com, talkingpointsmemo.com, and huffingtonpost.com—ranked third, tenth, and fourteenth, respectively. (This comparison does not include the more popular news and opinion Web sites such as cnn.com, nytimes.com, or drudgereport.com, since none of them are primarily blogs.)

Air America: Struggling to Get Airborne
In the late 1980s, when the talk radio format became popular again in the United States, conservatives rushed to dominate the revived medium (Laufer 1995). Both the most popular hosts and those who tuned in to their radio shows displayed a distinct ideological and demographic identity: mostly middle-aged white males holding generally conservative views (Owen 1996).

Table 4.4 Top-Ranked Political Bloggers, February 25, 2008

1.	www.michellemalkin.com
2.	www.dailykos.com
3.	tmz.com
4.	wwwinstapundit.com
5.	littlegreenfootballs.com
6.	slashdot.org
7.	powerlineblog.com
8.	captainsquartersblog.com
0.	feverishthoughts.com
10.	hotair.com
11.	www.talkingpointsmemo.com
12.	realclearpolitics.com
13.	politico.com
14.	www.bitter-girl.com/
15.	jihadwatch.org
16.	boingboing.net
17.	volokh.com
18.	globalvoicesonline.com
19.	thinkprogress.org
20.	crooksandliars.com

Source: www.truthlaidbear.com (accessed February 25, 2008).

Early liberal talk show hosts, including former New York governor Mario Cuomo, one of the most eloquent Democratic politicians of his generation, failed to attract a mass audience.

Air America was a self-identified liberal radio network created shortly before the 2004 presidential election to offer a talk radio alternative (Oravec 2005). The radio network benefited from cross-references on liberal blogs, but the audience remained small because of the limited reach of the radio stations in the network (Jensen and Miller 2006; Oravec 2005). The liberal radio network suffered from low audience share, and by late 2006 found it necessary to file for bankruptcy, a sharp contrast from the high ratings and high profits enjoyed by conservative radio and television networks (Jensen and Miller 2006).

Humor That Stings: The Daily Show *and the* Colbert Report

More commercially successful news outlets that appeal to liberals include *The Daily Show* and the *Colbert Report,* late-night faux news programs provided on cable by the Comedy Central network. These programs are particularly popular with college-aged students who seem drawn to the sarcasm and irreverence found on the two half-hour programs.

A content analysis study found that the *Daily Show* was extraordinarily negative overall (97 percent negative) in its discussions of the 2006 midterm elections. "When compared to the traditional network news coverage over the years, this is more negative than coverage of the GOP during the Mark Foley scandal (88 percent negative) or Saddam Hussein during the first Gulf War (88 percent negative)" (Center for Media and Public Affairs 2006). But the program was not guilty of ideological bias: 98 percent of the reports on the Republicans were negative, as compared to 96 percent of the reports on the Democrats, a difference too small to be detected even by devoted viewers without formal content analysis (Center for Media and Public Affairs 2006).

These slight content differences, in other words, mean that conservative news outlets like Fox News do far more to help the Republicans than these youth-oriented comedy shows do to help the Democrats.

Mainstream Media Online Commentators

Between the ideological poles of the new media are the mainstream media, who have developed their own daily bloggers. The *Washington Post,* for example, has more than a dozen regular commentators/bloggers writing about news, sports, travel, food, and other issues. Ideologically speaking, they tilt left, right, and center. The more politically oriented blogs include Dan Froomkin, who writes about the White House in an online column called "White House Watch," Chris Cillizza, who writes an election-oriented column called "The Fix," and Howard Kurtz, a media writer at the paper who has an online column called "Media Notes." All are available at washingtonpost. com and are featured on the front page of the paper's Web site. Other media outlets, including the *New York Times,* also feature bloggers on the front page of their Web sites. These voices provide only a small fraction of the news outlets' online content, however.

The 2008 Democratic Presidential Candidates: Spin and Spun Upon

Marketing Character in an Online World

Presidential candidates in recent election cycles frequently have turned to new media outlets to promote themselves and connect with voters. Perhaps because they lack the mass media megaphone of a sitting president, candidates seem much more aggressive in relying on the Internet to sell themselves to citizens. Senator Hillary Clinton (D-NY), launched her 2008 presidential campaign with an e-mail message to her supporters and a video statement on her Web site (Balz 2007; Homaday 2007). Clinton, who led in early polls for the Democratic nomination, followed up her announcement with three evenings of online chats in late January 2007, timed to surround President George W. Bush's State of the Union speech (Allen 2007; Balz 2007). Clinton's Web campaign statement portrayed the senator seated in a gracious living room. This setting maximized Clinton's appearance as a confident, establishment figure, perhaps even looking rather presidential herself, a year before the Iowa Caucus.

Being a front-runner makes you a target, even online. During her first visit to Iowa as a presidential candidate, Hillary Clinton's off-key rendition of the national anthem, captured by a live microphone on stage, became one of that week's most popular YouTube videos, with 800,000 people tuning in, many of them after learning about the video clip from the *Drudge Report.* The Clinton campaign decided not to respond to the clip, and the story was not picked up by mainstream media outlets in the days after the January 27 campaign kickoff appearance, just as the Clinton team wished (Healy 2007). The nonresponsive response was similar to the approach her husband and George W. Bush would have used: ignoring as beneath them the criticism airing in online venues. Even trivial attacks, including one's ability to carry a tune, will get far more attention if a candidate responds.

Clinton's genteel campaign announcement online was a sharp contrast to that of former senator John Edwards (D-NC), who started his 2008 run via Web video from the still-devastated streets of New Orleans, looking like an earnest television correspondent reporting from the wreckage of the

Ninth Ward (Cillizza and Balz 2007; Homaday 2007). "'Our goal was to have people go and watch that video so they could hear directly from John what this campaign was about,' said Matthew Gross, chief Internet strategist for the Edwards campaign. 'Within the first 48 hours or so, 50,000 people had watched that video. Now it is over 100,000 people who have seen it'" (quoted in Cillizza and Balz 2007).

Edwards's announcement followed frequent postings of the candidate's musings released during 2006 and 2007 on YouTube, an effort to present the candidate as unscripted, captured on film during a candid moment. "The 2008 campaign is 'totally going to be on steroids this time in terms of what a candidate can do,' says Joe Trippi, who masterminded Howard Dean's Internet-driven bid in 2003 and 2004. 'You're going to see reality, and you're going to see savvy manipulation under the guise of something that's authentic and real.' But Trippi warns against candidates' secretly scripting such moments: 'If you get caught, you're dead'" (quoted in Kurtz 2007a).

Edwards was unusually active on the Web during the weeks before his campaign launch, posting pages on MySpace and Facebook, two Web sites popular with teens and young adults who want to tell the cyberworld about themselves and share their daily musings and activities. Edwards also answered questions posed by online questioners on dailykos.com (Kurtz 2007a).

Although his online media strategy was more aggressive and angry than Clinton's, an approach reporters have dubbed "Dean 2.0," Edwards also faced online attacks for non-policy-related matters. One of the most popular candidate YouTube videos during 2007 focused on Edwards's efforts to primp before a public appearance. At first Edwards ignored the clip, but during a July 2007 debate in which candidates answered video questions submitted online, Edwards offered a self-deprecating video about his hair (Rutenburg 2007; Stanley 2007).

In the early campaign activities for 2008, Senator Barack Obama (D-IL) also focused on Facebook, suggesting a greater hipness than that of more establishment candidates like Clinton. By early February 2007, more than 250,000 people joined two Facebook groups supporting an Obama presidential campaign (Goldfarb 2007). Facebook gives people an opportunity to express themselves about their favored presidential candidates (along with many other matters) and also to try to convince others to join the movement. Because Facebook postings are dominated by young adults, who generally are not political elites, Facebook postings offer a new opportunity for grassroots political participation. How effective Facebook Nation will be in the 2008 presidential election remains an open question.

The Web-based efforts are clearly designed to attract young voters to the candidates, but how well middle-aged candidates will adapt to these new media remains uncertain. Of course, as shown in Table 4.1, younger adults are more likely to be reached by online political messages than are older adults. In addition, those young voters transfer the information to each other rapidly through a variety of Internet communication mechanisms. "While politicians navigate the Googley highways and Wiki byways, looking about as comfortable as Barbara Bush at a rave, the young and the viral that they're trying so desperately to win over are ready to chew up and spit out anything that smacks of the inauthentic, the unhip or the analog" (Homaday 2007).

The 2008 Internet-heavy political strategies have been undertaken with a nod to the highly successful efforts of former Vermont Democratic governor Howard Dean, who used the Web four years earlier to bolster his long-shot candidacy (Trippi 2004). Dean's savvy campaign team used the Web to organize Meet-ups that built an army of volunteers and donors who pushed Dean from 1 percent in the polls to front-runner status in the weeks before the 2004 Iowa Caucus (Burden 2005; Faler 2003; Kerbel 2005). Despite his popularity on the Web, Dean lost to Kerry in Iowa and New Hampshire, two key states on the road to a presidential nomination (Burden 2005). The expansion of online activity in the years since Dean's campaign has lifted the hopes of some Democrats who believe that by 2008 liberal online activists will be powerful enough to determine the party's nominee and lift that person into the White House in January 2009.

The First Smear of the 2008 Campaign

But what can shine a light on a candidate can also burn that candidate. In mid-January 2007, *Insight,* a conservative online magazine owned by the Unification Church, reported that Obama, one of two leading Democratic presidential candidates for 2008, was raised as a Muslim and attended a Muslim religious school known as a madrassa, when he was six years old (Kurtz 2007b). The story, which included no source identified by name, was subsequently picked up by Fox News, which both reported the allegation and alleged that the report came from the office of Senator Hillary Clinton (D-NY) (Kurtz 2007b). The *New York Post,* which like Fox is owned by Rupert Murdoch, followed up with a banner headline: "'Osama' Mud Flies at Obama" (Kurtz 2007b). A day later, the deputy headmaster at the school Obama attended four decades before said that the school was a public institution, not a madrassa, and that it had a secular curriculum (Kurtz 2007c).

Not all reports on the *Insight* story were so accepting of its findings. CNN sent a reporter to the elementary school in question and found it was a secular, not religious, educational institution (Carter 2007). With that evidence, CNN aired negative reports on Fox's handling of the matter, and Fox fired back claiming that CNN was trying to generate publicity by attacking its cable rival. "Yet another cry for attention by the Paris Hilton of television news, Anderson Cooper," scoffed Irena Briganti, a Fox spokesperson (quoted in Carter 2007). The *Washington Times*, a conservative newspaper owned by the Unification Church led by the Reverend Sun Myung Moon, refused to report on the *Insight* article even though the online magazine is also owned by the church (Kirkpatrick 2007).

When accused of shoddy journalism, new media often fight back, and do so using the same techniques presidents employ to shape the story in a desired way. "*Insight*'s story was not thinly sourced," the Web magazine said in an online posting after the controversy over its report erupted. "Our reporter's sources close to the Clinton opposition research war room confirm the truth of the story. The Clinton camp's denial has as much credibility as the 'I never had sex with that woman' statement" (quoted in Kurtz 2007c). *Fox and Friends*, the Fox morning show that discussed the allegations when they first emerged, later aired a clarification saying that both the Obama and Clinton campaigns denied the allegations (Kurtz 2007c). These two campaigns claimed the reports were an irresponsible right-wing attempt to discredit both Democrats (Carter 2007; Kurtz 2007b).

> "The allegations are completely false," says Obama spokesman Robert Gibbs. "To publish this sort of trash without any documentation is surprising, but for Fox to repeat something so false, not once, but many times is appallingly irresponsible. This is exactly the type of slash-and-burn politics the American people are sick and tired of." Obama, aides note, is a Christian and belongs to a Chicago church.
>
> Clinton campaign officials were relieved that what they regard as an absurd allegation was not picked up more widely. "It's an obvious right-wing hit job by a Moonie publication that was designed to attack Senator Clinton and Senator Obama at the same time," says Clinton spokesman Howard Wolfson. *Insight*, like the *Washington Times*, is owned by a company controlled by the Rev. Sun Myung Moon. (Kurtz 2007b)

In his report on the unsubstantiated charges, which of course gave those claims a greater airing, *Washington Post* news media reporter Howard Kurtz observed:

> There was a time when major media outlets refused to touch unsubstantiated allegations. When Gennifer Flowers sold her account of an affair with Hillary Clinton's husband to the *Star* tabloid in 1992—allegations that turned out to be true, at least in part—some news organizations went with it and others shied away for days. These days, the time elapsed between a flimsy charge from some magazine or Web site and amplification by bigger media outlets is often close to zero. (Kurtz 2007b)

Rumors may travel faster than fact, and much faster than before. As a result, these two campaigns faced difficult challenges. Assuming the stories are false, the more the campaigns say beyond the denials, the larger they make the story. And any efforts to clear their names through lawsuits will keep the charges front and center in the public mind for years, long after the 2008 presidential election is completed.

The 2008 Republican Presidential Candidates: Spin and Spun Upon

The George Allen Collapse

For all the benefits the new media may give presidential candidates seeking to spin themselves, it can also destroy their campaigns, sometimes even before a candidacy gets off the ground. For Republicans, the first casualty in the character sweepstakes of would-be presidential candidates took place in 2006, more than two years before the subsequent presidential election. When 2006 dawned, Senator George Allen (R-VA) appeared likely to coast to reelection to a second term and into the 2008 presidential race. Christian conservative voters liked Allen a great deal, a huge advantage in the GOP primaries. The incumbent senator possessed a huge campaign war chest, making it look like the 2006 election would be little more than a warm-up exercise for the national campaign to follow. After every Democratic candidate who had ever waged a statewide race in Virginia passed on taking on Allen, the hapless Democrats settled on Jim Webb, a best-selling author who had served as Ronald Reagan's secretary of the navy. Webb, a decorated Vietnam War veteran, had broken with Republicans over the Iraq War and was willing to wage his first campaign for office against a highly popular incumbent (Toner 2006).

For Allen, the trouble began during summer 2006 when he said one little word, "macaca," which was captured on video and distributed worldwide via YouTube (Stout 2006). The grainy, amateur video showed Allen at his most harsh, "welcoming" an Indian American campaign worker for Webb to largely white rural Virginia. (It turned out that the campaign worker, unlike Allen, was a Virginia native). The word, it turned out, was a racial epithet commonly used in North Africa, where Allen's mother had lived before coming to the United States (Toner 2006). Unfortunately for Allen, the gaffe didn't go away in a few news cycles, as probably would have been the case a decade earlier. In a new example of how masses of citizens can shape the national news agenda, YouTube viewers kept the video front and center, creating a long-running crisis for Allen instead of a two-day story.

To make matters worse for Allen, subsequent news reports brought forth other allegations about Allen's alleged racial insensitivity, including claims that while a University of Virginia undergraduate Allen had used the "n word" and had stuffed a deer head into the mailbox of a Charlottesville-area African American family (Kirkpatrick 2006). Allen never regained his stride as the allegations piled up. He clumsily handled the question over whether he had Jewish ancestry, at first claiming he didn't and a few days later admitting that he did, ultimately explaining the discrepancy by saying he had never asked his mother about her ancestry (Hulse 2006).

As the election drew closer, the sinking Allen campaign sought to deflect attention onto Webb. The Allen campaign attacked Webb for his statement three decades earlier that the U.S. Naval Academy should not admit women, along with what the Allen campaign said were negative portrayals of women in Webb's novels (Toner 2006). But those efforts to change the subject, which included *Drudge Report* headlines reporting on Allen's attacks, failed to turn the tide. Allen lost his Senate seat by roughly 9,000 votes out of more than 2.3 million cast in Virginia (Broder 2006).

YouTube, and Trying Not to Be the Next George Allen

Allen's painful experience, the first likely 2008 presidential candidate whose hopes were destroyed by YouTube, created a new awareness of how a gaffe captured on the Web can kill a candidacy in its cradle. Candidates quickly realized that they must counterspin immediately or be forever spun by others, including their enemies, online. Former governor Mitt Romney (R-MA), a candidate for president in 2008, was one of the first to learn from Allen's online meltdown. In early January 2007, Romney campaign workers started hearing about video clips flying around the Internet that contained excerpts from Romney's 1994 U.S. Senate debate with Senator Ted Kennedy (D-MA). In that debate footage, which became a prominent item on YouTube, Romney declared his support for abortion rights and gay rights, positions he subsequently renounced (Cillizza and Balz 2007). Renounced or not, the statements could damage if not destroy Romney's standing among Christian conservative voters, the heart of the party's ideological base.

> Romney's political inner circle, alerted to the threat, decided to strike back quickly. Less than eight hours after the attack appeared, a video of Romney rebutting the charges was being sent to his supporters and to Republican blogs. "In a viral information age, a distortion of the record can quickly sink in as fact," [Romney communications aide Kevin] Madden said. "It was very important to show that what was an anonymous attack eventually became a moment of strength for the campaign." (quoted in Cillizza and Balz 2007)

Senator John McCain (R-AZ), one of the few Republicans publicly supporting a troop increase in Iraq in early 2007, was attacked on YouTube by moveon.org, a leading antiwar group. Moveon.org ran a television ad in Iowa and New Hampshire, traditionally the two most important states in the presidential nomination process, faulting McCain for his pro-Bush stance, and posted it on YouTube, where it could be seen at any time. The YouTube ad quickly became one of the most watched videos on the site during its first week, and moveon.org demonstrated how quickly and how inexpensively candidates can be attacked on YouTube (Cillizza and Balz 2007).

Spinning against the White House in the New Media

Citizen Voices

During the heady days of his 2004 presidential campaign, Howard Dean and his team spoke often of "people-powered politics" (Trippi 2004). Although the Dean campaign failed, the online movement he helped build convinced many activists that the Internet would become the great equalizer for citizen action. No longer would poorly funded and modestly staffed interest groups have to find the money for postage and paper to stay in touch with their membership. With the Web, citizen activists could send information to loyalists for virtually nothing, keeping people in touch with causes and encouraging them to support public interest activities with their money and their time and their Internet hits. They could even let the like-minded come to them after their Web page was operational.

The White House may dominate the mainstream media, but in the online world activists have long believed they have more of a chance to be heard. Indeed, the hints of this potential for citizen counterspin first appeared nearly a decade before Dean's historic rise and fall. The 1994 Zapatista uprising in the southern Mexican state of Chiapas marked a key early example of how activists, led by a Subcomandante Marcos, can use the Internet to make their case to the world. The uprising was in response to the North American Free Trade Agreement (NAFTA) and its likely consequences on the livelihood and well-being of indigenous peoples. Even more visible electronic activism took place five years later when demonstrators went online to coordinate demonstrations on a street-by-street basis against the World Trade Organization meeting in Seattle (Ayres 2005). Although protest groups may be more efficient organizers online, mainstream media coverage of their activities appears to have generated little support for their agenda.

The person-to-person nature of the Internet can also be used to attack mainstream media reports themselves, including those that relate to the White House. Frustrated with the coverage of the postinauguration audit of the Florida ballots of 2000, blogger Mickey Kaus sought to bring attention to thousands of "overvotes" that if counted would have given Gore the state and the presidency. Overvotes, where citizens marked the Gore box on the ballot and also wrote in Gore's name, should have been counted under the "clear intent of the voter" standard in Florida law, Kaus argued. Kaus and others complained that the *New York Times* and other mainstream media outlets refused to acknowledge the fact that Gore would have been president had there been a fair counting of the Florida ballots, largely because of the national crisis brought on by the terrorist attacks of 9/11 (Kaus 2001; Weisberg 2001). The rise of online politics probably meant that the charges received a wider hearing than they would have a decade earlier. But these online reports on protests, demonstrations, and the dubious vote-counting procedures in Florida in 2000 generated more heat than change.

Cindy Sheehan: The Poster Mother of the Iraq War

Cindy Sheehan, a mother who lost a son in Iraq, demonstrated to George W. Bush in 2005 that he was not the only person who could use the military to get a point across to the public. That summer, Sheehan camped alongside the road to Bush's Crawford, TX, ranch to condemn the policies that sent her son to die in Iraq and to build support for the end-the-war movement (Quintanilla 2006). "My son died for lies," she repeated to the many reporters who came to meet the activist and report on the one-woman counterspin machine (quoted in Quintanilla 2006).

Her visible location brought her massive media attention, and her online commentaries also drew greater public attention to her cause (Quintanilla 2006). After her first summer in Crawford, she was invited on a speaking tour, becoming one of the Bush's administration's most visible critics during late 2005 and 2006. In summer 2006, she returned to Crawford, TX, to renew her media-oriented vigil for peace in Iraq. Although her protests were not popular in that conservative community, Sheehan purchased land in Crawford through a surrogate so that she could continue her antiwar and media-friendly demonstrations in the town George W. Bush calls home (Stolberg 2006a).

Although she was criticized by war supporters for politicizing the death of her son, her family's sacrifice offered a powerful contrast to the president, who successfully avoided military service in Vietnam by joining the Texas Air National Guard, and the vice president, who successfully avoided military service altogether during the Vietnam era through the use of personal deferments. Sheehan was vilified by the president's online supporters, but her presence and her voice helped undermine White House spin about conditions in Iraq and about the validity of the administration's prewar claims. She was arguably a more effective countervoice than the entire Democratic legislative caucus during those years.

Posting Images from Iraq on the Web

As discussed throughout this book, the troubling and long-lasting birth pangs of the Iraqi government have vexed policymakers in Washington. For years the Bush administration rejected criticisms that the United States was losing the occupation, dismissed complaints that the Iraqis were not ready to take over their government, and denied that the sectarian violence in the country amounted to a civil war. But the sectarian violence and the mayhem in Iraqi political circles were reported regularly in U.S. media outlets. Those reports, together with the Internet postings of war critics, cast doubt on the administration's claims that things in Iraq were going far better than news reports indicated.

The Iraqi execution of former dictator Saddam Hussein on December 30, 2006 followed years of court proceedings and efforts by U.S. and Iraqi officials to demonstrate that he was a cold-blooded killer. The Iraqi "national unity" government insisted the hanging proceed despite legal concerns, some of them raised by Americans, that the execution could not legally occur during the Muslim holiday weekend, and despite the absence on the execution documents of the legally required signature of Iraq's president (Burns and Glanz 2007; Burns and Santora 2007). The Iraqi government's mismanagement of the execution triggered major rioting in the Sunni regions and suggested that the United States had allied itself with a sectarian faction that was unsavory, to say the least. It also did nothing to further U.S. claims that Iraq was a democracy, beholden to the rule of law. Due process, after all, is a key component of free societies.

As the *New York Times* reported on January 1, 2007:

> None of the Iraqi officials were able to explain why [Iraqi Prime Minister Nuri Kamal al-] Mr. Maliki had been unwilling to allow the execution to wait. Nor would any explain why those who conducted it had allowed it to deteriorate into a sectarian free-for-all that had the effect, on the video recordings, of making Mr. Hussein, a mass murderer, appear dignified and restrained, and his executioners, representing Shiites who were his principal victims, seem like bullying street thugs. But the explanation may have lain in something that Bassam al-Husseini, a Maliki aide closely involved in arrangements for the hanging, said to the BBC later. Mr. Husseini, who has American citizenship, described the hanging as "an Id [holiday] gift to the Iraqi people." (Burns and Santora 2007)

The U.S. government did try to limit public disclosure of Saddam Hussein's final moments by confiscating cell phones when the U.S. military transported Iraqi witnesses to the execution site. But clearly some cell phones with cameras were brought into the execution chamber, and the resulting videos soon spread widely across Iraq and the world on YouTube. The graphic images and mayhem clearly visible on the video recordings triggered renewed sectarian violence between Sunnis and Shiites (Burns and Glanz 2007). White House claims about a largely pacified Iraq could not compete with the chaotic images found on YouTube.

Two weeks later, additional botched hangings of Saddam Hussein's two top lieutenants by the Shiite-led government further inflamed Sunni-Shiite tensions, creating further impediments to the Bush plans to pacify Iraq and the region. New media images sent via cell phones and routinely available on the region's cable programming gave the videos of the executions a wide airing and made peaceful resolution of the Iraqi crisis more elusive (Burns and Glanz 2007; Slackman 2007). Most importantly, the widely disseminated images undermined White House claims that Iraq was led by a stable and just government.

Abu Ghraib

The execution videos were not the first time the Bush administration had to deal with ugly public images of the Iraq War that undermined White House efforts at spin. Unsavory photos of prison guards abusing inmates at the Abu Ghraib prison in Iraq were made public early during the U.S. occupation. In the pictures, the soldiers seemed to enjoy humiliating the prisoners: terrifying them with dogs, forcing them to pile on top of each other in human pyramids, or parading them around in dog collars (Wypijewski 2006). The photos, which bounced around the Internet almost immediately after becoming public, looked something like the prison guards' version of "trophy photos," where hunters and fishermen show off their prize conquests. Although many of the prison guards involved faced military discipline for their misconduct, the Internet's worldwide disclosure of such images greatly complicated U.S. efforts to pacify Iraq and to portray the U.S. military as a positive force in the region (Wypijewski 2006).

The Abu Ghraib scandal demonstrated powerfully how modern technology can undermine a president's ability to present a consistent message about U.S. intentions. Above all, the scandal demonstrated that private photos depicting newsworthy events—for example, the torture of prisoners of war by U.S. troops—do not always stay private. But more was to come.

Haditha

As 2007 began, another round of photos documenting the unsavory side of U.S. activities in Iraq was made public. U.S. Marines took photographs following the deaths of 24 civilians killed in Haditha, Iraq. The images were located by the U.S. Naval Criminal Investigative Service as part of the trial of four marines charged with murder over those deaths on November 19, 2006. Editors at the *Washington Post*, which obtained the photos, considered many of the pictures too graphic to publish in the paper, though some were available on the newspaper's Web site. "Among the images there is a young boy with a helicopter on the front of his pajamas, slumped over, his face and head covered in blood. There is a mother lying on a bed, arms splayed, the bodies of three young children huddled against her right side. There are men with gaping head wounds, and a woman and a child hunkered down on their knees, their hands frozen around their faces as if permanently bracing for an attack" (J. White 2007a).

As of this writing, the case remains in the courts. The marines have told investigators that they were following rules of engagement for hunting for insurgents, and that they believed they had permission from their superiors to fire at will inside two homes following the death of a marine corporal from a roadside bomb planted in that neighborhood (Carter 2008; White 2007a).

Conclusion

After watching D. W. Griffith's film *Birth of a Nation* in 1915, an astonished President Woodrow Wilson famously described the new technology of motion pictures as "writing with lightning." Given the early struggles of the 2008 candidates with the new media, it seems that Wilson's description would be equally apt for our latest new media technology. Campaigns are getting burned by the lightning strikes, and the new technology of YouTube claimed its first victim more than a year before the Iowa Caucus in would-be 2008 presidential candidate George Allen. Campaigns are struggling to avoid their own "macaca moments," sometimes fighting with online clip versus clip and at other times hoping the latest attack clip posted on YouTube dies a quiet death.

However the candidates approach these new media, Web sites such as YouTube have undermined politicians' ability to control campaign messages. The more people watch a particular segment and talk about it, the more others will watch. A clip that moves up in the rankings generates more attention and still more attention after that as the hours click by. Eventually even the candidates and the mainstream reporters can no longer avoid paying attention to what so many people are talking about. The news cycle no longer takes days to turn; now it completes its circuit in hours.

Presidents have new opportunities to dominate the political discourse in this environment. New media outlets provide presidents new vehicles to communicate messages to those who visit the White House Web page and other propresident sites, and presidents have an increased ability to tailor their messages to specific elements of their support base: different e-mails can go to gun lovers, prolife activists, and supporters of Iraq policies.

White House administrations tend to be rather insulated by their very nature, regardless of the shape of the media environment, and the Bush team has done little online to reverse that tendency. The Bush White House redesigned the White House Web site in a way that discourages mass participation; for example, there are no cast-your-vote icons that allow people to vote for or against policy ideas. There is no chat room for citizens to communicate with each other about the president's performance on the site. Although administration officials appear on the Web site from time to time to participate in "conversations" with viewers, the questions are all deliberately selected to maximize the administration's ability to promote its policies. Old strategies of White House media management, in other words, are applied to new technologies.

But the story does not end there. A president's critics also can utilize new media outlets to spin a story in a different direction than the White House wishes. But whether critics can command as large a share of the new media audience as propresident Web sites is an open question. The Web offers a powerful venue for undermining presidential spin, and Web users have already helped set the political agenda by making certain YouTube videos and online postings highly popular. Government elites and Washington correspondents can no longer determine the newsworthiness of events without taking into account citizens' own agenda-setting efforts, and the public's ability to help determine what the news is will only increase over time. As more people go online, they have more of a chance to spin the news for others. If a political video becomes highly popular online, traditional media outlets find it hard not to take notice.

Perhaps the next president will use the Internet differently than Bush has. But it seems likely that future presidents may find Bush's approach to the White House Web site to be the best approach, as it minimizes the ability of critics to use the page to undermine the president and the White House agenda. Of course a key factor affecting whether the next president will follow George W. Bush's online approach depends on who is elected in 2008.

At least one early favorite seems likely to follow his lead in crafting an online presidential news style. Hillary Clinton's carefully managed 2008 campaign Web presence seems much like the carefully managed public communication efforts during the Bill Clinton and George W. Bush presidencies. Her online conversations likewise are largely scripted affairs, designed to present the candidate in a favorable light. Like Bush, the Hillary Clinton campaign team does what it can to present itself as on message at every opportunity. Even her online video homage to *The Sopranos* cable program was designed to shape her image in a more common direction. But her conventional approach online did not allow her to convert her early front-runner stance into a clear path to her party's nomination.

The wide Democratic and Republican candidate fields of 2008 have given rise to different approaches to online communication, with some other candidates offering more freewheeling online content. Mitt Romney, the former Massachusetts Republican governor, appeared to be most effective at fighting back online, but he nevertheless fell behind Senator John McCain, who practices a cautious Internet communication strategy like that favored by Hillary Clinton. For the Democrats, Edwards and Obama offered a more renegade approach. But these approaches may be the result of being behind in the polls early on, and helped Obama erase Clinton's early advantages in political endorsements and money. In the next chapter, presidential spin and its policy consequences are discussed at greater length.

Chapter Five

The Consequences
of Presidential Spin

U.S. Presidents, who govern a nation of more than 300 million people, are immensely distant figures for nearly all citizens. Few Americans have met a president in person, and fewer still have had a conversation with a chief executive that lasted beyond the few words that can be exchanged during a receiving line. Even so, for many Americans the presidency is an immensely personal office. From childhood, Americans exhibit a deep personal attachment to the president, who is in many ways the approximation of a national parent (Easton and Dennis 1969).

In times of deep trouble, youngsters are not the only ones who look to the White House for leadership and direction. As 9/11 and previous crises have shown, citizens "rally 'round the flag" (and the president) when disaster looms or after it strikes (Dimock 2004; Nincic 1997). The intense loyalty felt for a president is greater than that felt for elected leaders in many other countries, in part because a U.S. president is both head of the government and head of state (Bowles 2003; Brooks 2006).

Television as a medium can make its subjects seem intensely personal, and the president's dominant role in news coverage of government makes him a well-known figure. Not only is a president the policymaker in chief, the first family is one of the longest-running dramas (or depending on the family—sitcoms) in U.S. history. From their regular "appearances" in our living rooms, we know an awful lot about presidents: the rough patches in their marriages, the hard-partying children, the results of presidential colonoscopies, how they pronounce the word "nuclear," and whether they like to binge at McDonald's or prefer to spend time on a mountain bike.

However distant they may be in reality, presidents like to give the impression that they have the common touch. Trying to market a president as an ordinary American when he or she is usually anything but is a tough task indeed. But it is a key part of White House media management no matter who sits in the Oval Office. Presidents and presidential candidates who are seen as somewhat disconnected from the lives of ordinary people—be it the 2004 image of the elitist windsurfer John Kerry or the image of George H. W. Bush as a clueless blue-blood as the economy soured around him a dozen years earlier—do not fare well politically. Americans tend to vote for candidates who at least appear to resemble themselves, including the plainspoken Ronald Reagan, Bill Clinton, and George W. Bush. These three presidents in particular made efforts to portray themselves as regular Joes, be it by clearing brush on the ranch, grabbing a cheeseburger, or enjoying a NASCAR race. Although these efforts sometimes appear forced, defining presidential character for the cameras is an important part of White House media management and presidential policy success.

Presidents try to be "of the people" by offering popular public policies, and if the public is not already behind an idea, the administration tries to build support for the initiative. In the main, these efforts involve communicating with the public through speeches by administration officials, presidential speeches in Washington, and—for the highest priority items and the toughest sells—presidential travel around the country. Most modern presidents believe they were elected to be trustees, to do what they think best for the country, rather than delegates, who repress their own judgments and simply govern consistently with the public will. As a result, modern presidents invariably try to use the mass media to shape public opinion to correspond with their own views.

The aggressive media management efforts of recent presidencies have deepened a central problem of modern administrations: a short-term focus that ignores the longer-term consequences of presidential actions. This is not a new problem. Richard Nixon, for example, was quite short-sighted in the domestic policy management of his administration. Richard Neustadt (1990), the dean of presidential scholars, faulted Nixon for failing to consider the road the president would have to take to achieve his ultimate goals, along with the unappealing and illegal steps required of the president and his team along the way to that destination.

All too often, the president's short-term personal goals conflict with the longer term best interests of the executive branch as an institution. To counter this problem, Neustadt (1990) encouraged what he called "backward mapping," a presidential process of taking the long view in evaluating possible approaches to issues. Perhaps the short-term presidential goal of spinning the news to win today's legislative skirmish seems less desirable when one considers the costs, the long-term consequences that follow from taking the necessary steps along the way to achieve that goal.

Although Neustadt is the most well-known presidential scholar of the past half century, the two most recent U.S. presidents have stumbled badly because they failed to heed his vital warning of the dangers of being short-sighted. And the nation, the world, and even the presidency itself have suffered as a result of White House focus on each day's spin cycle. Although a short-term focus has been a problem for many presidents, heightened public expectations of our most recent presidents—and the availability of ever-more advanced media outlets—have made a bad situation worse (Farnsworth and Lichter 2006a; Lowi 1985). Short-term manipulation of the public debate through secrecy and selective information disclosures paints a distorted picture of reality that undermines democracy. When the fraud is discovered, it weakens individual presidents and their presidencies—as demonstrated by Bill Clinton and George W. Bush. In other words, the normalization of presidential deceit through overspinning undermines effective lawmaking by all branches of government and makes it hard for citizens and lawmakers to determine the nation's best interests.

An Obsessive Short-Term Focus

A president who focuses on short-term media management strategies can remain popular, get relatively good news coverage, pass some legislation, and maybe even win a second term. And television, from which most citizens still get most of their news about politics, has a short attention span. Citizens learn from television news about what is important at any given moment, but the lack of context in most news stories creates a "now, this" mentality that discourages citizen evaluation of issues over the longer term (Iyengar 1991; Iyengar and Kinder 1987; Postman 1985). Television news itself likewise encourages the public to focus on trivial matters, such as the latest drunken celebrity, rather substantial policy concerns (Farnsworth and Lichter 2007; Iyengar et al. 2004). Given the great interest presidents have in going public to advance their agendas, administrations are often drawn into playing to the cameras. They count on brief public attention spans to limit the long-term consequences of their short-sighted governing.

For the modern White House, playing to the cameras means keeping it simple, keeping it lively, and keeping it focused on the short-term payoff (Hart 1994; Kerbel 1995, 2001, 2005; Lopez 2001; McChesney 1999). The administrations that don't make good television, like those of Jimmy Carter and George H. W. Bush, are cancelled in midseason like a bad sitcom (Brinkley 1998; Fitzwater 1995; Robinson and Sheehan 1983). Presidential candidates who present an unsettling mediated presence in U.S. living rooms—the Howard Dean "scream" of 2004 may be the most memorable recent example—may not even get to be president (Clancey and Robinson 1985; Eggerton 2004; Hershey 1989; Pomper 1989, 1997).

As a result, presidents have to tailor their political communication strategies to meet the needs of television. Most victorious campaigns have mastered this skill. If not, they were probably defeated by more media-savvy operations (Farnsworth and Lichter 2007). The most dangerous way presidents succumb to the siren song of favorable news coverage by going public is by oversimplifying issues. Encouraged by news coverage dynamics that favor the White House, presidents all too often focus on the "sellable" short-term policy that may be popular but can create long-term problems for the president, the country, and even the world.

The next section of this chapter looks at three examples of the dangers of a short-term policy focus and the resulting long-term consequences. Two powerful examples of this severe problem of modern governance from the George W. Bush presidency are the Iraq War and his tax cut initiatives. From the Clinton years, we look at the president's failed health insurance plan of 1994. These case studies demonstrate how short-term desires overrun long-term good judgment. These are not the only examples one could cite. A more comprehensive treatment of this pathological pattern would also include the damage to the Clinton presidency caused by the Clinton-Lewinsky scandal and the disinterest the George W. Bush administration showed in dealing with climate change even as the planet continues to warm rapidly (Blaney and Benoit 2001; Rosenthal and Revkin 2007). But the three examples considered here demonstrate the longer-term consequences of short-sighted governing by chief executives who see themselves more as spinners in chief than as trustees for the nation's future.

Clinton's Failed Health-Care Plan of 1994

When Bill Clinton first proposed national health insurance for all Americans, the idea enjoyed massive public approval. Citizens who worried that they would soon lose their jobs and thus their health care, coupled with the tens of millions of Americans without health insurance, hailed the idea.

Democrats had talked of government health insurance since the presidency
of Harry Truman decades earlier, and Clinton vowed he would succeed where
so many other Democratic presidents had failed. But Clinton's health-care
plan was on a road to ruin. Clinton made a number of early decisions that
seemed appealing in the short term but destroyed the plan's chance of
eventual passage. By placing the plan's development in the hands of First
Lady Hillary Clinton, and by keeping the health-care panel's deliberations
secret, Clinton helped build anxiety over the group's message and its messenger. By dealing with the controversial issue of the North American Free
Trade Agreement (NAFTA) before tackling health care, Clinton built up
resistance among Democrats, particularly among organized labor and envi-
ronmentalists who were angry about NAFTA. Thus they were less supportive
of Clinton in 1994 than they would have been without the controversial trade
agreement. To make matters worse, putting NAFTA first pushed the debate
over the health insurance plan too close to the 1994 elections to ensure
serious legislative consideration by distracted and often anxious lawmakers
on Capitol Hill. On matters other than trade, Clinton governed in a largely
partisan matter during his first two years, rebuffing potential Republican
ideas and supporters, an unwise approach given the minority party's ability to gum up the legislative process through the use of Senate filibusters
(Drew 1994; Skocpol 1997). All these short-term calculations undermined
the health-care bill's prospects for passage.

When the health-care plan began to generate resistance in both parties
on Capitol Hill in mid-1994, Clinton refused to compromise, warning that
he would veto any legislation that provided health-care coverage for most,
but not all, Americans (Skocpol 1997). The president was overconfident of
his ability to spin his way to legislative victory. His efforts to bully Congress
were counterproductive, stiffening the resolve of Republicans to defeat the
measure, reducing the interest some Democrats had in making a deal, and
encouraging administration critics to fund a major advertising campaign
(dubbed "Harry and Louise") to sow doubts about the health-insurance
proposal by "Slick Willie" (Jamieson and Cappella 1998; Skocpol 1997).
The president's Democratic supporters on Capitol Hill, fearful of the pending 1994 elections, decided it best to bottle up the legislation in committee,
hoping to set the issue aside until after lawmakers had won another term.
Many did not win another term, and the health-insurance program was
buried for the remaining six years of the Clinton presidency.

The long-term consequences for Democrats of Clinton's secretive, bul-
lying strategy became clear almost immediately (Burnham 1996). The
Republicans won the 1994 midterms in a landslide, winning the House for
the first time in a generation, and they kept control of the lower chamber
until the 2006 midterm elections. The Senate also went Republican that
year, and stayed in Republican hands until 2006 except for a brief period

from mid-2001 until the 2002 midterm elections (Broder 2006). However appealing it may have been for President Clinton to name the First Lady to chair the health-care task force (and given his frequent extramarital transgressions, one might suppose it would be hard for him to deny her such a request), a less polarizing figure might have made the plan more palatable (Jamieson and Cappella 1998; Skocpol 1997). Clinton's presidency was deeply wounded by the plan's failure, effectively forcing the president into playing defense against the Republican majorities for his final six years in the White House. Forward motion on any of his other policy priorities became difficult, if not impossible, after 1994.

The consequences for citizens of Clinton's failure to make more progress on his health-care plan are likewise apparent: the number of uninsured Americans grew by millions after the Clinton health-care plan failed. Since 1994 millions more uninsured families have been saddled with heavy medical bills that create deep anxieties and can bankrupt those unlucky enough to be without health insurance when a medical crisis strikes (Pear 2007a).

Government programs help pay for health care for senior citizens and the poor, and the tens of millions of Americans without health insurance generally are from working families, not on welfare but employed by a company that does not provide workers with access to affordable health insurance. Young adults who have just graduated from high school or college and who are entering the full-time permanent workforce for the first time may not find health care attached to their first job. Single parents who may not be able to work full-time because of child-care obligations and those with low levels of education or job training are also particularly likely to end up in jobs without health insurance.

The lack of a comprehensive health insurance program for all citizens is one of the major differences between the United States and the other advanced western democracies to which the nation compares itself, including Canada, Japan, the United Kingdom, France, and Germany. The comprehensive, taxpayer-financed national health insurance programs of these countries have their problems, including in some cases a shortage of high-tech equipment and long wait times for nonemergency procedures. But those nations and many others provide health insurance for all citizens for a smaller share of their economy than the United States spends on a health-care system that leaves tens of millions uninsured. Even though their countries spend far less, comparative statistics from the Organization for Economic Co-operation and Development (OECD) show that residents of many other advanced western democracies have better overall health care than Americans do.

The first column of Table 5.1 compares the total amount of public and private expenditure on health care in a variety of western democracies. As the table demonstrates, the United States devotes a far greater share of its

Table 5.1 International Health-Care Expenses and Indicators, 2003

	Total Public and Private Health-care Expenses as a Percentage of GDP	Life Expectancy at Birth (in years)	Number of Deaths of Children Aged under One Year per 1,000 Live Births[a]
Australia	9.2	80.3	4.8
Austria	9.6	78.8	4.5
Belgium	10.1	78.8	4.3
Canada	9.9	79.9	5.3
Czech Republic	7.5	75.4	3.9
Denmark	8.9	77.5	4.4
Finland	7.4	78.5	3.1
France	10.4	79.4	4.0
Germany	10.8	78.6	4.2
Greece	10.5	78.9	4.0
Hungary	8.3	72.6	7.3
Iceland	10.5	81.2	2.4
Ireland	7.2	78.3	5.1
Italy	8.4	79.7	4.2
Japan	8	81.8	3.0
Luxembourg	7.7	78	4.9
Mexico	6.3	74.9	20.5
Netherlands	9.1	78.6	4.8
Norway	10.1	79.6	3.4
Poland	6.5	74.7	7.0
Portugal	9.8	77.4	4.1
Slovak Republic	5.9	73.9	7.9
Spain	7.9	80.3	3.6
Sweden	9.3	80.2	3.1
Switzerland	11.5	80.6	4.3
Turkey	7.6	71	28.7
United Kingdom	7.8	78.5	5.3
United States	15.2	77.5	6.9

Note: Only OECD countries with complete 2003 data are included here
[a]In some countries, such as the United States, Canada, and the Nordic countries, very premature babies (with relatively low odds of survival) are registered as live births, which increases mortality rates compared with other countries that do not register them as live births.

Source: Organisation for Economic Co-operation and Development (OECD) Health Data. 2006. Health data, update of May 16, 2006. http://www.oecd.org/dataoecd/20/51/37622205.xls. (accessed February 1, 2007).

overall economy to health care than to any other advanced democracy—15.2 percent of all economic activity. The country with the second-highest share of its economy devoted to health care lags well behind the United States: the 11.5 percent in Switzerland. Germany ranks third, with health care composing 10.8 percent of its national economic activity, and Greece, Iceland, and France take the next three places. Of the twenty-eight relatively advanced countries listed in the table, twenty of them devote less than two-thirds as much of their spending to health care as does the United States.

As anyone who is ill will readily admit, there is nothing wrong with spending a lot of money on health care when necessary. A lot of people in a lot of countries probably wish their own societies devoted more resources to health care. But the more important issue is whether the money invested in the health of a country's citizens is spent wisely. For that comparison I use two widely accepted measures of a society's overall health: the average lifespan of its population and the number of babies (out of every 1,000 live births) who die before their first birthday.

As Table 5.1 shows, the much larger U.S. expenditures on health care than every other economically advanced nation here do not produce anything approaching the best health results. Even though we spend more than other comparable countries, our results are worse. The average American lives 77.5 years, longer than people in much poorer nations like the Czech Republic, Hungary, and Mexico, but not as long as those in most of the other countries examined here. Overall, people in six nations on this list live to see their eightieth birthday, with residents of Japan living the longest: an average of 81.8 years. (The other nations where the average lifespan is more than 80 years are Australia, Iceland, Spain, Sweden, and Switzerland.) Canadians live an average of 79.9 years, more than two years longer than average Americans. Residents of the United Kingdom, France, and Germany all live on average more than a year longer than Americans.

The second overall measure of health in Table 5.1—the number of deaths in the first year of life for every 1,000 live births—is a bit less reliable, but the United States again fares poorly. On this measure, the United States includes very premature babies (with relatively low odds of survival) and some other countries do not. But very premature babies represent a tiny fraction of live births, and so do not explain fully (or even mostly) the vast differences between the performance of the United States and other nations. Only five of the twenty-seven other countries in this comparison do worse than the United States, and once again they are much poorer nations that devote a much smaller portion of their much smaller economies on health care: Hungary, Mexico, Poland, the Slovak Republic, and Turkey. When the United States is compared with the other countries that include very premature births in their infant mortality statistics—Canada, Norway, and Sweden—the United States does far worse on this measure. A baby born in the United States is more than twice as likely to die in its first year of life as a baby born in Sweden or Norway. Survival rates are also considerably higher for babies born in nearby Canada.

These data could provide effective presidential sound bites. Imagine the French doing better than the U.S. of A.! Imagine the Germans! More babies die in their first year, and more elderly die sooner in nearly every advanced country with which the United States compares itself.

For the Clinton plan, the biggest obstacle to public acceptance and passage was the all-or-nothing campaign. Had the Clinton team focused more on politically possible improvements to the health-care system, a simpler plan that it could sell more effectively, or a more incremental plan it could pass in stages, the country would have been better off. So too would have been the Clinton presidency, assuming progress on health care would have preserved Democratic majorities in the House and Senate beyond 1994.

The Clinton administration also could have put health care first, ahead of NAFTA on the legislative calendar. This would have given lawmakers more time to deal with the plan before the 1994 elections. With a more long-term policymaking focus, with more adept timing, or even with a more comprehensible bill, more citizens might have had more health care and less financial anxiety. A big, complicated plan that failed helped no one get better health care. Fellow Democrats often attacked Clinton for favoring incremental approaches to policymaking, not doing enough to advance the party's issues with bold policies (Drew 1994; Reich 1998; Woodward 1994). Ironically, though, Clinton failed to reach for incremental improvements in his health-care plan, where modest advances in health-care financing for those without health insurance could have made life a lot better for some of the more than 45 million working Americans without public or private health insurance and tens of millions of other Americans who have inadequate coverage. (Clinton learned from his mistakes and secured passage of some modest health-care reforms later in his presidency). Only in 2007, more than a dozen years later, were Democrats and Republicans again talking seriously about a large-scale government program to help cover those roughly 45 million uninsured workers (Pear 2007a). But the pending presidential election means that the crisis will be one of the legacies that will be waiting for the president who takes office in January 2009.

George W. Bush's 2001 and 2003 Tax Cuts

Who doesn't like a tax cut? Not too many people, obviously. But when the president and Congress agree on tax cuts but do not cut spending as well, the result is an unbalanced budget. If the budget is already unbalanced, it becomes even more so if new tax cuts are not offset by new spending reductions. Bill Clinton is the only president since the mid-1960s to have presided over balanced budgets, with the greatest annual gaps between revenues and spending found in the budgets of Ronald Reagan, George H. W. Bush, and George W. Bush (Quirk and Nesmith 2006).

George W. Bush made tax cuts the centerpiece of his 2000 campaign. Vice President Al Gore, Bush's rival that year, complained that the benefits of the Bush plan would be limited to the very wealthy, and that those cuts would reverse the gains made in balancing the budget during the Clinton-Gore years (Ceaser and Busch 2001). Gore insisted that payments into the Social Security system be placed in a "lockbox" and set aside to help pay for the retirement of the Baby Boomers, the largest generation in U.S. history. Bush said during the campaign that he would preserve the payments for when the Baby Boomers retire, but when the budget fell into deficit in 2001 Bush raided the trust fund to pay for general government operations, as other presidents did before him (Campbell 2004a, 2004b; Suskind 2004).

After obtaining office, Bush moved aggressively to push his tax cut plan through the Republican-controlled chambers on Capitol Hill. Bush fought against efforts to include provisions for suspending the tax cut if the government were to fall into deficit, claiming that the nation was on the verge of economic crisis (Campbell 2004a, 2004b). Despite the concerns of many that it was too big, Bush signed a $1.35 trillion bill to cut taxes over ten years on June 7, 2001 (Suskind 2004).

Although the terrorist attacks of 9/11 led to major reconstruction expenses and major military operations, Bush did not propose rescinding the tax cuts to pay for these new obligations. Nor did he propose undoing the tax cuts when he insisted in 2002 that Saddam Hussein be driven from power with military actions. In fact, Bush called for even more tax cuts even as the government's military obligations grew and its deficits mounted (Quirk and Nesmith 2006). In 2003, Bush requested a ten-year plan for an additional $726 billion in tax cuts, which included the elimination of taxes on stock dividends. In the end Congress passed and the president signed a $320 billion tax cut plan, even less than a $350 billion tax cut plan Bush had derided as "a little bitty tax relief package" during negotiations over the bill (Edwards 2004, 33). Despite Bush's objections to the small size of the tax cut plan, the White House claimed victory anyway (Edwards 2004).

The year after Bush signed the latter tax cut bill, the deficit for fiscal year 2004 reached a new record: $412 billion. Even so, Bush kept pressuring Congress to make all those tax cuts permanent (Quirk and Nesmith 2006). During the years of GOP control of at least one chamber of Congress—the first six years of his presidency—George W. Bush did not exercise fiscal prudence and veto a single spending bill.

Although one might expect public opinion to be strongly in favor of tax cuts, a significant number of people recognize the problems with routine deficit spending by government. In four Gallup surveys taken during

February, March, and April 2001, when Bush was pitching his tax cut regimen most aggressively, support for the Bush plan ranged from 53 to 56 percent, barely a majority. Opposition ranged from 30 percent to 35 percent of those surveyed, with the rest uncertain, generally around 15 percent or so (Edwards 2004, 33). That is relatively modest support, particularly considering that Bush promised voters could have something for nothing. But Congress did not balk, and gave Bush nearly all of his original 2001 tax cut bill.

Presidents certainly find it easier to spin a tax cut as a good idea than as a bad one, as people are disposed to like more money in their pockets. But people also like many government programs and are willing to pay for them. In May 2003, a *Washington Post*/ABC News poll found that when the public was given the choice between further tax cuts and increased domestic spending, the public supported more government spending by a margin of 67 percent to 29 percent (Edwards 2004, 32).

Presidents of both parties have a stake in minimizing the apparent size of the federal deficit beyond the short-term benefits of enacting a popular program. So too do members of Congress hoping to secure their reelection through special government spending programs for their districts—programs that are easier to pass when the budget looks closer to being balanced. The smaller the deficit appears to be, the less pressure there is to curtail government policies that give citizens roughly $1.20 in services for every $1 paid to the federal government in taxes and fees. If you shrink the size of the deficit—at least on paper—tax cuts are more likely to pass, existing programs are more likely to remain in place, and new programs seem less painful to implement than they would be otherwise.

For these reasons, Democrats and Republicans have conspired to count Social Security payments as revenue against current year expenses. The Social Security system is now running a substantial surplus in contributions—$185 billion for fiscal 2006—largely because the Baby Boomers are in their peak earning years (U.S. Congressional Budget Office 2007). That will not last much longer—the oldest Baby Boomers turn sixty-five in 2011. Using the additional Social Security revenue to hide the true size of the budget deficit makes things look better than they are, albeit temporarily. When the problem becomes clearer, somebody else will be president.

By applying the temporary Social Security revenue surplus to the actual deficit, the government reported a budget deficit for fiscal year ended September 30, 2006, of $248 billion. A more accurate (but unpublicized) number for the fiscal 2006 budget is $433 billion. Table 5.2 shows how much worse the nation's financial standing would be if the government honestly reported its annual budget deficit.

The first column of Table 5.2 shows the official reported federal budget deficit or surplus for the past four presidents. Only four of the twenty-five

138

Table 5.2 Federal Budget Deficits, Reported and Actual, 1982–2006 (billions of dollars)

	Reported amount	Social Security "surplus"	"Honest budget" (excluding Social Security effects)
2006	−248	185	−433
2005	−318	174	−492
2004	−413	151	−564
2003	−378	156	−534
2002	−158	159	−317
2001[a]	128	163	− 35
2000	236	152	84
1999	126	125	1
1998	69	99	− 30
1997	− 22	81	−103
1996	−107	66	−173
1995	−164	60	−224
1994	−203	57	−260
1993[a]	−255	47	−302
1992	−290	51	−341
1991	−269	54	−323
1990	−221	58	−279
1989[a]	−153	52	−205
1988	−155	39	−194
1987	−150	20	−170
1986	−221	17	−238
1985	−212	9	−221
1984	−185	0	−185
1983	−208	0	−208
1982	−128	− 8	−120

Note: Figures are in billions of dollars for fiscal years ending September 30. Negative numbers are deficits; positive numbers are surpluses.

[a]A new president takes office on January 20, but the incumbent president approves the budget for the fiscal year that starts on October 1 of a presidential election year.

Source: U.S. Congressional Budget Office. 2007. "Historical Budget Data." http://www.cbo.gov/budget/historical.pdf (accessed January 30, 2007). Table E-1 is the source of columns 1 and 2. Column 3 was calculated by the author by subtracting the Social Security "surplus" from the official budget figures.

federal budgets starting with fiscal year 1982 were in surplus—and all four of those budgets were Bill Clinton budgets. Of the 21 budgets in deficit here, twelve of them were more than $200 billion in the red: three Reagan budgets, all four George H. W. Bush budgets, one Clinton budget (his first year), and four of the first five George W. Bush budgets. The second column shows the Social Security "surplus," though those figures do not take full account of the fact that the number of retirees will be exploding in the coming years. These figures come from the Congressional Budget Office (2007), a highly respected nonpartisan source of fiscal information on the government's performance. (With inflation, a $200 billion deficit today is less than it used to be, but the cumulative effect of all these large annual budget deficits means that the long-term federal debt has set a new record every year of the George W. Bush presidency.)

Prudent financial management would suggest putting money aside to pay for expanded costs associated with the aging of the Baby Boomers, the largest generation in U.S. history. More than 70 million Baby Boomers will be retiring in the coming decades, and those retirements will trigger massive increases in government spending to support a variety of government social programs including Medicare, Medicaid, and veterans' health-care benefits (Dye 2008). People paying into the Social Security system after the Baby Boomers retire will stagger under the weight of the increased obligations (Peterson 2004). Current government estimates predict the size of the U.S. workforce will increase by 0.4 percent a year for the next half century, but the number of retirees will increase by many times that amount, particularly if the average life span in the U.S. continues to lengthen (Panetta 2006).

If the United States had adopted Al Gore's "lockbox" strategy of saving Social Security funds for the bulge in retirements in the coming years, and if the retirement revenue were no longer used to hide the true size of the federal deficit, the result would be the third column of numbers—identified in Table 5.2 as the "honest budget" figures. (The numbers in the third column were calculated by subtracting the net revenue from Social Security of Column 2 from the official reported budget amount of Column 1.) With this adjustment, the number of budgets in balance over the past quarter century drops from four to two—though the remaining two still make Clinton the only president to have balanced a budget during this period. The government reported twelve budget deficits of more than $200 billion during this period; under these more accurate figures there were fifteen budget deficits of that magnitude. In Column 1, the largest deficit was the $413 billion deficit for fiscal 2004 (a George W. Bush budget). If you take out the impact of Social Security collections, the new record deficit is actually $151 billion more—up to a total of $564 billion for fiscal 2004.

There is an old saying that people in holes should stop digging, but the advice has not been taken by the White House and Capitol Hill. Rather than having money in the bank for these wholly anticipated retirement expenditures, government officials of both parties have raided the Social Security piggy bank and filled it with "IOUs." The consequences of this short-sighted approach will be severe, as massive benefit cuts or dramatically higher taxes will be needed to pay for the cost of Baby Boomer retirements. This won't help the stock markets or the U.S. economy either. Bush proposed dealing with this looming disaster by privatizing part of Social Security. Democrats did not like that idea, as they view Social Security as a vital safety net for all people, and do not want to see that net shredded by risky market investments. Bush vowed to veto an alternative solution, tax increases. In order to strengthen his hand, he defined a tax increase as including a failure to make permanent the temporary tax cuts of 2001.

Even if Bush had convinced Congress to support partial privatization, that approach would not have solved the problem according to Paul O'Neill, Bush's first treasury secretary. O'Neill noted that transitioning to Bush's new partially privatized system would have cost an additional $1 trillion at least, a dramatic increase in the nation's long-term debt (Suskind 2004). Bush never talked about how he would pay for those transition costs, perhaps because of the cost to the nation's total long-term debt. Presidential spinning, in part, means never having to talk about transition costs.

Bush's level of commitment to changing Social Security is a matter of debate, as he waited until his second term to draw much attention to the topic. By then, his appeals largely fell on deaf ears: citizens were far more concerned about Iraq than anything else, and Bush's second term credibility problems meant that few Americans would take him seriously on any policy matter. In addition, economic news is always a tough sell for U.S. mass media, making it even harder for Bush to direct the agenda toward changes in the Social Security system and to promote his plan to reform that entitlement program.

For those paying attention to economic matters, Bush had already bungled the deficit. When his first tax cuts were adopted in 2001, Bush said the country could afford them. Trillions of dollars in additional debt later, Bush still denied there was a problem. In effect, Bush's economic approach is for the Baby Boomers to party today, and leave the bill—the nation's long-term debt—to the later generations, including today's college students. Bill Clinton, who briefly reversed the nation's budgetary malpractice by balancing budgets in the late 1990s, and Al Gore, who in the 2000 election warned of the government's future fiscal problems relating to Baby Boomer retirements, were ridiculed by some Bush partisans as unrealistic worriers. Republicans who also saw the looming disaster, like former treasury secretary Paul O'Neill, were dismissed as insufficiently loyal during George W. Bush's first term. Presidential spinning means firing those who warn of future problems, guaranteeing that fewer discouraging (though accurate) statements will be heard in the future and that the covered-up problems will only get worse.

Efforts by the fiscally prudent of both parties to sound the alarm throughout the Bush years failed. Even presidential exhortations have a tough time making the evening news when the topic is difficult to present visually—and therefore difficult to excite viewers—as the government's budget deficit. It certainly is not a made-for-television story. No one in or out of the Oval Office has been effective in making budgetary responsibility a winning political issue or a high-profile media topic. Even talking about it makes many people want to vote for someone who tells them they can have their cake and eat it too.

Faith-based accounting may pay political dividends in the short term. But what are the long-term consequences?

> "Reagan proved deficits don't matter," Vice President Cheney told O'Neill during a policy argument near the end of O'Neill's tenure as treasury secretary (quoted in Suskind 2004, 291). Recalling the exchange later, O'Neill fumed about the costs of such intellectual dishonesty: "It's okay to wish for something that's, you know, outside of your fact realm. But it's not okay to confuse all that.... Ideology is a lot easier, because you don't have to know anything or search for anything. You already know the answer to everything. It's not penetrable by facts. It's absolutism" (quoted in Suskind 2004, 292).

How much will Bush's fiscal mismanagement cost the United States in the end? Who knows? It depends on how long it takes reporters to start covering the looming crisis with the attention it deserves, how long it takes citizens to start worrying about the deficit more, and how long it takes politicians to do more than make the problem worse before handing it off to their successors. If past experience is any guide, the nation's fiscal problems will get far worse before anything changes for the better.

Bush's Iraq War and Occupation

By focusing on what he said would be a quick military victory with a minimum number of troops in Iraq, Bush tried to minimize the consequences of the war both on soldiers' lives and the national economy. The longer-term consequences, the opposite of the prewar spin, are now obvious for all to see: the intractable occupation, the inability to prevent a civil war in Iraq, and the lack of a clear plan for managing the occupation in a way that will turn Iraq into a stable, self-governing nation. And the war has cost the United States far more in lives and money than government officials originally predicted.

But the ongoing mess in Iraq is not likely to be the most significant negative consequence of Bush's media-abetted focus of winning short-term battles over news coverage and public opinion. Although publics may have short attention spans, other governments do not. Although Iraq was easier to defeat militarily than either Iran or North Korea would be (both nations possess larger armies than did Saddam Hussein), the decision to invade Iraq probably accelerated programs to develop nuclear weapons in those other two nations. Indeed, the next few years may mark the end of relatively successful efforts since the 1960s to prevent the proliferation of nuclear weapons around the world, one of the key U.S. foreign policy goals of the past half century.

To see how this process may work in the coming years, imagine, for a moment, that you are the president of Iran. You know the U.S. president doesn't like you, and has invaded a neighboring country he hates about as much as he does yours. You notice that the president's first target was not North Korea, which at the time of the Iraq War was probably the furthest along of the three "axis of evil" nations in developing nuclear weapons. Do you want your country to be the next Iraq, invaded and occupied? Or would you prefer to be left largely alone, like North Korea? The answer is obvious, and any Iranian president with any sense would accelerate a national nuclear weapons program with the hopes of keeping the "infidels" away. Since the U.S. military is already stretched to the breaking point by the Iraq occupation, Bush cannot do much to stop Iran from pursuing that goal. The Europeans, even when they are united (which is not often), do not exactly instill fear in Tehran. Any Iranian promise to stop its nuclear weapons program should be viewed skeptically, given the advantages the current international environment provides to nuclear weapons states.

Turning to another oil-rich country, how happy would the Sunni leaders of Saudi Arabia be about a Shiite nuclear bomb in Iranian hands? Saudi rulers would insist on a nuclear weapons development program of their own, and given Saudi oil revenues there is no question they have the money to pay for it. The countries are longtime rivals in the region, and the normally poor relations between the two nations worsened as they support different factions in the now disorganized Iraq (Slackman and Fattah 2007).

Taking the argument a step further, the governments in Turkey and Syria, two other nations bordering Iraq, might think they need to go nuclear, also for reasons of self-defense and national pride. If Iran and Saudi Arabia are building nuclear weapons, can any self-respecting regional power afford to be left behind? (Any Middle East politician choosing a non-nuclear course in this environment may not stay in power for long. Other, more nationalistic politicians or military leaders would likely accuse that leader of failing to defend the national honor—sort of like the way Republicans in the United States attack Democrats for allegedly being weak on national security.)

A Persian Gulf bristling with nuclear weapons is far more threatening to U.S. national interests than the present situation in the region or the situation in Iraq before the U.S.-led invasion of 2003. By waging "preventive war" in Iraq—particularly without the existence of a credible threat posed by that nation—Bush has likely accelerated a race to develop nuclear weapons in several countries in the years ahead. From the perspective of the self-interest of the governments of Iran or nearby states, having nuclear weapons is the best way to keep yourself safe from a U.S. invasion and from a growing number of nuclear armed rivals at your doorstep. The Iranians, above all, saw what happened to Iraq. Having nukes is the only way to keep up with the Joneses, or more precisely, the mullahs.

Nuclear proliferation also appears more likely in the Far East, and for the same basic reasons. North Korea apparently accelerated its nuclear weapons program after the U.S. invasion of Iraq. Now that North Korea apparently has successfully tested a warhead, other nations in the region—including Japan, South Korea, and perhaps even Taiwan—may feel the best way to protect their security is to develop weapons programs of their own. And even if North Korea decides to cooperate with Washington, China is also rapidly modernizing and expanding its nuclear weapons and its conventional military forces. (Given the Bush administration's obsession with Iraq and its limited military successes in restoring order there, the so-called U.S. defense umbrella over its allies in the Asia-Pacific region may feel less comforting than it once was.)

Bush's presidential communication approach to foreign policy tries to tie U.S. enemies to the terrorist attacks of 9/11 whenever possible. Bush's marketing plan calls for optimism, perhaps even unrealistic optimism, at every turn. The potential negative consequences that result from today's actions do not appear to concern him, and they are certainly not something Bush talks about publicly.

Deep concerns over nuclear weapons proliferation cannot be dismissed as dovish paranoia. A bipartisan team of four of the nation's leading foreign and military policy thinkers—George P. Schultz (Reagan's secretary of state), William J. Perry (Clinton's defense secretary), Henry A. Kissinger (secretary of state for both Nixon and Ford), and former chairman of the Senate Armed Services Committee Sam Nunn (D-GA)—in January 2007 collaborated on an opinion column for the *Wall Street Journal* that offered a dire warning about the dangers to the United States of nuclear proliferation (Schultz et al. 2007).

> Unless urgent new actions are taken, the United States soon will be compelled to enter a new nuclear era that will be more precarious, psychologically disorienting, and economically more costly than even Cold War deterrence. It is far from certain that we can successfully replicate the old Soviet-American "mutually assured destruction" with an increasing number of potential nuclear enemies worldwide without dramatically increasing the risk that nuclear weapons will be used (Shultz et al. 2007).

Bush's invasion of Iraq, though it made for good television in the short term and probably helped Bush win reelection in 2004, comes with a high price tag. The costs of the U.S. occupation of Iraq are immense indeed for the families of the more than 4,000 servicemen and servicewomen killed in Iraq. The cost to U.S. standing in the world is high as well, as the United States now appears to have started a war on false premises. The mishandled occupation has led to a bloody civil war in Iraq that some experts say already has killed more Iraqis than the genocidal Saddam Hussein ever did (Tavernise 2007). Nuclear proliferation is likely to get worse not better, as a result of Bush's preventive war approach, as other countries feel they need to block preemption with nukes of their own.

The financial costs of waging war on a credit card—that is, without any government plan to pay for the war efforts except by expanding the federal debt—by the start of 2007 had already cost more in constant dollars than the Vietnam War. Since 9/11, the Bush administration has spent or budgeted more than $750 billion on the wars in Iraq and Afghanistan, increasing the long-term government debt that will be passed on to the next generation (Abramowitz and Montgomery 2007).

Bush's spin on Iraq has not succeeded internationally or domestically. In addition to low public approval numbers in the United States, anti-American sentiments have reached record levels around the world (Brooks 2006). But equally important is the fact that the problem-filled occupation of Iraq has reduced the chances that U.S. military threats will be taken seriously in the coming years, as the Bush administration has shown how incapable the United States is of managing military operations. Like some other presidents over the years, Bush may be better at starting wars than finishing them. But the most dangerous consequence may well be nuclear weapons proliferation on a scale that will make concerns over Saddam Hussein's alleged weapons of mass destruction look like a bad joke.

The Costs of the Spinner in Chief Presidency to U.S. Democracy

In many ways, this book makes the case that modern presidential political communication, as practiced by our two most recent presidents, is both deceitful and counterproductive. Clinton and Bush did not seek primarily to educate citizens on the concerns of the day, nor did they speak of the unpleasant trade-offs that come with difficult policy choices. For the White House, there is a great temptation to manipulate appearances and tell only the most favorable part of the story. Presidents can and do appear before invitation-only crowds asking preselected questions that praise the chief executive's wisdom and foresight.

Presidents likewise can appear before crowds of servicemen and service-women to create the images that suggest they are heroic and popular. People in uniform are hardly in a position to speak frankly to their commander in chief, and having all those uniformed personnel around the president can link the president to the military, a highly rated institution in public opinion. But good pictures only work for so long. Polls show that by January 2007 a majority of the military had turned against the war, but even so Bush and his plan to escalate the war received a polite response when he appeared before the troops at Fort Benning, Georgia, shortly after announcing his surge plan (Herbert 2007; Stolberg 2007). It may not have been as enthusiastic as the welcome Bush had received earlier in the occupation, but it was positive enough not to generate critical pictures on the evening newscasts (Stolberg 2007). In other words, presidents aim for the heart through emotional appeals rather than trying to help citizens come to intelligent judgment about tough policy alternatives.

Lessons for Presidents and Presidential Administrations

Technology has helped advance public disclosure, even within the government. Presidents have made use of the Internet to offer citizens and reporters direct access to important documents the government wants to make public. Under George W. Bush, the White House Web site has blossomed into a one-stop-shopping zone for the administration's views on the leading public policy debates. White House press briefings, presidential statements, and copies of testimony are readily available to citizens interested in the president's views on policy matters. For people who like their news unmediated by journalists, finding the administration's unfiltered commentary has never been easier. The relatively rare fireside chats of FDR's time and the televised prime-time news conferences of John F. Kennedy's time have been replaced by a mountain of White House material immediately available online to anyone with the interest and the free time to sort through it. For presidents, such direct access to the public is a great asset, particularly when they are going public to sell their policy proposals.

But technological improvements, by themselves, do not solve the problems caused by dishonest presidential marketing. The Bush administration's record of disclosure in particular was highly limited, self-serving, and ultimately counterproductive for an effective public discussion about foreign and military policy choices. Neustadt's idea of backward mapping is a particularly powerful lesson for presidents who may be tempted to lie or mislead for short-term advantage: the consequences of being caught deceiving one's own citizens—and administrations usually are caught, if not by Congress then by the courts—are severe. The link between the public and the president is a tentative one and can be broken by betrayal. Once severed, the links cannot quickly be restored, as Bush and Clinton both discovered during their presidencies.

Presidents who fail to tell the truth rarely get impeached as Bill Clinton did over the Clinton/Lewinsky scandal, and even he won an acquittal in the Senate. But their administrations can suffer deep wounds caused by their own dishonesty. Ronald Reagan was not impeached over the illegal activities of Iran-contra because prosecutors found it difficult to determine how much Reagan actually knew about what was going on in his own administration. But Reagan's presidency was effectively over after the public learned the president's team had been trading arms for hostages and negotiating with terrorists, two things the president had vowed he would never do (Neustadt 1990). Efforts by Reagan's aides to insulate the president from White House actions failed, as they always will. Presidents are responsible for what goes on in their administrations whether they approve of the specific actions in question or not. Presidents appoint the people who work for them, after all. There will always be loyal White House aides like G. Gordon Liddy or John Poindexter, willing to fall on their swords to protect a president. But their efforts are in vain—the buck really does stop at the president's desk (Neustadt 1990). The Watergate break-in was illegal, to be sure, but in the end Nixon's biggest problem occurred when the public heard the taped recordings in which the president directed his aides on how to cover up the crime (Bernstein and Woodward 1974; Woodward 1999).

The poisonous nature of presidential deceit can be seen most clearly in the George W. Bush administration's dubious claims of Iraq's weapons of mass destruction program and Saddam Hussein's link to 9/11 to trigger the U.S.-Iraq War of 2003. Even though the threat of nuclear-armed North Korea and Iran during Bush's second term may be far more real and far more dangerous to U.S. interests over the long term, the president is like "the boy who cried wolf" in the children's story, not to be taken seriously even though the wolf really may be at the door the next time. Bush's credibility became a major problem in late 2006 and early 2007 as he tried to focus U.S. and international attention on what he considered a nuclear weapons development program under way in Iran (Balz and Cohen 2007; Mazzetti 2007a, 2007b; Sanger 2007b; Weisman 2007). As a result of the way he spun public discussion of Iraq, Bush finds it much harder to build an international coalition or to develop an effective plan to deter Iran and other would-be nuclear powers.

In the struggle with Congress, there are certain things a media-savvy White House will be unwilling to live without. The president's news coverage advantages in particular are of great value. The next president almost certainly will rely, as Bush does, on tailor-made crowds to minimize the possibility of unpleasant questions and to reduce the media access of presidential critics. Presidents have to struggle so mightily to get anything out of Congress that every tool of media spin in the shed is likely to be employed. Even though the evidence that presidents "win" by going public is scant, presidents will likely to continue to try to move the public as a way of moving Congress. Going public is something presidents can do, and administrations argue that it probably does not make matters worse.

Future presidents would be wise to consider more seriously the long-term consequences that stem from overreaching short-term public relations strategies. Presidents who want to change the status quo, particularly on a domestic policy matter, have a hard climb ahead. Lawmakers in Congress have won elections on the current public policies, and they are loath to upset a status quo that has worked so well for them in the past.

Lessons for Reporters

Encouraging politicians to be more honest in their political communication may sound trite and unrealistic, and as an approach to governing it probably is. The Founders warned us that politicians would be sorely tempted to act in ways that benefit their own short-term advantage, whatever the long-term consequences to themselves or the country. As Hamilton, Madison, and Jay told us in the *Federalist Papers,* at least some politicians would readily deceive the public when it seems expedient, and they would focus on their own short-term interests no matter the long-term consequences for the country. Many politicians would be tempted to govern with divisive strategies that pit a national majority against an unpopular minority. To depend on enlightened officials always being at the helm, they warned, is a fragile form of government indeed. Such an expectation of selfless leadership is also breathtakingly unrealistic, as it runs counter to the experience of thousands of years of collective human political activity (Hamilton, Madison, and Jay 1990 [1787–1788]). Every form of government produces good leaders and bad leaders. To the Founders, the proper goal of a political system was to maximize the chances that good leaders would emerge and minimize the damage that bad leaders could cause.

So if presidents and other politicians cannot be relied upon to communicate honestly with the public, to govern in the nation's long-term interests, to be prudent when considering whether to wage a war, to increase the size of the budget deficit only in emergencies, or even to keep their zippers closed at the office, what is to be done?

This is where reporters come in. White House spin is most successful in the absence of counterspin. Although neither journalists nor citizens can compel presidents to govern responsibly, journalists can raise the costs of bad behavior. Presidents can and often do surround themselves with sheep, bleating in unison about the wondrous nature and sage judgment of the national shepherd (Neustadt 1990). The critical voices of people who question the conventional wisdom and who debate the national best interests of policy may not always be found in the West Wing. But they can be found elsewhere, such as in Congress, which should be treated by reporters as the equivalent branch the founders intended. Reporters would be well advised to worry about institutional bias in their coverage favoring the executive branch, a consistent problem in news coverage of government in recent decades (Farnsworth and Lichter 2006a).

In recent years, journalists have done a good job of raising the costs of presidential mismanagement on some issues, though their best reporting sometimes comes too late to affect ongoing policy debates. The Bush administration's current problems in Iraq are largely the result of extremely wishful imagining—if not deliberate deception—by the White House regarding issue after issue. This Bush White House's spin list is long: the alleged Iraqi weapons of mass destruction program, the alleged links between Saddam Hussein and Al-Qaeda, the willingness of allies in the region to support the invasion, the size of the occupation force necessary to pacify Iraq, the costs of the war and the subsequent occupation, the extent to which the "de-Baathification" of the Iraqi Army would create an effective armed resistance, the amount of armor that should be on a Humvee, the length of time it would take to build a democratic government in Baghdad from scratch, the extent to which the Bush administration's disregard of international legal standards in the treatment of prisoners would be reflected in the abuses at Abu Ghraib and Guantánamo, the extent to which unsavory images of this war would be photographed and videotaped and end up on the Web, the extent to which hiring reconstruction staff based on ideology (including their views on abortion) rather than on substantive experience in the region would hurt the reconstruction effort, the extent to which trigger-happy private contractors would undermine U.S. efforts to pacify Iraq, the magnitude of the hostility between Shiites and Sunnis in Iraq, the extent to which the Kurds want to separate from Iraq, the extent to which divisive religious leaders and their militias would control the post-Hussein government, and finally the extent to which regional powers such as Saudi Arabia and especially Iran would support the religious factions in Iraq that correspond to the dominant strains of Islam in their own nations (Chandrasekaran 2006).

We know about this staggering list of Bush administration misjudgments and delusions regarding Iraq because of the many reporters who have investigated government claims and even reflected on the sometimes unsatisfactory performance of news organizations when reporting on Iraq. In recent years, many reporters in this war zone have risked and in some cases lost their lives to report on a dangerous environment. But, as others have noted (Entman 2004; Orkent 2004), journalists did a far worse job of getting to the bottom of things beforehand, when it mattered most. In short, the president spun the people and the press and won.

There were relatively few serious investigations of the Bush administration's claims about Iraq before the war started (Orkent 2004). In the aftermath of 9/11, too many reporters and citizens were inclined to accept uncritically the government's claims. Although the Bush administration may be faulted for mismanagement of virtually all aspects of the Iraq mess, many journalists and citizens share the blame, as so many were willing to go along with extreme presidential spin and declined to raise serious questions before the war started.

At its best, journalism can be a key mechanism for government accountability. After the fact, many journalists have done an effective job of reporting the problems with the Bush administration's case for war and for its handling of that war. Reporters have faced considerable criticism from the administration and its partisan supporters for doing so. Although some may say that it may have been asking a great deal of reporters to apply the same level of critical analysis to the administration immediately after 9/11 as they did before, the consequences of the reduced scrutiny of the Bush administration are present for all to see.

Reporters did a far better job of telling Americans what they were getting ahead of time in the 1992 presidential campaign, which featured many stories about "Slick Willie," the Arkansas political operative who had what was once delicately referred to as "a zipper problem" (mainly, it won't stay closed). Sexual escapades ended Gary Hart's presidential aspirations in 1988 and nearly had the same effect on the Clinton campaign four years later. Given all the reporting on Gennifer Flowers, Paula Jones, and the rest, only the most delusional Americans would have been surprised when the Clinton-Lewinsky scandal emerged. News coverage did raise the cost of misbehavior ahead of time for Clinton, but he chose to ignore the lessons of the Hart campaign and his own nearly politically fatal experience in 1992. Republicans saw the danger to Clinton and the Democrats of this presidential misbehavior—as well as a chance to exploit the political indignation of religious conservatives for their own purposes—and the nation spent a year dealing with this sordid mess. As Entman (2004) observed, reporters are better at aggressive real-time coverage of less significant matters, such as personal scandals, than they are at challenging a commander in chief in time to affect the debate over whether the nation should go to war.

Journalists face a difficult balancing act: when does a reporter's aggressive treatment of political figures run the risk of being seen as a partisan attack? In fact, any criticism of political figures will be seen as partisan by some, as Bill Clinton's complaints about his alleged mistreatment by the press rival Bush's. Hostility to reporters, the old problem of blaming the messenger, is particularly apparent in today's political and media environment of heightened partisanship. The current political conversation in the United States, particularly online, is really more a shouting match between supporters and opponents of the president—be it Clinton or Bush—than a reasoned, effective debate about the country's future. It certainly isn't getting any easier to be a reporter, but the many sophisticated people looking over one's shoulder can make sure that any questions that arise with media reports can be dealt with quickly—such as the problematic *Sixty Minutes II* report during the 2004 campaign on Bush's National Guard service record (Rutenberg 2004; Rutenberg and Zernike 2004).

One particularly valuable service that reporters, particularly television reporters, can offer for citizens is to provide more context for ongoing news developments. Too often events are presented as isolated news bites, unconnected to the larger narrative of the long-term story (Iyengar 1991). This contextualization has been done more frequently online and in the print media, such as when reporters contrasted the *National Intelligence Estimate*'s bleak outlook on Iraq with Cheney's upbeat assessment, "The reality on the ground is, we have made major progress," a week earlier (Mazzetti 2007b). When Bush tries to argue that the administration's strategy has not been "stay the course," reporters can provide online links to the video clips to show how often he used exactly those words in describing his Iraq occupation policy (Froomkin 2006).

For busy news consumers, contextualization of events is essential to an understanding of presidential communication and the temptation to deceive through overspin. Most people do not remember what politicians said in the past, and it is an important public service to note how the administration's story has changed over time.

Lessons for Citizens

When one watches a film, one sometimes has to engage in what movie buffs call a suspension of disbelief, or the ability to consider, at least within the context of the film, that something outlandish on screen nevertheless makes some sense. Although presidential spin is not a movie, the same temptation may arise. With the political passions of our deeply divided times, many citizens have succumbed to the temptation to suspend disbelief when a favored politician starts to speak. Whether it was Democrats convinced that Bill Clinton was being set up in a phony sex scandal by neo-Puritans, or whether it was Republicans convinced that George W. Bush was the only thing that kept Saddam Hussein and Osama bin Laden from singing and dancing in a victory celebration on the National Mall, we the people have let presidents and their partisans get away with far too much. Repeatedly presidents have deceived us. They have shown callous indifference to the truth. They have failed to meet our most minimal demand: to behave responsibly as president.

Most of us don't get mad at first; in fact we even give them second terms. Then, maybe in year six or seven, many of us get really mad.

With their many advantages in the mass media, presidents are in an ideal position to win the marketing wars of modern U.S. politics. Although the media treat almost all political figures negatively, presidents do fare better than Congress in the battle for public attention: the executive branch gets far more coverage and distinctly less negative coverage than the legislative branch. Although the media can do more to even out these disparities, citizens need to be smart consumers as far as politicians are concerned. Presidents will try to manipulate the political conversation, as they are convinced it is in their advantage to do so. Like teenagers with a new driver's license, new presidents wonder just how far and how fast they can go. The result, all too often, is that citizens give them the keys, turn their attention to other matters, and before you know it, the car is in the ditch, totaled. We as citizens have to pay more attention to the spin, and consume enough news to recognize deceit when presidents and their teams are trying to get away with yet another fraud. Otherwise we will get more of the same in the years ahead.

Fool Me Once, Shame on You; Fool Me Twice . . .

This final chapter examined in depth several examples of how the modern presidency's focus on short-term advantages, a tendency made worse by the modern mass media, can exacerbate long-term national problems. Those issues in which the long-term consequences may be most severe are also the most complicated—ill-suited to lengthy discussion but amenable to half-baked sound bites. The price of living beyond one's financial means is expensive, as is clear to everyone who has bounced a check or had an overdue credit card bill. The government likewise cannot live beyond its means indefinitely any more than a family can, no matter what the tax-cut-happy politicians say. Americans are practical people, and we know this, but we suspend disbelief in response to appealing, aggressive marketing by the spinner in chief.

To make matters worse, the media and the public do not punish presidents for record deficits—though voters do punish the politicians who warn that financial recklessness is a problem (as they did Gore in 2000, Dukakis in 1988, and Mondale in 1984). When Reagan gets away with mortgaging the nation's future, it encourages future presidents to test the boundaries of reckless fiscal behavior—borrowing more than the government has borrowed before. As any parent knows, rewarded behavior is repeated behavior.

Economic stories are not seen as exciting, and they do not get much media coverage. Television reporters find it difficult to spend a lot of time on a story that does not generally provide good pictures. So citizens today do not focus on the deficit, and our children will curse us for the bills we are leaving for them to pay. Presidents do not want to talk about it; neither do most members of Congress. Reporters think the economy, especially the deficit, is too boring to cover, and that citizens won't be interested. We the people generally do not want to think about balancing the budget either. So the nation's long-term economic problems do not get covered extensively, do not get talked about, and nearly every year things get worse. The same goes for nuclear proliferation, a complicated matter that does not easily lend itself to sound bites and brief news items. It, too, is getting worse by the year.

The particulars of health insurance programs likewise are not a simple story, and not one easily told to citizens. Statistics may tell an amazing story, but that still does not make the facts a great read or allow for great video. How many current or former political science majors, after all, know that the performance of our overall health-care system lags so far behind so many other countries? For people who have health insurance tied to their workplaces—generally middle-class people who are most likely to vote and to give money to politicians—the issue of a national government health-care program is not a central one.

The modern media environment and the president's ever-growing advantages in the public debate require an ever-more vigilant citizenry. Presidents have more of an ability to dominate the discourse than ever before, and the growing sophistication of White House spin efforts makes it harder for Congress to assert its place as a full partner in policymaking. The problem of president-dominated political conversation is intensified in the foreign policy realm, where the president's political role as commander in chief and his or her cultural role as the equivalent of a national parent create an environment far too friendly to presidential leadership.

In time, perhaps, Congress will reassert its policy prerogatives, as it did after the high water marks of presidential power experienced during the Lincoln, FDR, Nixon, and Reagan presidencies. Perhaps the next president will be as constrained by Congress as Jerry Ford and Jimmy Carter were, though that seems less likely than was the case in the past, during far less mediated times. Never before has the White House played such a dominant role in political discourse, and future presidents of whatever party will be tempted to take up where the George W. Bush presidency left off in terms of aggressive and deceptive media management. In other words, the ability of Congress to rejuvenate itself may be harder than ever, even after January 20, 2009.

Citizens, therefore, must be particularly vigilant regarding White House media messages. The new media have offered presidents new, ever-expanding opportunities to spin and to enlist allies in the administration's cause. Recent presidents have been quite willing to deceive the country to win political marketing disputes. In the end, citizens have to be smart consumers of government, being skeptical of the spin and being their own editors in the free-for-all online and offline worlds of modern political communication.

Counterspin Cookbook

Have a Healthy News Media Diet

- **Vary media format.** Do not consume only print reports or television news (or the online versions of either).
- **Limit your consumption of junk-food journalism.** Print news reports, PBS programming, and cable documentaries often provide more informational nutrients than the largely headline-oriented services of many network television and cable newscasts.
- **Focus on news, not opinion.** Use ideologically oriented media (including bloggers) as a side dish, not a main course.
- **When you do indulge, sample a range of ideologically oriented media.** Even if you are a strong partisan, it is good to learn what people of opposite views are thinking.
- **Sample non-U.S. media sources regularly.** International reporters often have different sources and report from different perspectives than their U.S. counterparts. In addition, U.S. coverage generally says little about what is going on in the world beyond our borders as well as how others view us. You might even like more exotic media choices.

Digest News Reports Critically

- **Weigh the evidence.** The best way to counter emotionally and ideologically driven policymaking is to insist on evidence, not rhetoric, then examine that evidence and seek out more information if the politicians and the news media don't satisfy. Some of the country's biggest problems occur when politicians appeal to our emotions rather than to our reasoning. In other words, read the fine print on the label.
- **Follow the money and the power.** All too often government officials make decisions by focusing too much on how they—rather than the country as a whole—benefit by their actions. Be particularly skeptical of government officials' marketing gimmicks, particularly those made right before elections.
- **Watch for short-term-itis.** Reporters and politicians often think only of the short term, and fail to discuss policies in a longer-term context. Be your own editor and get more information about whether the feel-good policymaking of today will cause severe indigestion later.

continues

Counterspin Cookbook (continued)

- **Seek out the undercovered stories.** Remember that television reporters hate to tell stories that lack excitement and good pictures. Be particularly aggressive in seeking out economic news and other government policy news that lacks the spiciness reporters think we want.
- **Correct for the propresidency bias.** Remember that the federal government includes more than the White House. Search for competing voices, particularly those coming from Capitol Hill, if you don't hear a full policy debate from your media sources.

References

Abramowitz, Michael, and Jon Cohen. 2008. "U.S. Concern over Economy Is Highest in Years." *Washington Post,* February 4.

Abramowitz, Michael, and Jonathan Weisman. 2007. "Bush's Iraq Plan Meets Skepticism on Capitol Hill." *Washington Post,* January 12.

Abramowitz, Michael, and Lori Montgomery. 2007. "Bush to Request Billions for Wars." *Washington Post,* February 3.

Abramowitz, Michael, and Peter Baker. 2007. "Embattled, Bush Held to Plan to Salvage Iraq." *Washington Post,* January 20.

Abramson, Paul R., John H. Aldrich, and David W. Rohde. 1982. *Change and Continuity in the 1980 Elections.* Washington, DC: Congressional Quarterly Press.

———. 1999. *Change and Continuity in the 1996 and 1998 Elections.* Washington, DC: Congressional Quarterly Press.

———. 2002. *Change and Continuity in the 2000 Elections.* Washington, DC: Congressional Quarterly Press.

Adatto, Kiku. 1990. "Sound Bite Democracy." Research paper, Kennedy School Press Politics Center, Harvard University, June.

Aitken, Jonathan. 1993. *Nixon: A Life.* Washington, DC: Regnery.

Alford, C. Fred. 1988. "Mastery and Retreat: Psychological Sources of the Appeal of Ronald Reagan." *Political Psychology* 9 (4): 571–589.

Allen, Mike. 2003. "Bush Cites 9/11 on All Manner of Questions." *Washington Post,* September 11.

———. 2007. "Senator Soothing: Hillary Clinton Can Be Warm, Casual." *Politico,* January 23. http://www.politico.com/news/stories/0107/2421.html (accessed January 23, 2007).

Alterman, Eric. 2000. *Sound and Fury: The Making of the Punditocracy.* Ithaca, NY: Cornell University Press.

———. 2003. *What Liberal Media?* New York: Basic Books.

———. 2006. "Liar. Liar?" *Nation,* December 11.

Alterman, Eric, and Mark Green. 2004. *The Book on Bush: How George W. (Mis)leads America.* New York: Viking.

Andrews, Edmund. 2007. "Bush Says Plan Would Balance Budget by '12." *New York Times,* January 3.

Asher, Herb, and Mike Barr. 1994. "Popular Support for Congress and Its Members." In *Congress, the Press, and the Public,* ed. Thomas E. Mann and Norman Ornstein, 15–44. Washington, DC: American Enterprise Institute/Brookings Institution.

Auletta, Ken. 2004. "Fortress Bush: How the White House Keeps the Press under Control." *New Yorker,* February 19.

Ayres, Jeffrey. 2005. "Transnational Activism in the Americas: The Internet and Innovations in the Repertoire of Contention." *Research in Conflicts in Social Movements and Change* 25: 35–61.

Bai, Matt. 2006. "What Are the Lieberman Foes For?" *New York Times,* August 20.

Baker, Nancy V. 2002. "The Impact of Anti-Terrorism Policies on Separation of Powers: Assessing John Ashcroft's Role." *Presidential Studies Quarterly* 32 (4): 765–778.

Baker, Peter. 2007a. "General Is Front Man for Bush's Iraq Plan." *Washington Post,* February 7.

———. 2007b. "The Image Bush Just Can't Escape." *Washington Post,* May 4.

———. 2007c. "White House Manual Details How to Deal with Protesters." *Washington Post,* August 22.

Balz, Dan. 2006. "Edwards Formally Joins 2008 Race." *Washington Post,* December 28.

———. 2007. "Hillary Clinton Opens Presidential Bid." *Washington Post,* January 21.

Balz, Dan, and Jon Cohen. 2006. "Independent Voters Favor Democrats by 2 to 1 in Poll." *Washington Post,* October 24.

———. 2007. "Confidence in Bush Leadership at All-Time Low, Poll Finds." *Washington Post,* January 22.

Barber, James David. 1992. *Presidential Character: Predicting Performance in the White House.* Englewood Cliffs, NJ: Prentice Hall.

Barringer, Felicity. 2005. "Public Relations Campaign for Research Office at E.P.A. May Involve Ghost-Written Articles." *New York Times,* July 18.

Barstow, David, and Robin Stein. 2005. "The Message Machine: How the Government Makes News; Under Bush, a New Era of Pre-packaged News." *New York Times,* March 13.

Baum, Matthew A., and Samuel Kernell. 1999. "Has Cable Ended the Golden Age of Presidential Television?" *American Political Science Review* 93 (1): 99–114.

Becker, Elizabeth, and David Sanger. 2005. "Wolfowitz Gets Bush Nomination for World Bank." *New York Times,* March 17.

Bennett, James. 1998. "Bad Vibes from the Heartland Launch Fleet of Finger-Pointers." *New York Times,* February 19.

Bennett, W. Lance. 2005. *News: The Politics of Illusion.* 6th ed. New York: Pearson Longman.

Berman, Larry, and Emily O. Goldman. 1996. "Clinton's Foreign Policy at Midterm." In *The Clinton Presidency: First Appraisals*, ed. Colin Campbell and Bert A. Rockman, 290–324. Chatham, NJ: Chatham House.

Berman, William C. 2001. *From the Center to the Edge: The Politics and Policies of the Clinton Presidency*. Lanham, MD: Rowman and Littlefield.

Bernstein, Carl, and Bob Woodward. 1974. *All the President's Men*. New York: Warner Books.

Beschloss, Michael. 2002. *The Conquerors: Roosevelt, Truman, and the Destruction of Hitler's Germany, 1941–1945*. New York: Simon and Schuster.

Binder, Sara A., and Steven S. Smith. 1997. *Politics or Principle? Filibustering in the United States Senate*. Washington, DC: Brookings Institution.

Blaney, Joseph R., and William L. Benoit. 2001. *The Clinton Scandals and the Politics of Image Restoration*. Westport, CT: Praeger.

Blumenthal, Mark. 2005. "Toward an Open-Source Methodology: What We Can Learn from the Blogosphere." *Public Opinion Quarterly* 69 (5): 655–669.

Blumenthal, Ralph. 2005. "Web Site Owner Says He Knew of Reporter's Two Identities." *New York Times*, February 20.

Blumenthal, Sidney. 2003. *The Clinton Wars*. New York: Farrar, Straus and Giroux.

Bonner, Raymond, and Jane Perlez. 2007. "British Report Criticizes U.S. Treatment of Terror Suspects." *New York Times*, July 28.

Bonner, Raymond, and Sara Rimer. 2000. "Executing the Mentally Retarded Even as Laws Begin to Shift." *New York Times*, August 7.

Bowles, Nigel. 2003. "Comparing the Core Executive in Britain, France, and the United States." In *The Presidency and the Political System*, ed. Michael Nelson, 7th ed., 29–47. Washington, DC: Congressional Quarterly Press.

Bremer, Paul (with Malcolm McConnell). 2006. *My Year in Iraq: The Struggle to Build a Future of Hope*. New York: Simon and Schuster.

Brinkley, Douglas. 1998. *The Unfinished Presidency: Jimmy Carter's Journey beyond the White House*. New York: Penguin.

———. 2007. "Reckless Abandonment." *Washington Post*, August 26.

Broder, John M. 2006. "Democrats Take Senate: Concession in Virginia Completes Midterm Sweep." *New York Times*, November 10.

———. 2007. "Filling Gaps in Iraq, Then Finding a Void at Home." *New York Times*, July 17.

Brody, Richard A. 1991. *Assessing the President: The Media, Elite Opinion, and Public Support*. Stanford, CA: Stanford University Press.

Brooks, Stephen. 2006. *As Others See Us: The Causes and Consequences of Foreign Perceptions of America*. Peterborough, ON: Broadview.

Brown, Cynthia, ed. 2003. *Lost Liberties: Ashcroft and the Assault on Personal Freedom*. New York: New Press.

Brown, Janelle. 2001. "Nostradamus Called It! Internet Conspiracy Theories Are Having a Field Day after the Attacks." *Salon.com*, September 17. http://archive.salon.com/tech/feature/2001/09/17/kooks.print.html (accessed May 29, 2008).

Bugliosi, Vincent. 2001. *The Betrayal of America: How the Supreme Court Undermined the Constitution and Chose Our President*. New York: Avalon/Nation Books.

Bumiller, Elizabeth. 2002. "Bush Urges Nation to Follow His Lead and Get Fit." *New York Times,* June 21.

———. 2003. "Keepers of Bush Image Lift Stagecraft to New Heights." *New York Times,* May 16.

———. 2004. "Bush Backs Ban in Constitution on Gay Marriage." *New York Times,* February 25.

———. 2005a. "Evicted 'Denver Three' Gain Support in Quest." *New York Times,* June 27.

———. 2005b. "Cheney Sees 'Shameless' Revisionism on Iraq War." *New York Times,* November 22.

Burden, Barry C. 2005. "The Nomination: Technology, Money, and Transferable Momentum." In *The Elections of 2004,* ed. Michael Nelson, 18–41. Washington, DC: Congressional Quarterly Press.

Burke, John P. 2006. "The Institutional Presidency." In *The Presidency and the Political System,* ed. Michael Nelson, 8th ed., 383–409. Washington, DC: Congressional Quarterly Press.

Burnham, Walter Dean. 1996. "Realignment Lives: The 1994 Earthquake and Its Implications." In *The Clinton Presidency: First Appraisals,* ed. Colin Campbell and Bert A. Rockman, 363–396. New York: Chatham House.

Burns, James MacGregor, and Susan Dunn. 2001. *The Three Roosevelts: Patrician Leaders Who Transformed America.* New York: Atlantic Monthly Press.

Burns, John F., and James Glanz. 2007. "Iraq to Review Hussein Execution." *New York Times,* January 3.

Burns, John F., and Marc Santora. 2007. "U.S. Questioned Iraq on the Rush to Hang Hussein." *New York Times,* January 1.

Burns, John F., and Sabrina Tavernise. 2007. "In Baghdad, Bush Policy Is Met with Resentment." *New York Times,* January 12.

Burns, John F., Sabrina Tavernise, and Marc Santora. 2007. "U.S. and Iraqis Are Wrangling over War Plans." *New York Times,* January 15.

Busch, Andrew E. 2004. "On the Edge: The Electoral Career of George W. Bush." In *Considering the Bush Presidency,* ed. Gary Gregg II and Mark J. Rozell, 177–200. New York: Oxford University Press.

Campbell, Colin. 2004a. "Managing the Presidency or the President?" In *The George W. Bush Presidency: Appraisals and Prospects,* ed. Colin Campbell and Bert A. Rockman, 1–15. Washington, DC: Congressional Quarterly Press.

———. 2004b. "Unrestrained Ideological Leadership in the Bush II Advisory System." In *The George W. Bush Presidency: Appraisals and Prospects,* ed. Colin Campbell and Bert A. Rockman, 73–104. Washington, DC: Congressional Quarterly Press.

Campbell, James. E. 1992. "Forecasting the Presidential Vote in the States." *American Journal of Political Science* 36 (2): 386–407.

———. 2001. "The Referendum That Didn't Happen: The Forecasts of the 2000 Presidential Election." *PS: Political Science and Politics* 34 (1): 33–38.

Carey, George W. 1989. *The Federalist: Design for a Constitutional Republic.* Urbana: University of Illinois Press.

Carter, Bill. 2007. "Rivals CNN and Fox News Spar over Obama Report." *New York Times,* January 24.

Carter, Chelsea. 2008. "Marine General to Testify in Haditha Case." Associated Press Online. http://www.washingtonpost.com/wp-dyn/content/article/2008/05/30/AR2008053002447.html (accessed June 2, 2008).

Cavanaugh, Tim. 2002. "Another Voice: Net Generates Sound and Fury." *Online Journalism Review,* April 2. http://www.ojr.org/ojr/ethics/1017782089.php (accessed May 30, 2008).

Ceaser, James. 1988. "The Reagan Presidency and American Public Opinion." In *The Reagan Legacy: Promise and Performance,* ed. Charles O. Jones, 172–210. Chatham, NJ: Chatham House.

Ceaser, James, and Andrew Busch. 1993. *Upside Down and Inside Out: The 1992 Elections and American Politics.* Lanham, MD: Rowman and Littlefield.

———. 1997. *Losing to Win: The 1996 Elections and American Politics.* Lanham, MD: Rowman and Littlefield.

———. 2001. *The Perfect Tie: The True Story of the 2000 Presidential Election.* Lanham, MD: Rowman and Littlefield.

———. 2005. *Red over Blue.* Lanham, MD: Rowman and Littlefield.

Center for Media and Public Affairs. 2006. "'Daily Show:' Night-Time Nabobs of Negativity?" News Release, December 20.

Chandler, Michael A. 2007. "A President's Illness Kept under Wraps." *Washington Post,* February 3.

Chandrasekaran, Rajiv. 2006. *Imperial Life in the Emerald City: Inside Iraq's Green Zone.* New York: Knopf.

———. 2007. "Back on Capitol Hill, Bremer Is Facing a Cooler Reception." *Washington Post,* February 6.

Cillizza, Chris, and Dan Balz. 2007. "On the Electronic Campaign Trail, Politicians Realize the Potential of Web Video." *Washington Post,* January 22.

Clancey, Maura, and Michael J. Robinson. 1985. "General Election Coverage." In *The Mass Media in Campaign '84,* ed. Michael J. Robinson and Austin Ranney, 27–33. Washington, DC: American Enterprise Institute.

Clarke, Richard A. 2004. *Against All Enemies: Inside America's War on Terror.* New York: Free Press.

Cohen, Jeffrey E. 2002a. "The Polls: Policy-Specific Presidential Approval, Part I." *Presidential Studies Quarterly* 32 (3): 600–609.

———. 2002b. "The Polls: Policy-Specific Presidential Approval, Part II." *Presidential Studies Quarterly* 32 (4): 779–788.

Cohen, Jon, and Dan Balz. 2008. "U.S. Outlook Is Worse Since '92, Poll Finds." *Washington Post,* May 13.

Confessore, Nicholas. 2005. "Going for Broke May Break Bush." *New York Times,* February 6.

Cook, Corey. 2002. "The Contemporary Presidency: The Permanence of the 'Permanent Campaign': George W. Bush's Public Presidency." *Presidential Studies Quarterly* 32 (4): 753–764.

Cook, Timothy E. 1989. *Making Laws and Making News.* Washington, DC: Brookings Institution.

———. 2005. *Governing with the News: The News Media as a Political Institution.* 2nd ed. Chicago: University of Chicago Press.

Cooper, Helene. 2007. "With Rumsfeld Gone, Critics of War Look to Rice." *New York Times,* February 4.

Cooper, John M. Jr. 1983. *The Warrior and the Priest: Woodrow Wilson and Theodore Roosevelt.* Cambridge, MA: Harvard University Press.

Cronin, Thomas E., and Michael A. Genovese. 2004. *The Paradoxes of the American Presidency.* 2nd ed. New York: Oxford University Press.

Dallek, Robert. 2007. *Nixon and Kissinger: Partners in Power.* New York: Harper-Collins.

Dautrich, Kenneth, and Thomas H. Hartley. 1999. *How the News Media Fail American Voters: Causes, Consequences and Remedies.* New York: Columbia University Press.

Davis, Richard. 1994a. *Decisions and Images: The Supreme Court and the Press.* Englewood Cliffs, NJ: Prentice Hall.

———. 1994b. "Supreme Court Nominations and the News Media." *Albany Law Review* 54: 1061–1079.

———. 1999. *The Web of Politics: The Internet's Impact on the American Political System.* New York: Oxford University Press.

Davis, Richard, and Diana Owen. 1998. *New Media and American Politics.* New York: Oxford University Press.

Dean, John W. 2004. *Worse Than Watergate: The Secret Presidency of George W. Bush.* Boston: Little, Brown.

Dimock, Michael. 2004. "Bush and Public Opinion." In *Considering the Bush Presidency,* ed. Gary Gregg II and Mark J. Rozell, 69–97. New York: Oxford.

Dionne, E. J. 2007. "Reagan Democrat." *Washington Post,* January 25.

Dowd, Maureen. 2005. "The United States of Shame." *New York Times,* September 3.

Drew, Elizabeth. 1994. *On the Edge: The Clinton Presidency.* New York: Simon and Schuster.

Drezner, Daniel, and Henry Farrell. 2004. "Web of Influence." *Foreign Policy* 145 (November–December): 32–40.

Druckman, James N. 2003. "The Power of Television Images: The First Kennedy-Nixon Debate Revisited." *Journal of Politics* 65 (2): 559–571.

Drudge, Matt. 2000. *Drudge Manifesto.* New York: New American Library.

Dye, Thomas R. 2008. *Understanding Public Policy,* 12th ed. Upper Saddle River, NJ: Pearson Longman.

Easton, David, and Jack Dennis. 1969. *Children in the Political System.* New York: McGraw-Hill.

Easton, Nina J., Michael Kranish, Patrick Healy, Glen Johnson, Anne E. Kornblut, and Brian Mooney. 2004. "On the Trail of Kerry's Failed Dream." *Boston Globe,* November 14.

Edwards III, George C. 1989. *At the Margins: Presidential Leadership of Congress.* New Haven, CT: Yale University Press.

———. 1996. "Frustration and Folly: Bill Clinton and the Public Presidency." In *The Clinton Presidency: First Appraisals,* ed. Colin Campbell and Bert A. Rockman, 234–261. New York: Chatham House.

———. 1997. "Aligning Tests with Theory: Presidential Approval as a Source of Influence in Congress." *Congress and the Presidency* 24 (2): 113–130.

———. 2000. "Campaigning Is Not Governing: Bill Clinton's Rhetorical Presidency." In *The Clinton Legacy,* ed. Colin Campbell and Bert A. Rockman, 33–47. New York: Chatham House.

———. 2003. *On Deaf Ears: The Limits of the Bully Pulpit.* New Haven, CT: Yale University Press.

———. 2004. "Riding High in the Polls: George W. Bush and Public Opinion." In *The George W. Bush Presidency: Appraisals and Prospects,* ed. Colin Campbell and Bert A. Rockman, 16–45. Washington, DC: Congressional Quarterly Press.

———. 2006. "The Illusion of Transformational Leadership." Paper delivered at the annual meeting of the American Political Science Association, Philadelphia, September 1.

Eggen, Dan. 2008. "Ex-Colleagues Ask: 'What Happened?'" *The Washington Post,* May 29.

Eggerton, John. 2004. "Howard Dean: Scream Never Happened." *Broadcasting and Cable,* June 14.

Entman, Robert M. 2000. "Declarations of Independence." In *Decision-Making in a Glass House: Mass Media, Public Opinion, and American and European Foreign Policy in the 21st Century,* ed. B. L. Nacos, R. Y. Shapiro, and P. Isernia, 11–26. Lanham, MD: Rowman and Littlefield.

———. 2004. *Projections of Power: Framing News, Public Opinion, and U.S. Foreign Policy.* Chicago: University of Chicago Press.

Faler, Brian. 2003. "Web Site for the Like-Minded Turning into Boon for Dean." *Washington Post,* October 18.

Farnsworth, Stephen J. 1988. "Kansas City Pulls the Plug on Klan Access to Cable TV." *Chicago Tribune,* June 18.

———. 1989. "Kansas City Drops Fight to Keep Klan off Cable TV." *Chicago Tribune,* July 17.

———. 2001. "Patterns of Political Support: Examining Congress and the Presidency." *Congress and the Presidency* 28 (1): 45–60.

———. 2003a. "Congress and Citizen Discontent: Public Evaluations of the Membership and One's Own Representative. *American Politics Research* 31 (1): 66–80.

———. 2003b. *Political Support in a Frustrated America.* Westport, CT: Praeger.

Farnsworth, Stephen J., and S. Robert Lichter. 1999. "No Small-Town Poll: Public Attention to Network Coverage of the 1992 New Hampshire Primary." *Harvard International Journal of Press/Politics* 4(3): 51–61.

———. 2004. "New Presidents and Network News: Covering the First Year in Office of Ronald Reagan, Bill Clinton, and George W. Bush." *Presidential Studies Quarterly* 34 (3): 674–690.

———. 2006a. *The Mediated Presidency: Television News and Presidential Governance.* Lanham, MD: Rowman and Littlefield.

———. 2006b. "The Mediated Supreme Court Nomination Process: News Coverage of Presidential Nominees." Paper delivered at the annual meeting of the American Political Science Association, Philadelphia, September 2.

———. 2007. *The Nightly News Nightmare: Television's Coverage of U.S. Presidential Elections, 1988–2004.* 2nd ed. Lanham, MD: Rowman and Littlefield.

Farnsworth, Stephen J., and Diana Owen. 2004. "The Internet and the 2000 Elections." *Electoral Studies* 23 (3): 415–429.

Farrell, John A. 2001. *Tip O'Neill and the Democratic Century.* Boston: Little, Brown.

Feith, Douglas J. 2008. *War and Decision: Inside the Pentagon at the Dawn of the War on Terrorism.* New York: Harper.

Fenno, Richard F. Jr. 1975. "If, as Ralph Nader Says, Congress Is 'the Broken Branch,' Then How Come We Love Our Congressmen So Much?" In *Congress in Change: Evolution and Reform,* ed. Norman J. Ornstein, 277–287. New York: Praeger.

Fisher, Ian. 2006. "Italy Calls Iraq War 'Grave Error.'" *New York Times,* May 16.

Fisher, Louis. 2004. "The Way We Go to War: The Iraq Resolution." In *Considering the Bush Presidency,* ed. Gary Gregg II and Mark J. Rozell, 107–124. New York: Oxford University Press.

Fitzwater, Marlin. 1995. *Call the Briefing! Bush and Reagan, Sam and Helen: A Decade with Presidents and the Press.* New York: Times Books/Random House.

Fritz, Ben, Bryan Keefer, and Brendan Nyhan. 2004. *All the President's Spin: George W. Bush, the Media, and the Truth.* New York: Touchstone.

Froomkin, Dan. 2005. "Spinner in Chief." *Washingtonpost.com,* August 29. http://www.washingtonpost.com/wp-dyn/content/blog/2005/08/29/BL2005082900733.html (accessed May 30, 2008).

———. 2006. "White House Year in Review: Bush Loses His Parade." *Washingtonpost.com,* December 20. http://www.washingtonpost.com/wp-dyn/content/blog/2006/12/20/BL2006122000603.html (accessed February 5, 2007).

Frosch, Dan. 2007. "Two Ejected from Bush Speech Posed Threat, Lawyers Say." *New York Times,* April 15.

Frum, David. 2003. *The Right Man: The Surprise Presidency of George W. Bush. An Inside Account.* New York: Random House.

Genovese, Michael A. 2001. *The Power of the American Presidency, 1789–2000.* New York: Oxford University Press.

Gergen, David. 2000. *Eyewitness to Power: The Essence of Leadership.* New York: Simon and Schuster.

Germond, Jack, and Jules Witcover. 1993. *Mad as Hell: Revolt at the Ballot Box, 1992.* New York: Warner Books.

Gilbert, Robert E. 1989. "President versus Congress: The Struggle for Public Attention." *Presidential Studies Quarterly* 16 (3): 83–102.

Gillon, Steven M. 2002. "Election of 1992." In *History of American Presidential Elections, 1789–2001,* ed. Arthur M. Schlessinger Jr. and Fred L. Israel, vol. 11, 4327–4344. Philadelphia: Chelsea House.

Gingrich, Newt. 1995. *To Renew America.* New York: HarperCollins.

Goldberg, Robert, and Gerald J. Goldberg. 1995. *Citizen Turner.* New York: Harcourt Brace.

Goldfarb, Zachary. 2007. "Mobilized Online, Thousands Gather to Hear Obama." *Washington Post,* February 3.

Goldman, Emily O., and Larry Berman. 2000. "Engaging the World: First Impressions of the Clinton Foreign Policy Legacy." In *The Clinton Legacy,* ed. Colin Campbell and Bert A. Rockman, 226–253. New York: Chatham House.

Goo, Sara K. 2005. "List of Foiled Plots Puzzling to Some." *Washington Post,* October 23.

————. 2007. "Product Reviews and Links Turn Pages into Profit." *Washington Post,* January 11.

Goodnough, Abby. 2004. "Balancing Brotherly Love and a Duty to a Storm-Torn State." *New York Times,* October 31.

Goodwin, Doris Kearns. 1994. *No Ordinary Time.* New York: Simon and Schuster.

Goolsbee, Austan. 2006. "Lean Left, Lean Right? News Media May Take Their Cues from Customers." *New York Times,* December 7.

Gordon, Michael R. 2003. "Basra Offers a Lesson on Taking Baghdad." *New York Times,* April 3.

Graber, Doris. 2003. "Terrorism, Censorship, and the First Amendment: In Search of Policy Guidelines." In *Framing Terrorism: The News Media, the Government, and the Public,* ed. Pippa Norris, Montague Kern, and Marion Just, 27–42. New York: Routledge.

————. 2006. *Mass Media and American Politics.* 7th ed. Washington, DC: Congressional Quarterly Press.

Greenberg, David. 2003. "Calling a Lie a Lie." *Columbia Journalism Review,* September–October. http://cjrarchives.org/issues/2003/5/lie-greenberg.asp (accessed September 10, 2003).

Greenstein, Fred. 1982. *The Hidden-Hand Presidency: Eisenhower as Leader.* New York: Basic Books.

————. 2001. *The Presidential Difference.* Princeton, NJ: Princeton University Press.

Gregg, Gary L. 2004. "Dignified Authenticity: George W. Bush and the Symbolic Presidency." In *Considering the Bush Presidency,* ed. Gary Gregg II and Mark J. Rozell, 88–106. New York: Oxford University Press.

Grossman, Lawrence K. 1995. *The Electronic Republic: Reshaping Democracy in the Information Age.* New York: Penguin.

Grossman, Michael B., and Martha Joynt Kumar. 1981. *Portraying the President.* Baltimore: Johns Hopkins University Press.

Grynbaum, Michael. 2006. "Liberal Bloggers Come to the Fore." *Boston Globe,* August 8.

Halbfinger, David. 2002. "The 2002 Election: Georgia. Bush's Push, Eager Volunteers, and Big Turnout Led to Georgia Sweep." *New York Times,* November 10.

Hall, Jim. 2001. *Online Journalism: A Critical Primer.* London: Pluto Press.

Halperin, Mark, and John F. Harris. 2006. *The Way to Win: Taking the White House in 2008.* New York: Random House.

Hamilton, Alexander, James Madison, and John Jay. 1990 [1787–1788]. *The Federalist,* ed. George W. Carey and James McClellan. Dubuque, IA: Kendall-Hunt.

Han, Lori Cox. 2001. *Governing from Center Stage: White House Communication Strategies during the Television Age of Politics.* Cresskill, NJ: Hampton Press.

Hart, Roderick P. 1994. *Seducing America: How Television Charms the Modern Voter.* New York: Oxford University Press.

Healy, Patrick. 2007. "To '08 Hopefuls, Media Technology Can Be Friend or Foe." *New York Times,* January 31.

Herbert, Bob. 2007. "Another Thousand Lives." *New York Times,* January 4.

Hersh, Seymour M. 2005. *Chain of Command: The Road from 9/11 to Abu Ghraib.* New York: Harper.

Hershey, Marjorie Randon. 1989. "The Campaign and the Media." In *The Election of 1988*, ed. Gerald M. Pomper, 73–102. Chatham, NJ: Chatham House.

———. 2001. "The Campaign and the Media." In *The Election of 2000*, ed. Gerald M. Pomper, 46–72. New York: Chatham House.

Hertsgaard, Mark. 1989. *On Bended Knee: The Press and the Reagan Presidency.* New York: Schocken.

Hess, Stephen. 1981. *The Washington Reporters.* Washington, DC: Brookings Institution.

———. 1986. *The Ultimate Insiders: U.S. Senators in the National Media.* Washington, DC: Brookings Institution.

———. 1991. *Live from Capitol Hill!* Washington, DC: Brookings Institution.

———. 1996. *Presidents and the Presidency.* Washington, DC: Brookings Institution.

Hetherington, Marc J., and William J. Keefe. 2007. *Parties, Politics, and Public Policy in America.* 10th ed. Washington, DC: Congressional Quarterly Press.

Hiatt, Fred. 2007. "The Lives on the Line." *Washington Post,* January 15.

Hibbing, John R., and Elizabeth Theiss-Morse. 1995. *Congress as Public Enemy: Public Attitudes towards American Political Institutions.* Cambridge: Cambridge University Press.

———. 1998. "The Media's Role in Public Negativity toward Congress: Distinguishing Emotional Reactions and Cognitive Evaluations." *American Journal of Political Science* 42 (April): 475–498.

Hoge, Warren. 2006. "Official of U.N. Says Americans Undermine It with Criticism." *New York Times,* June 7.

Hollihan, Thomas A. 2001. *Uncivil Wars: Political Campaigns in a New Media Age.* Boston: Bedford / St. Martin's.

Homaday, Ann. 2007. "Throwing Her Hat on the Web." *Washington Post,* January 21.

Hulse, Carl. 2006. "Senator from Virginia Addresses Jewish Ancestry." *New York Times,* September 20.

———. 2007. "Leadership Tries to Restrain Fiefs in New Congress." *New York Times,* January 7.

Hulse, Carl, and Edmund L. Andrews. 2007. "House Approves Changes in Eavesdropping Program." *New York Times,* August 5.

Hulse, Carl, and Raymond Hernandez. 2006. "Top G.O.P. Aides Knew in Late '05 of Email to Page." *New York Times,* October 1.

Hunt, Albert R. 1981. "The Campaign and the Issues." In *The American Elections of 1980,* ed. Austin Ranney, 142–176. Washington, DC: American Enterprise Institute.

Isikoff, Michael. 2000. *Uncovering Clinton: A Reporter's Story.* New York: Three Rivers Press.

Iyengar, Shanto. 1991. *Is Anyone Responsible? How Television Frames Political Issues.* Chicago: University of Chicago Press.

Iyengar, Shanto, and Donald R. Kinder. 1987. *News That Matters.* Chicago: University of Chicago Press.

Iyengar, Shanto, Helmut Norpoth, and Kyu S. Hahn. 2004. "Consumer Demand for Election News: The Horserace Sells." *Journal of Politics* 66 (1): 157–175.

Jacobs, Lawrence R. 2006. "The Presidency and the Press: The Paradox of the White House Communications War." In *The Presidency and the Political System,* ed. Michael Nelson, 8th ed., 283–310. Washington, DC: Congressional Quarterly Press.

Jacobson, Gary. 2001. *The Politics of Congressional Elections.* 5th ed. New York: Addison Wesley Longman.

Jamieson, Kathleen Hall, and Joseph N. Cappella. 1998. "The Role of the Press in the Health Care Reform Debate of 1993–1994." In *The Politics of News, the News of Politics,* ed. Doris Graber, Denis McQuail, and Pippa Norris, 110–131. Washington, DC: Congressional Quarterly Press.

Jeffords, James M. 2003. *An Independent Man: Adventures of a Public Servant.* New York: Simon and Schuster.

Jensen, Elizabeth, and Lia Miller. 2006. "After Bankruptcy Filing, Recriminations Fly at Air America." *New York Times,* December 18.

Johnston, David. 2003. *Perfectly Legal: The Covert Campaign to Rig Our Tax System to Benefit the Super Rich—and Cheat Everybody Else.* New York: Portfolio.

———. 2004. "Judging Intelligence: Policy, Politics, and Pressure." *New York Times,* July 10.

Johnston, David, and Eric Lipton. 2007. "Ex-Justice Aide Admits That Politics Affected Hiring." *New York Times,* May 24.

Johnston, David, and Jim Rutenberg. 2007. "At the Libby Trial, Hints of Intrigue and Betrayal." *New York Times,* January 25.

Jones, Charles O. 1994. *The Presidency in a Separated System.* Washington, DC: Brookings Institution.

———. 1995. *Separate but Equal Branches: Congress and the Presidency.* Chatham, NJ: Chatham House.

Kaid, Lynda Lee, and Joe Foote. 1985. "How Network Television Coverage of the President and Congress Compare." *Journalism Quarterly* 62: 59–65.

Kaiser, Robert. 2007. "Trapped by Hubris, Again." *Washington Post,* January 14.

Kaplan, David. 1988. "Is the Klan Entitled to Public Access?" *New York Times,* July 31.

Kassop, Nancy. 2003. "The War Power and Its Limits." *Presidential Studies Quarterly* 33 (3): 509–529.

Kaus, Mickey. 2001. "Kausfiles: Everything the *New York Times* Thinks about the Florida Recount Is Wrong." *Slate,* November 13, 2001. http://www.slate.com/?id=2058603 (accessed November 14, 2001).

Kennedy, Robert F. 1969. *Thirteen Days: A Memoir of the Cuban Missile Crisis.* New York: Norton.

Kerbel, Matthew Robert. 1995. *Remote and Controlled: Media Politics in a Cynical Age.* Boulder, CO: Westview.

———. 1998. *Edited for Television: CNN, ABC, and American Presidential Elections.* 2nd ed. Boulder, CO: Westview.

———. 2001. "The Media: Old Frames in a Time of Transition." In *The Elections of 2000,* ed. Michael Nelson, 109–132. Washington, DC: Congressional Quarterly Press.

———. 2005. "The Media: The Challenge and Promise of Internet Politics." In *The Elections of 2004,* ed. Michael Nelson, 88–107. Washington, DC: Congressional Quarterly Press.

Kernell, Samuel. 2007. *Going Public: New Strategies of Presidential Leadership.* 4th ed. Washington, DC: Congressional Quarterly Press.

Kinsley, Michael. 2003. "An Apology Would Help." *Washington Post,* September 12.

Kirkpatrick, David D. 2006. "Two Ex-Acquaintances of Senator Allen Said He Used Slurs." *New York Times,* September 26.

―――. 2007. "Feeding Frenzy for a Big Story, Even if It's False." *New York Times,* January 29.

Klein, Joe. 2002. *The Natural: The Misunderstood Presidency of Bill Clinton.* New York: Doubleday.

Klotz, Robert J. 2004. *The Politics of Internet Communication.* Lanham, MD: Rowman and Littlefield.

Kolbert, Elizabeth. 1994. "Frank Talk by Clinton to MTV Generation." *New York Times,* April 20.

Kornblut, Anne. 2005a. "Third Journalist Was Paid to Promote Bush Policies." *New York Times,* January 29.

―――. 2005b. "Doubts on White House Reporter Are Recalled." *New York Times,* February 18.

Kristof, Nicholas D. 2004. "Dithering as Others Die." *New York Times,* June 26.

Krugman, Paul. 2006. "The Crony Fairy." *New York Times,* April 28.

Kumar, Martha Joynt. 2001. "The Office of the Press Secretary." *Presidential Studies Quarterly* 31 (2): 296–322.

―――. 2002. "Recruiting and Organizing the White House Staff." *PS: Political Science and Politics* 35 (1): 35–40.

―――. 2003a. "The Contemporary Presidency: Communications Operations in the White House of President George W. Bush: Making News on His Terms." *Presidential Studies Quarterly* 33 (2): 366–393.

―――. 2003b. "Source Material: The White House and the Press. News Organizations as a Presidential Resource and as a Source of Pressure." *Presidential Studies Quarterly* 33 (3): 669–683.

Kurtz, Howard. 1992a. "The Pundits, Eating Crow after a Clinton Comeback." *Washington Post,* March 18.

―――. 1992b. "Networks Adapt to Changing Campaign Role." *Washington Post,* June 21.

―――. 1994. *Media Circus: The Trouble with America's Newspapers.* New York: Times Books/Random House.

―――. 1998. *Spin Cycle: Inside the Clinton Propaganda Machine.* New York: Free Press.

―――. 2000. "The Shot Heard Round the Media: Bush's Off-Mike Crack Could Cut Both Ways." *Washington Post,* September 6.

―――. 2002. "Troubled Times for Network Evening News." *Washington Post,* March 10.

―――. 2005. "Network Fires Four in Wake of Probe." *Washington Post,* January 11.

―――. 2007a. "A Candidate's Not So Candid Camera?" *Washington Post,* January 8.

―――. 2007b. "Campaign Allegation a Source of Vexation." *Washington Post,* January 22.

―――. 2007c. "Headmaster Disputes Claim that Obama Attended Islamic School." *Washington Post,* January 23.

———. 2007d. "Journalist Forced to Reveal Her Methods." *Washington Post,* January 31.

Laufer, Peter. 1995. *Inside Talk Radio: America's Voice or Just Hot Air?* Secaucus, NJ: Carol Publishing.

Lazare, Daniel. 1996. *The Frozen Republic: How the Constitution Is Paralyzing Democracy.* New York: Harcourt Brace.

Leonnig, Carol D., and Amy Goldstein. 2007. "Ex-Aide Says Cheney Led Rebuttal Effort." *Washington Post,* January 26.

Lewis, David. 2006. "Presidents and the Bureaucracy: Management Imperatives in a Separation of Powers System." In *The Presidency and the Political System,* ed. Michael Nelson, 8th ed., 410–429. Washington, DC: Congressional Quarterly Press.

Lewis, David, and Roger Rose. 2002. "The President, the Press, and the War-Making Power: An Analysis of Media Coverage Prior to the Persian Gulf War." *Presidential Studies Quarterly* 32 (3): 559–571.

Lewis-Beck, Michael S., and Tom W. Rice. 1992. *Forecasting Elections.* Washington, DC: Congressional Quarterly Press.

Lewis-Beck, Michael S., and Charles Tien. 2001. "Modeling the Future: Lessons from the Gore Forecast." *Political Science and Politics* 34 (1): 21–23.

Lichtblau, Eric. 2007. "Senator Threatens to Charge White House with Contempt." *New York Times,* August 21.

Lichtblau, Eric, and David Johnston. 2007. "Court to Oversee U.S. Wiretapping in Terror Cases." *New York Times,* January 18.

Lichter, S. Robert, and Daniel Amundson. 1994. "Less News Is Worse News: Television News Coverage of Congress." In *Congress, the Press, and the Public,* ed. Thomas E. Mann and Norman Ornstein, 131–140. Washington, DC: American Enterprise Institute/Brookings Institution.

Lichter, S. Robert, and Stephen J. Farnsworth. 2003. "Government in and out of the News." A report to the Council for Excellence in Government. Washington, DC: Center for Media and Public Affairs.

Lindsay, James M. 2003. "Deference and Defiance: The Shifting Rhythms of Executive-Legislative Relations in Foreign Policy." *Presidential Studies Quarterly* 33 (3): 530–546.

Lipton, Eric. 2006a. "White House Declines to Provide Storm Papers." *New York Times,* January 25.

———. 2006b. "Lawmakers Agree to Spend $1.2 Billion Tightening Border." *New York Times,* September 26.

Lopez, Steve. 2001. "You Gotta Admire TV's Commitment to Meaninglessness." *Los Angeles Times,* November 26.

Lowi, Theodore J. 1985. *The Personal President: Power Invested, Promise Unfulfilled.* Ithaca, NY: Cornell University Press.

Maltese, John A. 1995. *The Selling of Supreme Court Nominees.* Baltimore: Johns Hopkins University Press.

———. 2000. "The New Media and the Lure of the Clinton Scandal." In *The Clinton Scandal and the Future of American Government,* ed. Mark J. Rozell and Clyde Wilcox. Washington, DC: Georgetown University Press.

Mann, Thomas E., and Norman J. Ornstein. 2006. *The Broken Branch: How Congress Is Failing America and How to Get It Back on Track*. New York: Oxford University Press.

Margolis, Michael, and David Resnick. 2000. *Politics as Usual: The Cyberspace "Revolution."* Thousand Oaks, CA: Sage.

Massing, Michael. 2004. "Now They Tell Us." *New York Review of Books*, February 26.

Mayer, Jane, and Jill Abrahamson. 1994. *Strange Justice: The Selling of Clarence Thomas*. New York: Houghton Mifflin.

Mayhew, David. 1991. *Divided We Govern*. New Haven, CT: Yale University Press.

Mazzetti, Mark. 2006a. "Spy Agencies Say Iraq War Worsens Terror Threat." *New York Times*, September 24.

———. 2006b. "Combative Bush Releases Parts of Terror Study." *New York Times*, September 27.

———. 2007a. "Leading Senator Assails President on Iran Stance." *New York Times*, January 20.

———. 2007b. "Analysis Is Bleak on Iraq's Future." *New York Times*, February 3.

———. 2007c. "Report Offers Grim View of Iraqi Leaders." *New York Times*, August 24.

McChesney, Robert W. 1999. *Rich Media, Poor Democracy: Communication Politics in Dubious Times*. New York: New Press.

McClellan, Scott. 2008. *What Happened: Inside the Bush White House and Washington's Culture of Deception*. New York: Public Affairs.

McCullough, David. 1993. *Truman*. New York: Simon and Schuster.

McGinniss, Joe. 1969. *The Selling of the President, 1968*. New York: Trident Press.

McLean, Renwick. 2004. "Old Friends U.S. and Spain Weather a Time of Tension." *New York Times*, October 17.

Mermin, Jonathan. 1997. "Television News and the American Intervention in Somalia: The Myth of a Media-Driven Foreign Policy." *Political Science Quarterly* 112 (Fall): 385–402.

Milbank, Dana. 2003. "Amid Iraq Policy Shift: Refusal to Admit Change Is a Constant." *Washington Post*, September 9.

———. 2004a. "Bush Was Surprised at Lack of Arms." *Washington Post*, February 9.

———. 2004b. "The Administration versus the Administration." *Washington Post*, June 29.

———. 2007. "Rice, a Uniter of the Divided." *Washington Post*, January 12.

Milbank, Dana, and Claudia Deane. 2003. "Hussein Link to 9/11 Lingers in Many Minds." *Washington Post*, September 6.

Milbank, Dana, and Walter Pincus. 2003. "Cheney Defends U.S. Actions in Bid to Revive Public Support." *Washington Post*, September 15.

Milbank, Dana, and Jim VandeHei. 2004. "From Bush, Unprecedented Negativity." *Washington Post*, May 31.

Milkis, Sidney. 2006. "The Presidency and Political Parties." In *The Presidency and the Political System*, ed. Michael Nelson, 8th ed., 341–382. Washington, DC: Congressional Quarterly Press.

Minoian, Valerie. 2001. "Acquiring a Sense of Citizenship: A Civic Contribution from the Official Site of the Executive Power." M.A. thesis, Georgetown University, Washington, D.C.

Minutaglio, Bill. 1999. *First Son: George W. Bush and the Bush Family Dynasty*. New York: Times Books.

Miroff, Bruce. 2006. "The Presidential Spectacle." In *The Presidency and the Political System*, 8th ed., Michael Nelson, ed. 255–282. Washington, DC: Congressional Quarterly Press.

Mooney, Chris. 2004. "Did Our Leading Newspapers Set Too Low a Bar for a Preemptive Attack? *Columbia Journalism Review*, March–April.

Morris, Irwin L. 2002. *Votes, Money, and the Clinton Impeachment*. Boulder, CO: Westview.

Mucciaroni, Gary, and Paul J. Quirk. 2004. "Deliberations of a 'Compassionate Conservative': George W. Bush's Domestic Presidency." In *The George W. Bush Presidency: Appraisals and Prospects*, ed. Colin Campbell and Bert A. Rockman, 158–190. Washington, DC: Congressional Quarterly Press.

Mueller, John. 2006. *Overblown: How Politicians and the Terrorism Industry Inflate National Security Threats, and Why We Believe Them*. New York: Free Press.

Nagourney, Adam. 2004. "Kerry Might Pay Price for Failing to Strike Back Quickly." *New York Times*, August 21.

———. 2005. "Hard Hit: Putting It Back Together Again." *New York Times*, October 30.

———. 2006. "Democrats Looking to Use Katrina Like the G.O.P. Used 9/11." *New York Times*, April 22.

Nagourney, Adam, and Janet Elder. 2006a. "Only 25% in Poll Voice Approval of Congress." *New York Times*, September 21.

———. 2006b. "Poll Shows Foley Case Is Alienating Public from Congress." *New York Times*, October 10.

Nagourney, Adam, Carl Hulse, and Jim Rutenberg. 2006. "Bush Immigration Plan Stalled as GOP Grew Anxious." *New York Times*, June 25.

Nelson, Michael. 2006. "Evaluating the Presidency." In *The Presidency and the Political System*, ed. Michael Nelson, 8th ed., 1–27. Washington, DC: Congressional Quarterly Press.

Neustadt, Richard E. 1990. *Presidential Power and the Modern Presidents*. New York: Free Press.

Newman, Brian. 2002. "Bill Clinton's Approval Ratings. The More Things Change the More They Stay the Same." *Political Research Quarterly* 55 (4): 781–804.

Nincic, Miroslav. 1997. "Loss Aversion and the Domestic Context of Military Intervention." *Political Research Quarterly* 50 (1): 97–120.

9/11 Commission. 2004. *Final Report of the National Commission on the Terrorist Attacks upon the United States*. Authorized ed. New York: Norton.

Norris, Pippa, Montague Kern, and Marion Just. 2003. "Framing Terrorism." In *Framing Terrorism: The News Media, the Government, and the Public*, ed. Pippa Norris, Montague Kern, and Marion Just, 3–23. New York: Routledge.

O'Brien, David M. 1996. "Clinton's Legal Policy and the Courts: Rising from Disarray or Turning Around and Around?" In *The Clinton Presidency, First Appraisals*, ed. Colin Campbell and Bert A. Rockman, 126–162. Chatham, NJ: Chatham House.

———. 2005. *Storm Center: The Supreme Court in American Politics.* 7th ed. New York: Norton.

Oldfield, Duane, and Aaron Wildavsky. 1989. "Reconsidering the Two Presidencies." *Society* 26 (July–August): 54–59.

Oravec, Jo Ann. 2005. "How the Left Does Talk Radio." *Journal of Radio Studies* 12 (2): 190–203.

Organisation for Economic Co-operation and Development (OECD). 2006. Health data, update of May 16, 2006. http://www.oecd.org/dataoecd/20/51/37622205. xls (accessed February 1, 2007).

Orkent, Daniel. 2004. "Weapons of Mass Destruction? Or Mass Distraction?" *New York Times,* May 30.

Owen, Diana. 1995. "The Debate Challenge: Candidate Strategies in the New Media Age." In *Presidential Campaign Discourse: Strategic Communication Problems,* ed. Kathleen E. Kendall, 135–156. Albany: State University of New York Press.

———. 1996. "Who's Talking? Who's Listening? The New Politics of Talk Radio Shows." In *Broken Contract? Changing Relationships between Americans and Their Government,* ed. Stephen Craig, 127–146. Boulder, CO: Westview.

———. 2000. "Popular Politics and the Clinton/Lewinsky Affair: The Implications for Leadership." *Political Psychology* 21 (1): 161–177.

Page, Benjamin I., and Robert Y. Shapiro. 1992. *The Rational Public: Fifty Years of Trends in American Policy Preferences.* Chicago: University of Chicago Press.

Panetta, Leon. 2006. "Politics of the Federal Budget Process." In *Rivals for Power: Presidential-Congressional Relations,* 3rd. ed., ed. James A. Thurber, 209–232. Lanham, MD: Rowman and Littlefield.

Pareles, John. 1992, "Dissing the Rappers Is Fodder for the Sound Bite." *New York Times,* June 28.

Patterson, Thomas E. 1994. *Out of Order.* New York: Vintage.

Pear, Robert. 2004. "U.S. Videos, for TV News, Come under Scrutiny." *New York Times,* March 15.

———. 2007a. "Experts See Peril in Bush Health Proposal." *New York Times,* January 27.

———. 2007b. "Bush Directive Increases Sway on Regulation." *New York Times,* January 30.

Pear, Robert, and Sheryl Gay Stolberg. 2004. "Inquiry Ordered on Medicare Official's Charge." *New York Times,* March 17.

Pelofsky, Jeremy. 2007. "Democrats Refuse to Budge on Iraq Plan Opposition." Reuters, in *Washingtonpost.com,* January 20. http://www.washingtonpost.com/ wp-dyn/content/article/2007/01/20/AR2007012000646.html (accessed January 22, 2007).

Peterson, Peter G. 2004. *Running on Empty: How the Democratic and Republican Parties are Bankrupting Our Future and What Americans Can Do about It.* New York: Farrar, Straus, and Giroux.

Pew Research Center for the People and the Press. 2000. "Some Final Observations on Voter Opinions." December 21. http://people-press.org/reports/display. php3?ReportID=20 (accessed May 30, 2008).

———. 2001. "Terror Coverage Boosts News Media's Images." November 28. http://people-press.org/reports/display.php3?ReportID=143 (accessed May 30, 2008).

———. 2004a. "News Audiences Increasingly Politicized." June 8. http://people-press.org/reports/display.php3?PageID=833 (accessed May 30, 2008).

———. 2004b. "Voters Liked Campaign 2004, but Too Much 'Mud-Slinging.'" November 11. http://people-press.org/reports/display.php3?ReportID=233 (accessed May 30, 2008).

———. 2006. "Online Papers Modestly Boost Newspaper Readership." July 30. http://people-press.org/reports/display.php3?ReportID=282 (accessed May 30, 2008).

———. 2007. "Election 2006 Online." Pew Internet and American Life Project Report. January 17. http://www.pewinternet.org/pdfs/PIP_Politics_2006.pdf (accessed January 31).

Pfiffner, James P. 2004a. *The Character Factor: How We Judge America's Presidents.* College Station: Texas A&M University Press.

———. 2004b. "Introduction: Assessing the Bush Presidency." In *Considering the Bush Presidency,* ed. Gary Gregg II and Mark J. Rozell, 1–20. New York: Oxford University Press.

———. 2006. "Partisan Polarization, Politics, and the Presidency. Structural Sources of Conflict." In *Rivals for Power: Presidential-Congressional Relations,* ed. James A. Thurber, 33–58. Lanham, MD: Rowman and Littlefield.

Polsky, Andrew J. 2006. "The Presidency at War." In *The Presidency and the Political System,* ed. Michael Nelson, 8th ed. 557–575. Washington, DC: Congressional Quarterly Press.

Pomper, Gerald M. 1985. "The Presidential Election." In *The Election of 1984: Reports and Interpretations,* ed. Gerald M. Pomper, 60–90. Chatham, NJ: Chatham House.

———. 1989. "The Presidential Election." In *The Election of 1988: Reports and Interpretations,* ed. Gerald M. Pomper, 129–152. Chatham, NJ: Chatham House.

———. 1997. "The Presidential Election." In *The Election of 1996: Reports and Interpretations,* ed. Gerald M. Pomper, 173–204. Chatham, NJ: Chatham House.

Popkin, Samuel. 1991. *The Reasoning Voter.* Chicago: University of Chicago Press.

Postman, Neil. 1985. *Amusing Ourselves to Death.* New York: Penguin.

Power, Samantha. 2002. *"A Problem from Hell": America and the Age of Genocide.* New York: Basic Books.

Purnick, Joyce. 2006. "In a G.O.P. Stronghold, Three Districts in Indiana Are Now Battlegrounds." *New York Times,* October 21.

Quintanilla, Ray. 2006. "Cindy Sheehan: In Losing Son, She Inspired a Movement." *Chicago Tribune,* August 6.

Quirk, Paul. 2006. "Presidential Competence." In *The Presidency and the Political System,* ed. Michael Nelson, 8th ed., 136–169. Washington, DC: Congressional Quarterly Press.

Quirk, Paul, and Bruce Nesmith. 2006. "Divided Government and Policy-Making: Negotiating the Laws." In *The Presidency and the Political System,* ed. Michael Nelson, 8th ed., 508–532. Washington, DC: Congressional Quarterly Press.

Rainey, James. 2007. "The Times Shifts Its Focus to the Web." *Los Angeles Times,* January 25.

Reich, Robert. 1998. *Locked in the Cabinet.* New York: Vintage.

Remini, Robert V. 1967. *Andrew Jackson and the Bank War.* New York: Norton.

Rich, Frank. 2005a. "The White House Stages Its 'Daily Show.'" *New York Times,* February 20.

———. 2005b. "Falluja Floods the Superdome." *New York Times,* September 4.

Rieff, David. 2003. "Blueprint for a Mess." *New York Times Magazine,* November 2.

Rimer, Sara. 1994. "Vineyard Vacation: 'Veg Out.'" *New York Times,* August 28.

Risen, James. 2006. *State of War: The Secret History of the CIA and the Bush Administration.* New York: Free Press.

Risen, James, and Eric Lichtblau. 2007. "Concerns Raised on Wider Spying under New Law." *New York Times,* August 19.

Robinson, Michael J., and Margaret Sheehan. 1983. *Over the Wire and on TV.* New York: Russell Sage Foundation.

Rockman, Bert A. 2006. "The American Presidency in Comparative Perspective: Systems, Situations, and Leaders." In *The Presidency and the Political System,* ed. Michael Nelson, 8th ed., 28–56. Washington, DC: Congressional Quarterly Press.

Rosenstiel, Tom. 1994. *Strange Bedfellows: How Television and the Presidential Candidates Changed American Politics, 1992.* New York: Hyperion.

Rosenthal, Elizabeth, and Andrew C. Revkin. 2007. "Science Panel Calls Global Warming 'Unequivocal.'" *New York Times,* February 3.

Rozell, Mark. 1994. "Press Coverage of Congress, 1946–1992." In *Congress, the Press, and the Public,* ed. Thomas E. Mann and Norman Ornstein, 59–130. Washington, DC: American Enterprise Institute/Brookings Institution.

Rutenberg, Jim. 2004. "CBS News Concludes It Was Misled on Guard Memos, Network Officials Say." *New York Times,* September 20.

———. 2006a. "In High Spirits, Bush Takes a Campaign Spin in the West." *New York Times,* June 17.

———. 2006b. "Conceding Missteps, Bush Urges Patience on Iraq." *New York Times,* October 26.

———. 2007. "Edwards Campaign Tries to Harness Internet." *New York Times,* August 1.

Rutenberg, Jim, and David Cloud. 2006. "Bush, Facing Dissent on Iraq, Jettisons 'Stay the Course.'" *New York Times,* October 24.

Rutenberg, Jim, and Kate Zernike. 2004. "CBS Apologized for Report on Bush Guard Service." *New York Times,* September 21.

Rutenberg, Jim, David E. Sanger, and Michael R. Gordon. 2007. "A Two-Month Debate on Iraq, Capped by 'the Big Push.'" *New York Times,* January 12.

Rutenberg, Jim, Sheryl Gay Stolberg, and Mark Mazzetti. 2007. "'Free Iraq' Is within Reach, Bush Declares." *New York Times,* August 23.

Sabato, Larry. 1993. *Feeding Frenzy: How Attack Journalism Has Transformed American Politics.* New York: Free Press.

Sabato, Larry, Mark Stencel, and S. Robert Lichter. 2000. *Peepshow: Media and Politics in an Age of Scandal.* Lanham, MD: Rowman and Littlefield.

Sanchez, Ricardo S., and Donald T. Phillips. 2008. *Wiser in Battle: A Soldier's Story.* New York: Harper.

Sanger, David. 2004. "War Figures Honored with Medal of Freedom." *New York Times,* December 15.

———. 2005. "The Reach of War: More Humble, Still Firm." *New York Times,* December 19.

———. 2007a. "Bush Plan for Iraq Requests More Troops and More Jobs." *New York Times,* January 7.

———. 2007b. "On Iran, Bush Faces Haunting Echoes of Iraq." *New York Times,* January 28.

Saulny, Susan. 2006. "Missouri Candidates Step Lightly on Stem Cell Measure." *New York Times,* October 15.

Schmitt, Eric. 2004. "Troops' Queries Leave Rumsfeld on the Defensive." *New York Times,* December 9.

Schmitt, Richard B. 2007. "Congress, Bush Poised for First Friction." *Los Angeles Times,* January 3.

Schudson, Michael. 2007. "Why Democracies Need an Unlovable Press." In *Media Power in Politics,* ed. Doris A. Graber, 5th ed. 36–47. Washington, DC: Congressional Quarterly Press.

Schultz, George P., William J. Perry, Henry A. Kissinger, and Sam Nunn. 2007. "A World Free of Nuclear Weapons." *Wall Street Journal,* January 4.

Scott, Ian. 2000. *American Politics in Hollywood Film.* Chicago: Fitzroy Dearborn

Scowcroft, Brent. 2007. "Getting the Middle East Back on Our Side." *New York Times,* January 4.

Seelye, Katherine. 2005. "Democrats Want Investigation of Reporter Using Fake Name." *New York Times,* February 11.

Sella, Marshall. 2001. "The Red State Network." *New York Times Magazine,* June 24.

Shane, Scott. 2007a. "As Trial Begins, Cheney's Ex-Aide Is Still a Puzzle." *New York Times,* January 17.

———. 2007b. "White House Retreats under Pressure." *New York Times,* January 18.

———. 2007c. "Former Press Secretary Dispels Many Illusions." *New York Times,* January 30.

Shane, Scott, and Adam Liptak. 2006. "Shifting Power to a President." *New York Times,* September 30.

Shane, Scott, and Eric Lipton. 2005. "Storm and Crisis: Federal Response, Government Saw Flood Risk but Not Levee Failure." *New York Times,* September 2.

Shane, Scott, and Neil Lewis. 2007. "Bush Commutes Libby Sentence, Saying 30 Months 'Is Excessive.'" *New York Times,* July 3.

Shane, Scott, and Ron Nixon. 2007. "Contractors Take On Biggest Role Ever in Washington." *New York Times,* February 4.

Shanker, Thom. 2007. "New Strategy Vindicates Ex–Army Chief Shinseki." *New York Times,* January 12.

Shanker, Thom, and David S. Cloud. 2007. "Bush's Plan for Iraq Runs into Opposition from Congress." *New York Times,* January 12.

Shear, Michael D. 2007a. "Va.'s Webb Offers a Blunt Challenge to Bush." *Washington Post,* January 24.

———. 2007b. "For Webb, Bouquets and a Few Brickbats." *Washington Post,* January 25.

Shenon, Philip. 2007. "As 'New Cop on the Beat,' Congressman Starts Patrol." *New York Times,* February 6.

Sinclair, Barbara. 2000. "Hostile Partners: The President, Congress, and Lawmaking in the Partisan 1990s." In *Polarized Politics: Congress and the President in a Partisan Era,* ed. Jon R. Bond and Richard Fleisher, 134–153. Washington, DC: Congressional Quarterly Press.

———. 2006. "Is Congress Gridlocked?" In *Readings in Presidential Politics,* ed. George C. Edwards III, 291–310. Belmont, CA: Wadsworth.

———. 2008. "Living (and Dying?) by the Sword: George W. Bush as Legislative Leader." In *The George W. Bush Legacy,* ed. Colin Campbell, Bert A. Rockman, and Andrew Rudalevige, 164–187. Washington, DC: Congressional Quarterly Press.

Sipress, Alan. 2007. "Too Casual to Sit on Press Row? Bloggers' Credentials Boosted with Seats at the Libby Trial." *Washington Post,* January 11.

Skocpol, Theda. 1997. *Boomerang: Health Care Reform and the Turn against Government.* New York: Norton.

Slackman, Michael. 2007. "Hangings Fuel Sectarianism: Botched Iraq Executions Split Sunnis and Shiites." *New York Times,* January 17.

Slackman, Michael, and Hassan M. Fattah. 2007. "In Public View, Saudis Counter Iran in Region." *New York Times,* February 6.

Slevin, Peter. 2004. "New 2003 Data: 625 Terrorism Deaths, Not 307." *Washington Post,* June 23.

Smith, Richard N. 2001. "'The President Is Fine' and Other Historical Lies." *Columbia Journalism Review* September–October: 30–32.

Stanley, Alessandra. 2007. "A Showcase for the YouTube Set Makes Voters the Stars." *New York Times,* July 24.

Stephanopoulos, George. 1999. *All Too Human: A Political Education.* Boston: Little, Brown.

Stevenson, Richard, and Anne Kornblut. 2005. "The Emergency Relief Agency: The Director of FEMA Stripped of Role as Relief Leader." *New York Times,* September 10.

Stolberg, Sheryl Gay. 2006a. "A Year after March against Iraq War, Another Try." *New York Times,* August 6.

———. 2006b. "Buzzwords: The Decider." *New York Times,* December 24.

———. 2007. "The Reach of War: Bush Speaks and Base Is Subdued." *New York Times,* January 12.

Stolberg, Sheryl Gay, and Anne Kornblut. 2006. "Antiwar Protester Arrested before Speech but Her Presence Looms Large." *New York Times,* February 1.

Stolberg, Sheryl Gay, and Jim Rutenberg. 2006. "Rumsfeld Resigns." *New York Times,* November 9.

Stout, David. 2006. "Senator Says He Meant No Insult by Remark." *New York Times,* August 16.

Sullivan, Terry. 1991. "A Matter of Fact: The Two Presidencies Thesis Revisited." In *The Two Presidencies: A Quarter Century Assessment,* ed. Steven Shull, 143–157. Chicago: Nelson-Hall.

Sunstein, Cass R. 2001. *Republic.com.* Princeton, NJ: Princeton University Press.

Sunstein, Cass R., and Richard A. Epstein. 2001. *The Vote: Bush, Gore, and the Supreme Court*. Chicago: University of Chicago Press.

Suskind, Ron. 2004. *The Price of Loyalty: George W. Bush, the White House, and the Education of Paul O'Neill*. New York: Simon and Schuster.

Swartz, Jon. 2001. "Houston Citizens Get Free E-mail: Project Attempts to Close 'Digital Divide.'" *USA Today,* August 20.

Tapper, Jake. 2001. *Down and Dirty: The Plot to Steal the Presidency*. Boston: Little, Brown.

———. 2002. "Down and Dirty, Revisited: A Postscript on Florida and the News Media." In *Overtime: The Election 2000 Thriller,* ed. Larry Sabato, 206–217. New York: Longman.

Tavernise, Sabrina. 2007. "Iraqi Death Toll Exceeded 34,000 in 2006, U.N. Says." *New York Times,* January 17.

Toner, Robin. 2006. "In Bruising Virginia Senate Fight: Women May Make the Difference." *New York Times,* November 3.

Trippi, Joe. 2004. *The Revolution Will Not Be Televised: Democracy, the Internet, and the Overthrow of Everything*. New York: HarperCollins.

Tulis, Jeffrey K. 1987. *The Rhetorical Presidency*. Princeton, NJ: Princeton University Press.

Tyson, Ann. 2007. "Democrats Vow to Resist Buildup." *Washington Post,* January 8.

U.S. Congressional Budget Office. 2007. "Historical Budget Data." http://www.cbo.gov/budget/historical.pdf (accessed January 30, 2007).

VandeHei, Jim. 2005. "Bush Paints His Goals as 'Crises.'" *Washington Post,* January 8.

Waterman, Richard W., Robert Wright, and Gilbert St. Clair. 1999. *The Image-Is-Everything Presidency*. Boulder, CO: Westview.

Wayne, Stephen J. 2000. "Presidential Personality and the Clinton Legacy." In *The Clinton Scandal and the Future of American Government,* ed. Mark J. Rozell and Clyde Wilcox, 211–224. Washington, DC: Georgetown University Press.

———. 2006. "Presidential Leadership of Congress: Strategies and Structures." In *Rivals for Power: Presidential-Congressional Relations,* ed. James A. Thurber, 3rd ed., 59–84. Lanham, MD: Rowman and Littlefield.

Webb, James. 2003. "Down and Dirty: The War in Iraq Turns Ugly. That's What Wars Do. *New York Times,* March 30.

Weisberg, Jacob. 2001. "Gore Wins after All." *Slate,* November 13, 2001. http://www.slate.com/id/2058631 (accessed May 30, 2008).

Weisman, Jonathan. 2002. "Remember Fiscal Discipline?" *Washington Post,* August 9.

———. 2007. "Democrats Revise Agenda to Deal with War in Iraq." *Washington Post,* January 8.

Weisman, Stephen. 2007. "Europe Resists U.S. Push to Curb Iran Ties." *New York Times,* January 30.

West, Darrell M. 2001. *Air Wars: Television Advertising in Election Campaigns, 1952–2000*. Washington, DC: Congressional Quarterly Press.

White, Josh. 2007a. "Marine Photos Provide Graphic Evidence in Haditha Probe." *Washington Post,* January 7.

————. 2007b. "Casey Urges Patience in Securing Baghdad." *Washington Post,* January 20.

White, Theodore H. 1961. *The Making of the President, 1960.* New York: Atheneum.

Wilgoren, Jodi. 2004. "Truth Be Told, the Vietnam Crossfire Hurts Kerry More." *New York Times,* September 24.

Williams, Bruce, and Michael DelliCarpini. 2004. "Monica and Bill All the Time and Everywhere." *American Behavioral Scientist* 47 (9): 1208–1230.

Wilson, Woodrow. 1885. *Congressional Government.* New York: Meridian Books.

Wines, Michael. 1992. "Political Memo: The Hurricane and Bush. An Opportunity Missed?" *New York Times,* August 29.

Wittes, Benjamin. 2006. "Judging the Hearings." *Washington Post,* July 30.

Wlezien, Christopher. 2001. "On Forecasting the Presidential Vote." *PS: Political Science and Politics* 34 (1): 25–31.

Woodward, Bob. 1994. *The Agenda: Inside the Clinton White House.* New York: Simon and Schuster.

————. 1999. *Shadow: Five Presidents and the Legacy of Watergate.* New York: Simon and Schuster.

————. 2002. *Bush at War.* New York: Simon and Schuster.

————. 2006. *State of Denial.* New York: Simon and Schuster.

Wypijewski, JoAnn. 2006. "Where's the Outrage? As America's Politicians, Media, and Citizens Get Used to War and Abuses, Horrific Policies Get a Pass." *Los Angeles Times,* September 30.

Zaller, John R. 1998. "Monica Lewinsky's Contribution to Political Science." *PS: Political Science and Politics* 31 (2): 554–557.

Zeleny, Jeff. 2007. "In Remarks, Democrats Put Fresh Face Forward." *New York Times,* January 24.

Zernike, Kate. 2006. "Bush's Use of Authority Riles Senator." *New York Times,* June 28.

Index